没後30年

木下佳通代

KAZUYO KINOSHITA

A Retrospective

展覧会

没後30年 木下佳通代

大阪中之島美術館
2024年5月25日[土]－8月18日[日]
主催　大阪中之島美術館
協賛　株式会社アサヒグラフィック、株式会社エグザイルス、国土防災技術株式会社
協力　カゴヤ・アセットマネジメント株式会社
助成　公益財団法人 小笠原敏晶記念財団

埼玉県立近代美術館
2024年10月12日[土]－2025年1月13日[月・祝]
主催　埼玉県立近代美術館
協力　カゴヤ・アセットマネジメント株式会社
広報協力　JR東日本大宮支社、FM NACK5
助成　公益財団法人 小笠原敏晶記念財団

Exhibition

KAZUYO KINOSHITA: A Retrospective

Nakanoshima Museum of Art, Osaka
May 25, 2024 – August 18, 2024
Organized by　Nakanoshima Museum of Art, Osaka
Sponsored by　ASAHI GRAPHIC Inc., exiles Inc., JAPAN CONSERVATION ENGINEERS & CO., LTD.
Cooperated by　KAGOYA Holdings inc.
Granted by　Toshiaki Ogasawara Memorial Foundation

The Museum of Modern Art, Saitama
October 12, 2024 – January 13, 2025
Organized by　The Museum of Modern Art, Saitama
Cooperated by　KAGOYA Holdings inc.
Cooperated in public relations by　East Railway Company Omiya Branch Office, FM NACK5
Granted by　Toshiaki Ogasawara Memorial Foundation

KAZUYO KINOSHITA

A Retrospective

Kazuyo Kinoshita

AKAAKA

木下佳通代
Kinoshita Kazuyo
1987

謝辞

本展開催にあたり、
右記の機関や個人の方々、
ならびにここに記すことを
差し控えさせていただいた方々に
ご支援、ご協力を賜りました。
深く感謝の意を表明します
（順不同、敬称略）。

Acknowledgements

We would like to express our
profound gratitude to
the following individuals and
organizations for their generosity
support and cooperation in
realizing this exhibition
(honorifics omitted).

玉田美智子
木下桂子
玉田聖

京都国立近代美術館
京都市美術館
国立国際美術館
静岡県立美術館
東京国立近代美術館
名古屋市美術館
西宮市大谷記念美術館
兵庫県立美術館
和歌山県立近代美術館

植松奎二
ギャラリー島田
ギャラリーヤマキファインアート
AD&A
The Estate of Kazuyo Kinoshita

株式会社アサヒグラフィック
株式会社エグザイルス
国土防災技術株式会社
カゴヤ・アセットマネジメント株式会社
公益財団法人 小笠原敏晶記念財団

ギャラリー開
ギャラリー16
成安造形大学
トアロード画廊
村松画廊
Yumiko Chiba Associates

相川裕司
浅田陽子
天野一夫
石橋宗明
伊藤治美
井上道子
今井祝雄
今村誠子
上田佳奈
植野比佐見
植松篤
内村周
宇野君平
榎本実
大石一義
大屋菜々子
小川絢子
小川綾子
奥村一郎
尾﨑登志子

越智久美子
蔭山リエチ
影山侑恵
勝田琴絵
加藤綾乃
喜夛孝臣
北川貞大
熊田司
駒田哲男
近藤将人
佐々木弥生
佐藤亜貴夫
佐原しおり
島田誠
島田容子
鈴木慈乃
鈴木俊晴
髙橋イロ
武田毅
竹葉丈
竹村楊子
千葉由美子
辻裕
寺内成仁
中山摩衣子
西田桐子
野口雅彦
橋詰英樹
長谷川新
牧口千夏
松島正典
光田由里
森下明彦
山木加奈子
山本友輔
横田直子
渡辺信子

ごあいさつ

大阪中之島美術館と埼玉県立近代美術館ではこのたび、展覧会「没後30年 木下佳通代」を開催いたします。神戸に生まれ、関西を中心に活躍した木下佳通代(きのした・かずよ、1939–1994)の没後30年の節目に開かれる本展は、国内の美術館では初の個展となります。

京都市立美術大学(現・京都市立芸術大学)で絵画を学んだ木下は、在学中から展覧会活動を開始しました。1960年代には、神戸で結成された前衛美術集団・グループ〈位〉に影響を受け、制作を通して「存在」に対する関心を掘り下げていきます。1970年代には、写真を用いてイメージと知覚、あるいは物質との関係を考察する作品を数多く手がけました。「絶対的存在と相対的存在はありながらも、存在はひとつでしかない」という考えを明確に表した写真のシリーズは、その極めて理知的なアプローチによって国内外で高く評価されます。同時代のアートの世界的潮流とも呼応し、1981年にはドイツのハイデルベルクで個展を開催しました。

　海外での初個展と時を同じくして、木下は作品そのもののコンセプトを変えずに、写真以外の手段で作品制作が可能か試行します。80年代に入ってパステルを用いた作品によって素材と表現の相性を模索した後、再び絵画の制作に回帰します。「存在そのものを自分が画面の上に作ればいい」と考えるに至った木下は、図式的なコンセプトから脱却することに成功します。シリーズの最初の作品に《'82-CA1》と名付けて以降、アップデートを続ける筆致とともに、画面上の「存在」はたびたびその表情を変えていきます。1990年にがんの告知を受けると、治療法を求めて何度もロサンゼルスを訪れ、現地でも絶えず制作を続けます。1994年、木下は神戸で55年の生涯に幕を下ろします。再び絵画へ立ち返った1982年以降だけでも、700点以上の絵画、ドローイングを制作しました。

本展は、活動時期をたどるように3つの章で構成しています。公開の機会があまりなかったごく初期の作品から、国内外で高く評価された写真作品、そして1982年以降ライフワークとなった絵画作品によって、その活動の全貌を探ります。木下が一貫してテーマとした「存在とは何か」という問いは、現代においても尚、色褪せず強烈に響きます。

　最後になりましたが、本展の開催にあたって惜しみないご尽力を賜りました玉田美智子氏をはじめ、貴重な作品をご出品いただきました美術館および所蔵者の皆様、そしてご協力くださいました関係各位に心より御礼申し上げます。

主催者

Introduction

Nakanoshima Museum of Art, Osaka, and the Museum of Modern Art, Saitama, are excited to present "KAZUYO KINOSHITA: A Retrospective." This exhibition three decades after the passing of Kinoshita Kazuyo (1939–1994), who was born in Kobe and based in Kansai for most of her career, is the first hosted by a Japanese museum to be dedicated entirely to her work.

Studying painting at Kyoto University of the Arts, Kinoshita began exhibiting while still a student. During the 1960s, influenced by the avant-garde art collective Group "i" gathering of artists in Kobe, she began to explore more deeply her burgeoning interest in questions of existence. In the 1970s she produced numerous works that used photography to ponder the relationship between image and perception, and image and matter. Kinoshita's photo series, lucid expressions of her idea that "while there is absolute existence and relative existence, there can be only one existence," earned her high acclaim at home and abroad for their distinctly cerebral approach. It was an approach also in keeping with currents in international art during this period, leading to a solo exhibition for Kinoshita in Heidelberg in 1981.

Coinciding with this first overseas solo outing, Kinoshita undertook a series of experiments to see if it were possible to make works using a method other than photography, without changing her actual concept. The early '80s saw her wielding pastels in works that explored compatibility of material and expression, before returning once more to painting. Having reached the conclusion that the best approach would be to personally create existence itself on the picture plane, Kinoshita succeeded in breaking away from schematic concepts. After naming the first work in this new series *'82-CA1*, Kinoshita altered the look of "existence" on the picture plane frequently, with each new iteration of her ever-changing brushwork. On receiving a cancer diagnosis in 1990 she visited Los Angeles several times seeking treatments, continuing to work untiringly during her sojourns in the city. In 1994 Kinoshita passed away in Kobe, at the age of fifty-five, leaving a legacy of paintings and drawings numbering over 700 just since her return to painting in 1982.

This exhibition is composed of three chapters tracing different periods of Kinoshita's career, exploring every facet of her practice via very early works rarely or never shown in public, the photographic works that made her name in Japan and further afield, and the paintings that became her life's work after 1982. The constant, underlying theme of Kinoshita's practice — interrogating the nature of existence — resonates as strongly in today's world as it did during her lifetime.

In closing, allow us to express our heartfelt thanks to Tamada Michiko, for her tireless assistance with the staging of the exhibition; to the museums and collectors that generously loaned their precious works; and to everyone else without whom "KAZUYO KINOSHITA: A Retrospective" would not have been possible.

The organizers

目次

Contents

今、再び、「みる」ことについて ── 木下佳通代の作品と活動

大下裕司 大阪中之島美術館学芸員

0. はじめに

木下佳通代(1939–1994)は神戸を拠点に活躍した、戦後関西を代表する美術家のひとりである。1970年代に写真を用いた幾何学的な表現で注目を浴び、1982年からは抽象絵画の制作を開始。1994年に55歳で亡くなるまでに1,200点以上を制作したと言われ、関西の美術館を中心に多くの作品がコレクションされている[*1]。

　しかしながら、木下を代表する1970年代の写真作品の評価や研究に比べて、1980年以降の絵画作品を含む総合的な検証は未だ為されていない。加えて、彼女の作品が、どのような思考のもと生み出され、そして変化していったのかも、詳らかにされていない。再び注目されつつある本作家の位置づけを、近年新たに発見された作品や資料と照らし合わせながら、再考するべき時が来ているのではないだろうか。

　本稿では、展覧会「没後30年 木下佳通代」に出品される作品を軸に、当時の展評や作家の言葉を手がかりにしながら、時系列に作家像を再検証していく[*2]。

1. 1939–1962

木下佳通代は1939年、兵庫県神戸市林田区(現・長田区)で建具店を営む両親のもとに長女

Fig. 1
《題不詳》制作年不詳|サイズ不詳
油彩, カンヴァス|個人蔵

Fig. 2
京都市立美術大学(当時)での様子
撮影年・撮影者不明

Fig. 3
《題不詳》1964年|サイズ不詳|水性ペン

として生まれた。幼い頃から絵を描くのが好きだった木下は、よく港を訪れては舟の絵を描いていたという*3。親和学園親和中学校2年生で油絵具のセットを購入してもらい、美術部に入部。当時、題材に選んでいたのは身近な人物や風景が多い。母や妹、友人をよく描いていた [Fig. 1]。同時にバレーボール部やコーラス部でも活動するなど、様々なものに関心を持っていた様子がうかがえるが、早くから美術の道に進むことを決心するなど*4、後年作品にも垣間見える芯の強さは、すでに持ち合わせていたようだ。高校でも美術部に属し、この頃に最初の配偶者となる河口龍夫と出会っている*5。1958年、京都市立美術大学（現・京都市立芸術大学）の西洋画科に入学 [Fig. 2]。黒田重太郎や須田国太郎らに師事している。在学中の1960年、グループ展に参加*6。記録として残る最初の展覧会参加である。同展に出品されたかどうかは分からないものの、同年に描かれた《題不詳 / む76》(cat.no.1) には、アカデミックな画風が見て取れる。

2. 1962-1969

大学を卒業した1962年には、植物をモチーフとした抽象画を描き始める。やや暗い画面に、植物の茎、葉、蔦などを思わせる形が描かれている。「最初のころは、地面・地球の中へどんどん関心をよせていってその中にある生命体を描こうとしていた。次に、植物の形を借りて、その生命体が自在に存在する・出来るというメッセージを絵にし始めました」*7とするこの時期の作品にはすでに、木下が生涯テーマにする「存在」への関心が滲んでいる。若くして宇宙の「境界と無限」を看取した早熟だった木下は、目に見える世界を再現的に描くのではなく、見えないものへと関心を向ける。1963年、京都アンデパンダン展に参加した記録が残るが、作品のタイトルしか分からない*8。同年に制作された作品が確認できないため、作風の変化に謎は残るが、1964年に制作されたとされる作品 [Fig. 3] には、小さな円が画面上に多数描かれている。《無題》(1962年、cat.no.7) にも見られる表現で、植物の雌しべや花被、あるいは蕾の断面を思わせる。この画風がその後どのように変化していったのかは不明である。

　前衛美術集団・グループ〈位〉*9 が結成された1965年は、木下にとって大きな変化を伴う1年だった。当時夫だった河口や、グループ〈位〉の活動に協力する。木下はグループの活動を「自分の一部として考えてやって」きたと晩年振り返っており、その影響は「強かった」と述べる*10。メンバーにこそ加わらなかったものの、そこで交わされた「存在」についての議論は木下にとっても肯定できるものであったという。しかし、この時期の作品については記録がほぼ残っておらず、グループ〈位〉がどう彼女の作品に影響を与えたかは、定かではない。1966年に神戸のウィンナ画廊で初の個展を開催したという情報が年譜に記録されている限りで、当時は生活が大変だったとも語られているが*11、1965年から1970年までの作品について詳しいことは分からない。

3. 1970 / 境界の思考

奥田善巳と再婚した1970年、作風はがらりと変わり、直方体や矩形を用いた作品が登場する。立体を描いたはずの線が、透視図法的な消失点に至る前に別の線や面に変わってしまう。画面上で二次元と三次元の境界を曖昧にさせる本シリーズは「境界の思考」(cat.nos. 8-13) と名付けられた。そのうちのAからCをジャパン・アート・フェスティバルに、DからFの3点を毎日現代美術展[12]に応募したと思しき裏貼りが残る。親交の深かった植松奎二によれば、これらの作品は選外となり、その後は発表されていない。資金がなく画廊を借りられなかった木下は、あらゆるコンクールに出したがほとんど落選したとも語っている[13]。なお、タイトルは《無題》となっているが、同じスタイルの作品 [Fig. 4] を1971年3月の京都アンデパンダン展に出品している[14]。

4. 1971 / 滲触 (Saturation)

1971年の京都アンデパンダン展のあと、図形を描いた作品から、グリッド上に朧げな輪郭を持った単色の塗りを見せる作品に変わる。1970年の「境界の思考」シリーズの示すものが二次元と三次元の境界であったとすれば、「滲触 (Saturation)」と名付けられたこのシリーズ[15]は、グリッドが持つ精緻な二次元平面と、濃淡のある色彩が備える質量や空間によって境界はぼかされている。「滲触」は、制作から年を跨いだ1972年2月、東京のシロタ画廊[16]にて行った奥田との二人展で発表された。主に50号から100号までのカンヴァスで約20点が制作された[17]。「滲触」でものにした表現を木下自身は好んでいた[18]ものの、このシロタ画廊での展示と同年7月のギャラリー16での個展[19]で発表したのみで、以降は制作していない。当時、「方眼紙のアミ目を拡大したような線条が画面の前景にあり、その奥に青い浮き雲やシミを思わすフォルムが手仕事の跡を残す。手描きによるウエットな"抽象風景"に、無表情のアミ目をかぶせることによって生じる心理的ゆらぎ」[20]と評されたが、こうした反応を木下は「叙情的にとられた」と感じ、「我慢できなかった」[21]のかもしれない。これらはそのほとんどが所在不明となっていたが、本展のための調査によりロール状になって保管されていた6点が遺族のもとから発見された[22]。1年と少しという短い期間の制作であるが、1970年代の写真への転換点であると同時に、1980年以降の平面作品に現れる色面との共通性などを鑑みても、重要な初期作品である。

Fig. 4
《境界の意識》あるいは《無題》1971年
油彩, カンヴァス | 116.0×91.0 cm
1971年3月京都アンデパンダン展での展示風景
—
Fig. 5
《Wall》あるいは《壁面》1973年
紙・セロハン紙 | サイズ不詳
1973年2月京都アンデパンダン展での展示風景

Fig. 4

Fig. 5

これらの発表と並行して立体作品も多数制作した*²³。セロハン3000枚を使って「存在」を表現した*²⁴作品は、1973年の京都アンデパンダン展で発表された《Wall》[Fig.5]*²⁵や、1977年にギャラリーキタノサーカスで発表されたアクリル板やテープなどによる「Installation」のシリーズ（pp.102-103）など、透過する素材の選択や、平面作品での実践の立体的な展開にも共通性がある。展示ごとに異なるアプローチに挑戦しているため、当時、毎年のように作風が変わる移り気な作家と捉えられたかもしれない。しかしながら、みずからに課したテーマにあまりにも忠実に、最適な表現方法を忙しく試行する作家だったとも言える。

---

5. 1972-1973 / 写真作品

1971年、奥田とともに自宅の1階に絵画教室アートルーム・トーア*²⁶をオープンする。それ以前にも、奥田と二人で喫茶店*²⁷を経営していた時期があり、喫茶店や絵画教室のある自宅に集った作家も多かったようだ。トアロードに拠点を構えてから、写真の表現に移行していく。その経緯をたどりつつ、現れる疑問を紐解いていくことにする。

　1973年の京都アンデパンダン展の次に木下が出品しているのは、同年のギャラリー16での個展である。出品作は《Untitled / む38（花時計）》（cat.no.19）のみだったが、ここで2つの疑問が生じる。第一に、木下に対して語られてきた「70年代は写真の表現を行い…」という定型句の起点をどこに設定するべきなのかということ。もう一つは、果たして本作が制作・発表された最初の写真作品なのかということである。

生前のインタビューでは以下のようなやり取りがある。（p.207）

　　越智：1972年のギャラリー16の仕事は？
　　木下：71年のシリーズだったかもしれない。その頃までは油彩をやっていて、（…）その時期に、京都の若い男性の作家が何人か集まってグループで仕事をしないかと、誘われたから、[奥田と]二人で話し合って、何かプランを考えてそれを持って人を集めようかという事にしました。私は、自分で自分のコンセプトで写真のプランを作ったんですが、7-8人集めた中でひとり、女性は入れたくないという事が私のところに伝わって、それなら結構ですと断りました。それで、作家ではなくて、自分の友人を10人集めて、協力してもらいました。グループで協力して出来るプランだったので、とにかく10人必要で、その方法として写真を使うことを考え付いたんです。（…）

「71年のシリーズ」と彼女が呼ぶのは「滲触」のことで間違いない*²⁸。しかし、その後の流れで説明される、10人の協力が必要という作品は、この「花時計」であろう。《Untitled / む38（花時計）》は、当時神戸のシンボルでもあった花時計*²⁹の前にカメラを三脚に立て、そ

れを撮影していくというものだが、木下を含む10人が代わる代わる時間を空けてシャッターを切っていく。その姿を同時に撮影するというもので、友人らと撮影した10枚と、その様子を木下が収めた10枚の合計10組・20点の組み合わせとなる作品である。撮影者それぞれの視界で捉えた世界は個別に存在しているが、撮影者をさらに同時に撮ることによって、個々人が同一の世界線に存在していることをメタに表現していると言える[30]。このプランについて「とにかく10人必要で、その方法として写真を使うことを考え付いた」[31]と木下は話しているが、であれば制作年からこれに先行すると考えられてきた1972年作《Untitled-a / む102（本数冊）》(cat.no.17)と《Untitled-b / む103（壁のシミ（ブロック））》(cat.no.18)は、一体どのような目的で、どのようなタイミングで制作されたのか。最初期の写真作品である2点は、1974年に京都市美術館で開催された「シグニファイング、言語、事物 / 態度の表明とともに」展[32]の出品作だが[33]、なぜ制作から発表まで2年も空いているのか。その理由については、本作を焼き付けた植松奎二の言葉によって明らかになった。植松いわく、この2点はジャパン・アート・フェスティバルに出品するために制作されたと言う[34]。落選後、1974年の出品まで保管されていたと考えられる[35]。

　再び《Untitled / む38（花時計）》の話に戻る。この時点ですでに、「存在」が現実世界で持つ時間的な拘束を逆手にとった「同一性と差異」という構図を、写真というメディアの特性を活かして制作したのが分かる。「自分が伝えたいメッセージが平面の油彩画よりもイージーに伝わった」[36]という木下は、1973年のギャラリー16での個展を経て、そこから写真を用いた作品の制作を本格化させていくのである[37]。

　1974年の活動も非常に興味深い。上述した「シグニファイング、言語、事物 / 態度の表明とともに」展は11月に開催された展覧会であるが、同年、木下は京都と東京で1回ずつ個展を開催。加えて、京都にあったギャラリーシグナムで2つのグループ展にも参加した[38]。開催順[39]に出品作品を検証していく。

6. 1974 / 映像作品

1974年1月に参加したギャラリーシグナムでの「PHOTO / ARTS −方法としての写真−」は、写真を用いてコンセプチュアルな表現に取り組んでいた作家によるグループ展であった。ここで発表された《Untitled / む59（腕時計）》(cat.no.20)は、腕時計を写した5枚の写真からなる作品だ。時計の針は5枚とも同じ時刻を示しているが、日付が異なっている。時計を介して時間の経過を知ることはできるが、「時間」そのものを見ることは誰にもできない。知覚することと見ることの違いを表現した作品である。この展覧会への参加と並行して、木下はギャラリー16で個展も開催している[40]。個展では《Untitled / む60（ビーカー）》(cat.no.21)を発表。これも同様に、温度計によって温度変化を見ることはできるが、「温度」そのものを見ることはできない。「存在の中に時間も入ってくるし、時間そのものが存在であ

る」*41と言うように、「存在」を表現するにあたり、「時間」を直接的に扱うようになっていく。4月には再びギャラリーシグナムで「ヴィデオ / 京都 / 1974」展に参加。ここで初めて、そして唯一の映像作品《題不詳》(cat. no. 23)を発表する。カメラの画角に収まる範囲に、オブジェが一点ずつ置かれていき、ピークを越して一点ずつ取り除かれていく様子が淡々と写っている。物が一点もない空間から始まり、画面が埋め尽くされた後、何もない空間へと戻っていく。物が置かれて取り除かれた時間とその事実によって、映像の最初と最後の空間は、映像上は同一の空間に見えるが、異なるものであると言える*42。映像作品の発表は生涯でこの1点のみであったが、同年9月の村松画廊の個展で映像作品から展開した写真作品《む61（物の増加と減少）》(cat. no. 22)*43を発表している。

7. 1975–1976 / シルクスクリーン

1975年にはシルクスクリーンによる作品を試行する。同一のイメージを十数点刷り出したものに、目で認識したものから順にフェルトペンで塗り込んでいく《無題》(cat. no. 24)をギャラリー16の個展*44で発表。その後、村松画廊の個展*45では、1枚に同じ写真を複数刷り、フィルムのコマ送りを想起させる映像的*46な表現 (cat. nos. 26-34) を採っている。シルクスクリーンをフェルトペンで塗りつぶし、視点を「増加」させる作品はこの1年のみの展開であったが、1976年からは、「存在」を表現するにあたり時間ではなく、より構造的な視点の取り方へと発展していくことになる。

　1976年2月、木下はギャラリー16の個展*47でシルクスクリーンによる作品ではなく、再び写真作品を発表。ビデオフィードバックを思わせる《Untitled (Some profile or some consciousness)》(cat. no. 35) や、カメラのフォーカスをずらすことによって、視覚の移動を強制的に起こさせる組写真が展示された [Fig. 6]。より三次元の空間へと意識が向けられている*48。認識の恣意性や限界をめぐるアプローチである。ただ、人間の視覚はレンズやビデオとは異なるため、あまりに比喩的で、すぐに別の手法へ移ったのも頷ける。以降、写真を用いる若い作家が増えてきたこともあって、CHペーパーにフェルトペンで加筆する作品へ移っていく。同年に制作されたフォトコラージュの《む36》(cat. no. 36) などは、翌1977年に高橋亨が企画した「自画像 '77」*49に出品された*50。

Fig. 6
木下佳通代個展（1976年、ギャラリー16、京都）展示風景
左 |《む64（家と木）》1976年｜CHペーパー、5点組
右 |《む63》1976年｜CHペーパー、5点組
いずれもサイズ不詳、個人蔵

8. 1977-1983 / 「存在」そのものを描くまで

CHペーパーにフェルトペンで加筆する作品群は、円や三角などの図形を描くところを撮影し、さらにその印画紙の上に同じ図形を同サイズで描き直すというものだ。例えば、写真の被写体としては楕円に見える円も、認識の中では正円として「存在している」。こうした視覚と認識のズレを図式的に示すことで、木下は「存在」に近づこうとした[*51]。1977年には同手法を発展させ、写された紙と印画紙との差異をも扱うようになる。それにあたり、物理的な紙の折れやシワ、歪みなどがより彼女の意図に合致したようだ。同年の「第13回現代日本美術展」[*52]で《作品 '77-D》(cat.no.48)が兵庫県立近代美術館賞を受賞する。コンテストに応募しては落選してきた初期のことを思えば、やっとという思いはあったであろう[*53]。1978年には、その差分を示すものとして、線が用いられるようになった。また、そのズレを色によっても表現するようになる。この線や折り、色との関係性は80年代の紙作品、そしてパステルによる絵画へと繋がっていく。

　1977年から1979年にかけては京都・神戸に限らず多くの個展[*54]、グループ展に参加している。特筆すべきは、1977年に神戸のギャルリーキタノサーカスで行われた個展[*55]であろう。この個展は、初期に立体作品も作っていたという木下の姿が垣間見えるという意味でも貴重である。「Installation '77」と題し、AからFまでの6点を出品[*56]。アクリル板と紙、テープを用いて、平面上で行っている認識のズレを空間で展開しようとした。これらに関するプランドローイングが多数残されており、発表したインスタレーション以外にも、やや大掛かりな作品を構想していたことがうかがえる[*57]。1978年にもう1点だけアクリル板を用いた《'78-A》[Fig.7]を出品しているが、それ以降はこのタイプの作品を発表していない[*58]。

　1979年に入ると、線を引いて平面性を意識させるものから、印画紙と撮影された紙のズレ、それを指し示す色面が前面に現れるようになる。ムラなく画面を作るために、フェルトペンではなくアクリル絵具を用いている。また、折った紙を撮影し、それを印画紙と重ねることでズレを認識させていた手法から、実際に折った紙そのものに着色する「fold」シリーズへと発展していく。1980年の京都アンデパンダン展ではすでにこのシリーズが展示されている[Fig.8]。こうした折りの作品を写真に収めた上で、印画紙と対照するのではなく、ドローイングとして元の形を描き加える《Ph '80-5》(cat.no.70)などの作品もある。これらの折りは感覚的に試しながら作られたのではなく、計算されて作られた[*59]。「fold」シリーズは1979年から1980年にかけて制作されるが、折った紙を開いたときにできる裂け

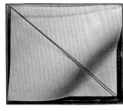

Fig. 7

Fig. 8

Fig. 7
《'78-A》1978年 | 紙・ビニールテープ・アクリル板
21.0×25.5×3.5 cm

Fig. 8
左 | 《Pa-fold '80-22》1980年
鉛筆・アクリル、紙 | 96.5×187.5 cm
1980年3月京都アンデパンダン展での展示風景

目に線を引くことで、画面を二重化する効果を狙った。この線はパステルで引かれるようになり、やがて描線から塗り込みへ変わる。紙を折ることからだんだんと離れ、《Pa-C '80-111》(cat.no.84)のように、パステルの色面と画面をジグザグに切る線の共存が、描かれたズレを引き受ける。この頃には、より柔らかく色を平面に浸透させるべくパステルを用いるようになった*60。そして、色や線そのものの構成によって画面を作る抽象絵画へと大きく切り替わっていくのである。1981年にはついに、油彩作品に回帰した。パステルで捉えた色と線の展開を、油彩でも取り組もうとしたのである。このパステルから油彩へ移行した直後の作品は、同年の京都アンデパンダン展 [Fig. 9]、第7回汎瀬戸内現代美術展 (p.212)などで発表され、翌1982年の京都アンデパンダン展まで続く [Fig. 10]。しかし、彼女の作品の変遷を考える上で一つの契機となるこの時期の作品は、1983年6月に起きたアトリエの火災により、そのほとんどが焼失してしまった*61。

9. 1981–1982 / ハイデルベルク

作品の転換を考えるにあたり、時を少し遡る。線から色へ、パステルそして油彩へと向かう1981年には、木下にとって非常に重要な展示があった。植松奎二の紹介もあり、ハイデルベルク・クンストフェラインで個展を開催したのである。当時すでに写真や紙の作品から油彩による抽象絵画に関心は移りつつあったが、同館の館長ハンス・ゲルクが評価したのは、旧作である写真作品だった。思うところはあったようだが、最終的には方向性の違う作品を混在させず、1976年から1980年の作品を総括する展覧会となった。この展覧会を開催するにあたり、木下はただ声がかかるのを待っていたわけではない。展覧会を実現するために、様々な海外の美術関係者へ送った交渉の書簡が残されている。当時デュッセルドルフに在住していた植松の助力もあるが、本人のこうした働きかけが大きかったに違

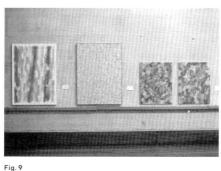

Fig. 9

Fig. 11

Fig. 10

Fig. 9　一番左 |《Ca-C '81-3》1981年 | 油彩, カンヴァス | 130.0×97.0 cm
　　　　1981年3月京都アンデパンダン展での展示風景

Fig. 10　《Ca-C '81-13》1981年 | 油彩, カンヴァス | 162.2×130.3 cm
　　　　1982年3月京都アンデパンダン展での展示風景

Fig. 11　1977年 | ドクメンタ6、フリデリチアヌム美術館の前にて

いない。木下は欧米での日本人作家の境遇や評価を嘆いており*62、その扉を開くべく世界中の美術関係者に書簡を送ったとも考えられる。1982年の書簡では、同時代の動向であるニューペインティングの流行に驚きつつ、「私自身はあまり肯定的ではない」と記している。以前から海外の動向には関心があったのか、1977年にドクメンタ6を訪れている[Fig.11]。

　ハイデルベルクでの展示を経て、1983年のレンバッハハウス美術館クンストフォルムでの展覧会の話も立ち上がったが、予算の都合で白紙となってしまった*63。この展覧会のために、ハイデルベルクで実現できなかった新作を構想していたことが書簡や写真からも見えてくる[Fig.12, 13]。木下は、線と色による1981年から1982年にかけての絵画を、インスタレーションとして発展させようとしていたのだ*64。

---

10. 1982−1994 / 油彩への回帰、ロサンゼルス、絶筆

パステルから油彩へ転換するにあたり、一種の行き詰まりを覚えたところに、ハイデルベルクでの展示、ミュンヘンでの企画の頓挫などが重なった。「存在」に対する考え方に自由をなくしつつあり、別の方法を模索する必要があった木下は、「存在」を表現するコンセプトを変えずに、手法を変えることで新しい表現にたどり着く。その記念すべき作品が《'82-CA1》(cat. no.90)である。筆で描いた画面を布で拭うことで、カンヴァスの持つ平面性と、絵具によって描かれる平面性を等価にする試みである。1983年に制作された《'83-CA74》(cat.no.94)や《'83-CA77》(cat.no.95)は、カンヴァスの面に対して絵具による面が斜めに傾き、1978年頃の作品を思わせるようなズレが見られる。1984年から1985年にかけては、拭き取りによる表現が線のような効果を持ち始め、塗り込みと拭き取りの関係性が逆転し始める。

　瀑布を思わせる表現がピークに達したこの時期、木下は奥田善巳とともに、自身最大の作品《'86-CA323》(cat.no.105)に取り組むことになる。この作品は、大阪のAD&Aによるコミッションワークとして実現した。AD&Aは、同志社大学ラーネッド記念図書館に設置する目的で二人に作品を依頼したのである。同図書館が改修される2017年頃まで多くの学生を見守ってきた本作は、「森下調査」で確認されて以降、長らく同大学の別キャンパスに移動され、非公開となっていた。今回、本展のための調査で所蔵者が代わっていることが判明し、作品の修復が行われた[Fig.14]*65。様々な彩度の青を用いて、空気遠近法的な効果で奥行きを表現した本作は、初期の「滲触」を思い出させる。

Fig.12　　　　　　　　　Fig.13　　　　　　　　　Fig.14

Fig.12　1982年11月25日付｜ヘルムート・フリーデル宛の書簡

Fig.13　レンバッハハウス美術館クンストフォルムのためのマケット（1982年）

Fig.14　作品修復は横田雅人氏（有限会社一風堂）が担当した

1986年から1987年にかけては、1980年以降画面を「塗り込んできた」色面は後退していく。《'86-CA350》(cat.no.107)のように、段々と筆致が強調されるようになる。色彩については《'86-CA358》(cat.no.108)のように色の明暗の前後関係を逆転させて、表現の違いを検証している。1988年に入ると「塗り込む」表現は完全に筆によるストロークを見せる描き方に変化した。制作スピードは加速度的で、1990年にはすでに《'82-CA1》から数えて600点以上を制作している。作家としての新しい扉を開き、その表現の技術開発が最高潮に達した1990年9月、木下は乳がんの告知を受けることになる。発見された時にはがんは進行しており、手術をしても助からない可能性があると知った木下は、外科手術以外の治療を希望し、治療法を求めて各地の病院を訪ねるようになる。1991年、知人を頼ってロサンゼルスに渡り、いくつかの病院を訪ねた。翌92年には約半年にわたってロサンゼルスに滞在し、様々な民間療法を試しながら現地でも制作を行った。この時期の作品が《LA '92-CA681》(cat.no.120)などのLAシリーズである。日本とは異なる環境に影響を受け、作品が持つ空気感も軽やかなものとなった[66]。帰国後も制作を止めず、ロサンゼルスと行き来しながらの生活であったが、1994年9月19日に神戸アドベンチスト病院のホスピスでその55歳の生涯に幕を下ろした。病床で描いた《無題(絶筆・未完)》(cat.no.133)は、1982年以降の制作において800作目にあたる。もし完成してタイトルが付けられていれば、「'94-Pa800」となっていたのだろうか[67]。

11. タイトルとサイズ

以上、木下の作家活動を時代順につぶさに振り返った。しかしながら、未だいくつかの疑問が残る。初期作品のタイトルはそのほとんどが不明である。「境界の思考」は作品裏面に残るコンテストへの応募票に依拠している。続く「境界の意識」「Saturation」は木下が整理した資料を参照した。1972年以降の写真作品においては「無題」「Untitled」「UNTITLED」「untitled」などの表記揺れが、作家が残した資料内でも散見される。コンセプチュアルな試みそのものがタイトル代わりになることもあり、それほどタイトルに拘ってはいなかったのかもしれない。制作年については、1976年以降「制作年－制作順」で表記されている。1976年はアルファベット順、1977年はAからZまで作られた後、足りなくなったのかその後は数字で「27」からカウントを進めている。1978年はすでに1作目から《'78-1》(cat.no.57)と数字によるカウントになった。1979年も同様であるが、制作順の後ろにアルファベットが付記されるケースがある。これはどうやらプリント順であり、サイズの異なるバリエーションとして制作されたものにアルファベットが付記されている。1979年は別のタイトルのルールも見受けられる。《Pa-fold '79-21》(cat.no.66)のように「支持体－加工－制作年－制作順」のような表記である。「Pa」は紙(Paper)、「Ph」は写真(Photograph)であり、「fold」は折りのことを指す。1982年以降の絵画については「制作年－支持体－制作順」となる。《'82-

CA1》以降、制作年が変わっても制作順はリセットされず通番になり、1994年の799まで制作された。「CA」はカンヴァス(Canvas)、「LA」は制作地のロサンゼルスのことのようだ。ひとつ表記ルールを読み取れないのは《Pa-C '80-99》(cat.no.83)などのパステル作品に入る「C」である。同系の各作品に共通しているのは、塗り込みの境目がジグザグに画面を裂いていることであり、「Cut」のCと考えられる。そして最大の謎は「む」で始まるタイトルである。これは晩年、病床で木下自身がまとめた作品ファイルに登場し、1962年以前の作品にまで付されている。「む」は恐らく、「無題」の「む」なのではないかと考えられる。ただ、制作時期の近い《ビーカー》と《花時計》の間に20番以上の開きがあることから、制作順とは異なるルールが存在すると思われる。

　また、十分に調査できなかったのが、1982年以降に絵画と並行して制作された水彩作品である。本展ではわずかに《'89-Pa537》(cat.no.113)と《無題(絶筆・未完)》(cat.no.133)を紹介するのみに留まるが、1984年以降の制作の通番を考えると、かなりの水彩作品が1994年までに制作されている。どうやら木下は、メディウムが変わっても作品の精度を下げないための検証を、制作を重ねながら行っていたと推測される。ほとんどの水彩作品にタイトルが与えられていることから、油彩作品のためのエスキースやアイデアドローイングではなく、自律した作品としての実践的検証だったことは判断がつき易い。実際、水彩作品と油彩及びアクリル絵具による作品の画面構成に差は少なく、メディウムと支持体が異なるにもかかわらず、支持体の平面とメディウムの生む面を等価に扱う表現が成立している。また、これは作品サイズの検証にも関係する。木下は《'85-CA267》(cat.no.103)や《'91-CA645》(cat.no.118)のような、極端に小さい作品も多数制作している[68]。これもまた、表現がサイズによって成立しているものではないことを示す実践的検証である。70年代の制作に使用したメモや折りの幅を試した資料からも、デッサンや下絵はそれとして分類されていることが分かる。そこからも、これら小さな絵画も、れっきとした1点ずつの作品であると分かる[69]。

12. むすび

木下佳通代の制作遍歴をたどりながら、どのような実践を重ねてきたかを確認してきた。なかでも、これまでの評価から零れ落ちてきた1971年の「滲触」シリーズや、1974年の映像作品の詳細が判明したことは大きな前進であり、その他の初期作品を理解する手立てとなる。加えて、1983年に焼失したと考えられてきた1981年作の油彩と思われる作品の発見によって、写真から絵画への転換点が唐突なものではなく、彼女が一貫して認識の問題に取り組んだ結果として自然に生じたことが明らかになった。一方で、作家の交友関係や、彼女が用いる「存在」という言葉の定義が年代ごとに変化している点については、引き続き調査・検証が必要であると言える。しかしながら、本展によって、これまで作品単位でしか捉えられなかった木下佳通代の作家活動が、一つの総体として浮かび上がったのではないだろうか。

*1 森下明彦「木下佳通代作品保存プロジェクト」報告書 (2017年、以降「森下調査」とする)による。

*2 その他、本稿は『木下佳通代 1939−1994』(1996年、AD&A発行)と、「森下調査」を基礎資料としている。

*3 令妹の玉田美智子氏への聞き取り調査による。当時のスケッチも現存する。

*4 木下佳通代・越智裕二郎・竹村楊子 (1994年)「インタビュー」『木下佳通代 1939−1994』、p.92

*5 熊田司編、年譜『木下佳通代 1939−1994』、p.96

*6 グループ〈ケゴ〉展 (会期及び木下以外の参加作家不明、京都書院画廊、京都)

*7 木下佳通代・越智裕二郎・竹村楊子 (1994年)、前掲書 (前掲記事)、p.91

*8 『京都アンデパンダンの20年 出品目録集』(1978年、京都市美術館)より。《植物界》及び《樹液》の2点を出品している。

*9 神戸在住の井上治幸、奥田善巳、河口龍夫、武内博州、豊原康雄、中田誠、向井孟、村上雅美、良田務によって結成された前衛美術のグループ。1960年代から70年代にかけて活動。兵庫県立美術館で2004年に開催された『小企画 グループ〈位〉展』カタログに詳しい。

*10 木下佳通代・越智裕二郎・竹村楊子 (1994年)、前掲書 (前掲記事)、p.92

*11 木下佳通代・越智裕二郎・竹村楊子 (1994年)、前掲書 (前掲記事)、p.92

*12 毎日新聞社が主催していた選抜美術展。1963年に国立近代美術館京都分館 (当時)で始まった「現代美術の動向」展とともに若手前衛作家の活躍の場だったとされる。坂上しのぶのwebサイトに詳しい (https://shinobusakagami.com/、2024年3月21日閲覧)。

*13 木下佳通代・越智裕二郎・竹村楊子 (1994年)、前掲書 (前掲記事)、p.91

*14 本作のタイトル《無題》は、後年に木下自身によってリネームされたと考えられる。同1971年の京都アンデパンダン展のパンフレットには《境界の意識》という作品名が確認できる。木下によるリネームは何度か行われた形跡があり、晩年にまとめられた資料には本作について《む84》というタイトルでも確認できる。

*15 このシリーズ名を日本語でどのように表記するか不明だったが、今回『三彩 1972年4月号』の展評に「滲触」と付記されていることが判明した。なお、作家は晩年のインタビューでも作品ファイルでも一貫して「Saturation」としている。

*16 「奥田善巳・木下佳通代展」(1972年2月7日−13日、シロタ画廊、東京)

*17 作家本人が残した作品ファイルによる (以降、「作家ファイル」とする)。作品タイトルに付されたナンバリングによって19点まで確認できる。

*18 熊田司編、年譜『木下佳通代 1939−1994』、p.96

*19 木下佳通代個展 (1972年7月11日−16日、ギャラリー16、京都)

*20 1972年7月14日京都新聞朝刊

*21 木下佳通代・越智裕二郎・竹村楊子 (1994年)、前掲書 (前掲記事)、p.92

*22 そのうちの1点が本展に際して修復され、展示される。

*23 木下佳通代・越智裕二郎・竹村楊子 (1994年)、前掲書 (前掲記事)、p.91

*24 木下佳通代・越智裕二郎・竹村楊子 (1994年)、前掲書 (前掲記事)、p.91。どのような作品かは写真などが残っていないため不明である。

*25 タイトルは晩年の作家ファイルに依る。1973年京都アンデパンダン展のパンフレットでは《壁面》となっている。

*26 熊田司編、年譜『木下佳通代 1939−1994』、p.96

*27 店名は「喫茶モア」。当時の建物が神戸市内に現存する。建物内には奥田善巳による壁画があると言われているが確認は出来ていない。

*28 1972年7月14日京都新聞朝刊の記述に詳しい。

*29 2019年に東遊園地南側エリアへ移設され、当時の撮影地には現存しない。

*30 1973年8月31日京都新聞朝刊は本作の表現に対し、「… 従来の『写真展』ではなく、一種の存在論を写真という視覚的な媒体によって考えさせるという観念思考の試みだ」としている。

*31 木下佳通代・越智裕二郎・竹村楊子 (1994年)、前掲書 (前掲記事)、p.92

*32 「シグニファイング、言語、事物 / 態度の表明とともに」展 (1974年11月6日−11日、京都市美術館、京都)、元 THE PLAYの水上旬が企画・主催。

*33 木下佳通代・越智裕二郎・竹村楊子 (1994年)、前掲書 (前掲記事)、p.92

*34 植松奎二氏インタビュー (2023年)、本書 p.220

*35 本人は「シグニファイング、言語、事物 / 態度の表明とともに」展に出品したと語るが、ジャパン・アート・フェスティバル応募については触れていない。なお「シグニファイング、言語、事物 / 態度の表明とともに」展への木下の参加は名簿から確認できるものの、管見の限り出品目録は確認できておらず検証が出来ていない。

*36 木下佳通代・越智裕二郎・竹村楊子 (1994年)、前掲書 (前掲記事)、p.92

*37 《Untitled／む38(花時計)》に対しては、『美術手帖 1973年11月号』の展評で平野重光が重要な指摘をしている。外なるものを相対的存在、あるいは客体とできるのは、絶対的対象や認識の総体や最大公約数として観念のなかでのみ成立する存在論であり、「方法論のなかだけで認識論や存在論が試みられるようなコンセプチュアルなやり方」について批判的であった平野であるが、翌年の《ビーカー》が出品された個展については「存在そのものに迫るには、もっと純粋に直覚的な方法をとることが望ましく、その意味では前回の風景写真の方が、もっと直接的であった」(『美術手帖 1974年4月号』)とも論じた。同時に「存在の様態を検証するしかたとして一つの見るべき形式を獲得したこともたしか」と評価している。この後の展開として、自らでシャッターを切ることやめ、外部を対象とするのをやめ、そして絵画の制作に回帰することで主体－客体の関係性に依拠する存在論から離れていったことを踏まえても、木下の方法論を考える上では興味深い。晩年の絵画がメディウム・スペシフィシティにおける等価性と差異を露わにしているのに対して、写真で扱った「見る－見られる」という関係性は後退していることにも関係するだろう。

*38 「PHOTO／ARTS－方法としての写真－」(1974年1月11日－19日)及び「ヴィデオ／京都／1974」(1974年4月28日－5月11日)の2つ。後者は企画に「ビデオひろば」が協力している。

*39 熊田司編、年譜『木下佳通代 1939－1994』、p.96などを参考にした。

*40 木下佳通代個展「『みる』ことについて」(1974年1月15日－20日、ギャラリー16、京都)

*41 木下佳通代・越智裕二郎・竹村楊子 (1994年)、前掲書 (前掲記事)、p.92

*42 本作は、「森下調査」でも言及がある(「おそらく作家が撮影したと推測される既存のスライド写真の、および、わずか1点ですが木下佳通代としては珍しいビデオ作品のデジタル化は完了しました」)。変換されたminiDVには余分な映像が含まれ、どこまでが上映された作品なのかを同定できずにいた。同作を出品した「ビデオ・新たな世界 ― そのメディアの可能性」展(1992年、○美術館、東京)を企画した天野一夫氏の協力により、作品部分が判明した。

*43 村松画廊での発表時は22点組で制作、発表されているが、1点(6枚目)が行方不明となり、現在は21点組で大阪中之島美術館のコレクションとなっている。木下の生前に失われたのか、没後に失われたのかは不明。

*44 木下佳通代個展(1975年2月25日－3月2日、ギャラリー16、京都)

*45 木下佳通代個展(1975年9月8日－14日、村松画廊、東京)

*46 「映像的」と論じたのは藤慶之(『美術手帖 1975年5月号』)。一方、木下自身はこの作品について1994年のインタビューで「一箇所見ることによって色を着けていく、最終的には、全て認識する…(中略)知覚して認識するということで、それを広げていけば存在が増えていくということでもある」とし、存在は認識によって成り立つのではなく、見ようが見まいが同じものとして存在すると述べる。

*47 木下佳通代個展(1976年2月24日－29日、ギャラリー16、京都)

*48 美術評論家・高橋亨は『美術手帖 1976年5月号』で本作で時間の要素が抜かれていることを指摘している。その上で記憶は時間を伴った作用であるとして、写真を用いることが適当か疑問を寄せる。

*49 アート・コア現代美術 '77シリーズ「自画像 '77展」(1977年5月17日－22日、アート・コアギャラリー、京都)。高橋亨による企画。

*50 作品の制作年は、作家ファイルによれば1976年3月である。また「自画像 '77展」に向けて制作されたわけではないことが『木下佳通代 1939－1994』掲載のインタビューからも分かる。

*51 木下佳通代・越智裕二郎・竹村楊子 (1994年)、前掲書 (前掲記事)、p.93

*52 4月28日から5月14日まで東京都美術館で開催され、6月1日から12日まで京都市美術館で開催されている。

*53 1977年6月1日毎日新聞の取材に、受賞に際して「慣れているんです、落選に」と答えているが、心に期するものはあったに違いないと書かれている。

*54 1994年インタビューでも言及のあるギャラリーU(1977年、名古屋)での個展のほか、乾由明の企画による今橋画廊でのドローイング展(1978年、大阪)、靭ギャラリーの個展(1979年、大阪)、ギャラリーウエストベスでのグループ展(1979年、名古屋)などがある。

*55 木下佳通代展(1977年11月1日－12日、ギャルリーキタノサーカス、神戸)

*56 本書pp.102-103を参照。

*57 インタビューには「フランス人が同じ事をしていたのでやめました」とある。また、これらアクリル板を用いた作品を「全て残っている」とする木下だが、2020年の時点ではその所在は不明である。

*58 作家ファイルに残る写真から、1978年12月に酒房ぼんくら(神戸)で開催されたグループ展に出品したのが最後と考えられる。

*59 生前、木下がAD&Aに託した資料群による。本書pp. 122-123など。大阪中之島美術館アーカイブ室蔵。

*60 木下佳通代・越智裕二郎・竹村楊子(1994年)、前掲書(前掲記事)、p.93

*61 木下佳通代・越智裕二郎・竹村楊子(1994年)、前掲書(前掲記事)、p.93。また、1982年10月9日付前野寿邦宛書簡の下書きの文中に「放火ではないかと思われます」と記している。

*62 「ドクメンタやヴェネツィア(・ビエンナーレ)、パリ・ビエンナーレやNYの情報を知ると、日本の位置を思い知らされる」などとある。1982年10月9日付前野寿邦宛書簡の下書きより。

*63 1982年11月25日付レンバッハハウス美術館のキュレーター(当時。後に館長)のヘルムート・フリーデルへの書簡より。展示が取りやめになったことに対して「来年Kunstforumであのプロジェクトを発表するという希望を捨てることは出来ません」として、詳しい理由を問い合わせている。現・マクシミリアンスフォルム。

*64 上記フリーデルへの書簡には、展示したいのはオイルペインティングではなく、会場に合わせたインスタレーション作品であると書かれている。

*65 大阪中之島美術館と成安造形大学、現所蔵者である北川貞大氏(カゴヤ・アセットマネジメント株式会社)の三者により、「作品修復プロジェクト」(2022年8月10日−10月31日、成安造形大学、滋賀)を実施した。

*66 木下佳通代・越智裕二郎・竹村楊子(1994年)、前掲書(前掲記事)、p.95

*67 本作はノマル・エディションの手で版画となり(Ed.120)、没後の偲ぶ会で関係者に配布されている。

*68 一方で、90年代に入ってからは300号の大型作品も制作した。きっかけとして、AD&Aギャラリーが大阪港の巨大なスペースへ移転したことが挙げられる。それ以前は100号を中心としていたが、AD&Aの新たな空間に刺激を受け、より大きな作品にも挑戦した。

*69 「森下調査」(2017年)が指摘するように、「AD」という記号が付されたものがある。確認できる範囲ではこれらには木下のサインがない。これらを本展では資料として扱った。

On "seeing," revisited — Works and practice of Kinoshita Kazuyo

Oshita Yuji Associate Curator, Nakanoshima Museum of Art, Osaka

Introduction

Kobe-based Kinoshita Kazuyo (1939–1994) was one of the leading postwar artists of the Kansai region. Coming to notice in the 1970s for her geometric expression using photography, from 1982 she began producing abstract paintings. By the time of her death in 1994 at the age of 55, her output numbered over 1200 works, many of which have ended up in collections, chiefly those of museums in her native Kansai.[1]

However in contrast to the appraisal and study of the 1970s photographic works for which Kinoshita is best known, a truly comprehensive survey of her career including her paintings since the 1980s is yet to be completed. The thinking on which her works were based, and which influenced their evolution over the decades, also awaits detailed elucidation. The time has come to examine the more recently discovered works and other relevant materials of this artist whose career is now attracting renewed attention, and to reconsider her place in the Japanese art world.

This essay reexamines the figure of the artist chronologically, in a discussion revolving round the works in the exhibition "KAZUYO KINOSHITA: A Retrospective," also finding clues in contemporary reviews, and Kinoshita's own words.[2]

1. 1939–1962

Kinoshita Kazuyo was born in 1939, the eldest daughter of a family of joiners in Hayashida-ku (now Nagata-ku) in the city of Kobe, Hyogo Prefecture. Kinoshita loved drawing even as a young girl, and would often go down to the harbor to draw pictures of the ships.[3] In her second year at Shinwa Girls' Junior High School she acquired a set of oil paints and joined the art club. Her early output was dominated by landscapes and portraits of loved ones, her mother, sister, and friends frequent subjects [Fig. 1]. The young Kinoshita also belonged to the school choir and volleyball clubs, so evidently had a wide range of interests, but her early resolve to make a career in art[4] suggests she already possessed the inner strength glimpsed in her later works. She joined the art club again on progressing to high school, around this time also encountering Kawaguchi Tatsuo, who would become her first husband.[5]

In 1958 Kinoshita began studying Western-style painting at the Kyoto City University of Arts [Fig. 2], where her teachers included artists Kuroda Jutaro and Suda Kunitaro. In 1960 while still at university she took part in a group show[6] that would be her first documented exhibition. Though unclear whether it was shown at this exhibition, *Title Unknown / Mu 76* (cat. no. 1), painted the same year, is very much academic in style.

2. 1962–1969

In 1962, the year she graduated from university, Kinoshita began producing botanical-themed abstract paintings, somewhat darkish in tone, featuring forms reminiscent of plant stems and leaves, and vines. Of the works from this period, the artist said, "Early on I was fascinated by the ground and the earth's interior and tried to depict life in there. Then borrowing plant forms, I started imbuing my paintings with the message that those life forms can and do exist freely."[7] These works are already steeped in the concern with "existence" that would become her life-long theme. The intellectually precocious Kinoshita had noted the "boundaries and infinity" of the cosmos while still in her teens, and turned her attention to painting the invisible rather than reproducing what the eye can see. In 1963 she is recorded as taking part in the Kyoto Independents Exhibition, but all we know about the works today is their titles.[8] With no way of identifying works made by her that year, any changes in style also remain a mystery, however a work [Fig. 3] deemed to be from 1964 consists of numerous small circles painted on the canvas. This look is also found in *Untitled*

Fig. 1
Title Unknown, date and size unknown,
Oil on canvas, private collection

Fig. 2
At Kyoto City University of Arts
Date and photographer unknown

Fig. 3
Title Unknown, 1964, size unknown,
Water-based ink

(1962, cat.no.7), and calls to mind the pistils and petals of flowers, or cross-sections of buds. It is unclear how Kinoshita's style of painting changed after this.

1965, when the avant-garde art collective Group "i"**9** was formed, was a transformative year for Kinoshita. She cooperated in the activities of then-husband Kawaguchi, and of Group "i." In later years Kinoshita reflected that she had always thought of the group's activities as part of herself, stating that she was "greatly influenced" by them.**10** Though never a member as such, the group's discussions on questions of existence were, Kinoshita said, something she could readily embrace. Of her own output during this period however there is almost no record, and it is uncertain exactly how Group "i" influenced her works. Mention of a first solo exhibition in 1966 at the Wiener Gallery in Kobe in a career timeline is the sole record from this period, and Kinoshita herself is also on record as saying this was a time when she had her own struggles with making ends meet.**11** The fact is that little is known of her works between 1965 and 1970.

---

3. 1970 / Boundary Thinking

—

In 1970, the year Kinoshita married for a second time, to Okuda Yoshimi, her art underwent a complete transformation with the appearance of works featuring the likes of oblong solids and rectangles. Lines supposedly depicting solids morph into different lines and planes before heading toward perspective vanishing point. This series blurring the boundary between second and third dimensions on the picture plane was duly titled "Boundary Thinking" (cat. nos. 8-13). Labeling on the back of these works indicates that A to C were entries in the Japan Art Festival, and D to F the Mainichi Contemporary Art Exhibition.**12** According to Uematsu Keiji, a close friend of Kinoshita's, these works did not make the cut in either case, and were never shown again. Kinoshita said that lacking funds to rent gallery space, she entered every competition she could, but was largely unsuccessful.**13** She also submitted a work of the same style [Fig. 4] albeit titled *Untitled*, to the Kyoto Independents Exhibition in March 1971.**14**

Fig. 4
Boundary Consciousness or *Untitled*, 1971,
Oil on canvas, 116.0 × 91.0 cm
Installation view, Kyoto Independents Exhibition
(March, 1971)

—

Fig. 5
Wall or *Hekimen*, 1973,
Paper, cellophane paper, size unknown
Installation view, Kyoto Independents Exhibition
(February, 1973)

Fig. 4

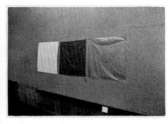

Fig. 5

4. 1971 / Saturation

Following the Kyoto Independents Exhibition in 1971, Kinoshita switched from works depicting mathematical figures, to works featuring soft-edged fields in a single color, on grids. If the "Boundary Thinking" series of 1970 showed the boundary between the second and third dimensions, this series dubbed "Saturation"[15] is about blurring boundaries, expressed by combining the two-dimensional precision of the grid with the mass and space conveyed by color of varying intensity. "Saturation" was unveiled in February 1972, early in the year after its production, at an exhibition staged with Okuda at the Shirota Gallery in Tokyo.[16] Around 20 works were produced in the series, mainly on canvases of No. 50 to 100 in size.[17] Despite Kinoshita herself liking the expression she made her own in "Saturation,"[18] the series was only ever exhibited at this Shirota Gallery show, and a solo outing at galerie 16 in July the same year,[19] and she never returned to it. A reviewer at the time noted, "Striations resembling the enlarged squares of graph paper make up the foreground of the picture plane, behind them blue forms reminiscent of drifting clouds or stains, displaying vestiges of handwork. Placing expressionless grid over aqueous hand-painted, 'abstract landscape' gives these works a psychologically unsettling quality,"[20] but Kinoshita felt a response of this nature pointed to her work being seen as "having a certain lyricism," which to her was "intolerable."[21] The whereabouts of most of these works was unknown until six were found rolled up and stored with Kinoshita's family during research for this exhibition.[22] "Saturation" was only produced for a short time, a little over a year, but its pivotal role in Kinoshita's shift to photography in the 1970s, and the qualities it shares with the color fields that appear in her two-dimensional works from 1980 onward, make it an important early series.

In parallel with these exhibitions of "Saturation," Kinoshita also made numerous sculptural pieces.[23] In the choice of a transparent material, and in its extension to three dimensions of her practice involving two-dimensional works, the object she made using 3000 sheets of cellophane to express "existence"[24] shares much for example with *Wall* [Fig. 5][25] unveiled at the Kyoto Independents Exhibition in 1973 and the *Installation* series (pp.102-03) made from sheets of acrylic, tape etc. exhibited in 1977 at Gallery Kitano Circus. Due to her custom of taking a different approach to each exhibition, back then Kinoshita may have been seen as a capricious artist who changed style almost every year. But she could also be seen as an artist steadfastly true to the theme she had set herself, assiduously searching for the optimal way to express it.

5. 1972—1973 / Photographic works

In 1971 Kinoshita and Okuda opened the painting school Art Room Tor[26] on the ground floor of their home. The couple had previously operated a coffee shop[27] for a time, and this, and their home with the painting school, appear to have attracted a lot of artists. After acquiring the base on Tor Road, Kinoshita transitioned to working with photographs. Tracing the circumstances behind this, we shall unravel any questions that surface along the way.

Kinoshita's next showing of work after the 1973 Kyoto Independents Exhibition was a solo outing at galerie 16 the same year. This consisted solely of *Untitled / Mu 38 (Flower Clock)* (cat. no. 19), and here two questions arise. The first is, where to fix the starting point for the statement "During the 1970s she worked in photographic expression..." that invariably appears in discussion of Kinoshita. The other is whether *Untitled / Mu 38 (Flower Clock)* was in fact the first photographic work she made and exhibited.

This exchange is from an interview with Kinoshita not long before her death.

> Ochi: How about your work at galerie 16 in 1972?
> Kinoshita: That might have been the series from 1971. Up to then I'd been doing oils... During this period a number of young male artists from Kyoto came together and invited me to work with them as a group, so I discussed this [with Okuda], and we decided to come up with some kind of plan, then take that plan and try to get people together. I put together a plan for photography using my own concept, but on hearing that of the seven or eight who assembled, one didn't want to work with women, I said very well, thanks but no thanks. So instead of artists I assembled ten of my own friends and asked them to help. My plan was one that involved a group working together, and required ten people, so I came up with a method for it using photographs....

The "series from 1971" to which Kinoshita refers can only be "Saturation."[28] However the work requiring cooperation by ten people mentioned later in the course of this exchange, is likely to be her "flower clock." *Untitled / Mu 38 (Flower Clock)* was made by setting up a camera on a tripod in front of the floral clock that was a symbol of Kobe,[29] and photographing it over time, ten people taking turns to press the shutter, with pauses in between. The work involved simultaneously photographing the photographers, and consists of ten sets totaling 20 photos: ten taken of the clock by friends, and ten taken by Kinoshita of the photos being taken. A separate world exists in each photographer's field of vision, but photographing the photographers at the same time could be described as a meta expression of the fact that individuals exist on the same world line.[30] Kinoshita has said of this plan that it "required ten people, and I came up with a method for it using photography,"[31] but this being the case, for what purpose exactly, and when, were 1972's *Untitled-a / Mu 102 (Books)* (cat. no. 17) and *Untitled-b / Mu 103 (Stains on the wall (blocks))* (cat. no. 18) made, going by year of production, preceding *Flower Clock* ? These earliest photographic works[32] appeared in the "Signifying: Language / Thing—with the Manifestation of Attitude" exhibition[33] at Kyoto City Museum of Art in 1974, but why the two-year gap between making and showing? The answer was revealed by Uematsu Keiji, who printed the works. According to him they had been made for the Japan Art Festival,[34] and one suspects that having been rejected, they were put aside until their presentation in 1974.[35]

Returning to *Untitled / Mu 38 (Flower Clock)*, it is evident that by this time, Kinoshita was already making use of the properties of photography as a medium to put together compositions of "identity and difference" that subvert real-world temporal constraints on existence. Noting that the message she wanted to convey was "communicated more readily than with a two-dimensional painting,"[36] following her 1973 solo exhibition at galerie 16 Kinoshita threw herself fully into the production of works using photographs.[37]

Her activities in 1974 are also intriguing. The aforementioned "Signifying" show was staged in November, but in the same year Kinoshita staged one solo exhibition each in Kyoto and Tokyo, adding two group shows at Kyoto's Gallery Signum for good measure.[38] Let us examine the works in these exhibitions, from first to last.[39]

6. 1974 / Work on video

The "Photo / Arts — Photography as method" exhibition Kinoshita took part in at Gallery Signum in January 1974 was a group show by artists engaged in photography-based conceptual expression. Kinoshita's contribution, *Untitled / Mu 59 (Watch)* (cat. no. 20) is a work consisting of five photographs of a watch. The hands on the watch show the same time in each photo, but the dates are different. A timepiece may inform us of the passing of time, but "time" itself is visible to no one. *Untitled / Mu 59 (Watch)* demonstrates the difference between perceiving and seeing. Kinoshita had a concurrent solo show at galerie 16,[40] at which she presented *Untitled / Mu 60 (Beaker)* (cat. no. 21). Here, similarly, the thermometer allows us to see changes in temperature, but "temperature" itself remains unseeable. In her expression of "existence" the artist comes to deal with "time" directly, in accordance with her assertion that "Time is also part of existence, and time itself is existence."[*41] In April, Kinoshita took part in "Video / Kyoto / 1974," once again at Gallery Signum, presenting her first and only work on video, *Title Unknown* (cat. no. 23). Here, objects are shown being placed one by one within the camera's angle of view, then having peaked in number, being removed one by one, all this being documented in matter-of-fact style. The video begins with a space containing nothing whatsoever, and returns to bare space after the screen has been filled. The time taken to place and remove the objects, and the fact of this process, mean that the spaces at the start and finish of the video appear on the video to be the same space, yet the assertion is that they are different.[*42] This was the only video released by Kinoshita during her lifetime, although in September of the same year at a solo outing at the Muramatsu Gallery, she presented the photographic work *Mu 61 (Increasing and decreasing of things)* (cat. no. 22), which evolved out of it.[*43]

---

7. 1975−1976 / Silkscreen

In 1975 Kinoshita experimented with silkscreen works. At a solo exhibition at galerie 16 she presented *Untitled* (cat. no. 24), for which she made a dozen or so prints of the same image, and used felt pens to color in parts in the order that she became aware of them.[*44] Then at a Muramatsu Gallery show[*45] she printed a single photo multiple times onto one sheet, adopting a filmic[*46] mode of expression evoking the frame-by-frame advance of a movie (cat. nos. 26-34). This was the only year in which she colored in silkscreen images to "increase" viewpoints, and from 1976, when it came to expressing "existence" there is a notable shift from the use of time to a more structural way of adopting a viewpoint.

In a solo exhibition at galerie 16 in February 1976,[*47] Kinoshita did not present silkscreen works, but returned to photography, showing *Untitled (Some profile or some consciousness)* (cat. no. 35), which calls to mind video feedback, plus composite photographs that force the vision to move by shifting the camera focus [Fig. 6]. Greater consciousness of three-dimensional space is evident in an approach embracing the arbitrary nature and limits of cognition.[*48] But because human sight is different to a lens or video, matters become so metaphorical here that one can see why Kinoshita quickly switched to a different technique. With the number of young artists employing photography also considerably larger by this point, Kinoshita moved on to adding felt pen annotations to photographs on Mitsubishi CH photographic paper. Works like the photo collage *Mu 36* (cat. no.

36) also made in 1976 were included in the "Self-Portraits '77" exhibtition[49] organized by Takahashi Toru the following year.[50]

8. 1977—1983 / Up to depicting existence itself

The works with felt pen annotations on CH photographic paper were made by photographing drawings of figures such as circles and triangles, then redrawing the same figure in the same size on top of the printed photograph. For example, a circle appearing to be an ellipse as the subject of the photograph also exists in our understanding as a perfect circle. By demonstrating in graphical terms this discrepancy between vision and cognition, Kinoshita attempted to grasp existence.[51] In 1977 she developed this methodology further, starting to deal also with the discrepancy between the paper appearing in the photo, and the photographic paper. When it came to doing this, the physical folding, crinkling and warping of paper seems to have fit her intentions. At the 13th Contemporary Art Exhibition of Japan[52] the same year, *Work '77-D* (cat.no. 48) won her the Hyogo Prefectural Museum of Modern Art Prize. Considering the number of competitions she entered in her early years without success, one can well imagine her feeling it was "about time."[53] In 1978, to show the difference between the two types of paper Kinoshita began using lines. She also began to use color to express these discrepancies. This relationship of lines, folding, and color would lead to her paper works of the 1980s, and paintings in pastels.

In the years 1977 to 1979 Kinoshita took part in numerous solo and group shows, not only in Kyoto and Kobe.[54] Of particular note is the solo exhibition at Kobe's Gallery Kitano Circus in 1977.[55] This show is also valuable in that it offers a glimpse of an earlier Kinoshita who also made three-dimensional pieces, in the form of "Installation '77" consisting of six works labeled A to F.[56] Here she employed sheets of acrylic, paper and tape in an attempt to take the cognitive discrepancies she was working with in two-dimensional form, and unfold them in space. Numerous plan drawings remain of these works, indicating that unsurprisingly, as well as this installation, Kinoshita was contemplating a slight-

Fig. 6
Installation view, "Kinoshita Kazuyo" exhibition
(1976, galerie 16, Kyoto)
Left: *Mu 64 (House and Tree)*, 1976, Photographic paper
(series of five photos)
Right: *Mu 63*, 1976, Photographic paper
(series of five photos)
Both size unknown, private collection

ly larger work.[57] In 1978 she unveiled just one additional work in acrylic, '78-A [Fig. 7], with no more following.[58]

By 1979 there is a move away from drawing lines to draw awareness to two-dimensionality, to a dominance of discrepancy between photographic paper and photographed paper, and using color fields to indicate this. Acrylic paint is used instead of felt pens to achieve a uniform picture plane. There is also a progression from the technique of photographing folded paper and superimposing it on photographic paper to draw attention to the discrepancies between them, to the "fold" series, in which coloring is added to the actual folded paper. This series appears already at the Kyoto Independents Exhibition in 1980 [Fig. 8]. There are also works, such as Ph '80-5 (cat. no. 70) in which having photographed the folded work, rather than contrasting it with the photographic paper, the original forms are drawn on. These folds were not made intuitively, by trying out different approaches, but carefully calculated.[59] The "fold" series was produced during 1979—1980, and by drawing a line in the cleft made when folded paper is opened up, Kinoshita was aiming for a doubling of the picture plane. She began to draw these lines in pastel, and eventually, switch from line drawing to coloring in. There is a shift little by little away from folding paper, to showing the depicted discrepancies by the coexistence of pastel color fields and lines that like Pa-C '80-111 (cat. no. 84) zig-zag across the picture plane. Around this time Kinoshita began using pastels as a way to permeate the plane with softer color.[60] What ensues is a significant switch to abstract painting in which the composition of the actual lines and colors themselves form the picture plane. In 1981, Kinoshita finally returned to oil painting, in an attempt to achieve in oils the development of color and line she had captured in pastels. Works made directly after this shift from pastels to oils were shown the same year at the Kyoto Independents Exhibition [Fig. 9], and at the 7th Pan-Setouchi Contemporary Art Exhibition (p. 259) then in 1982 once again at the Kyoto Independents [Fig. 10]. However most of Kinoshita's works from this transitional period in her art were unfortunately lost in a fire that broke out at her studio in June 1983.[61]

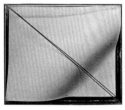

Fig. 7
'78-A, 1978,
Paper, plastic tape, acrylic plate,
21.0 × 25.5 × 3.5 cm

Fig. 8
Left: Pa-fold '80-22, 1980,
Pencil, acrylic on paper, 96.5 × 187.5 cm
Installation view, Kyoto Independents Exhibition
(March, 1980)

Fig. 7   Fig. 8

9. 1981—1982 / Heidelberg

To consider this turning point in Kinoshita's style more closely, let us go back in time a little. 1981, the year she moved from line to color, pastels then oils, was also the year of an extremely important exhibition for Kinoshita: her solo show organized at the Heidelberger Kunstverein (HdKV), in part courtesy of Uematsu Keiji's connections there. By this point Kinoshita's interest was already starting to shift from photographs and paper to abstract painting, but most acclaimed by HdKV director Hans Gercke were her older, photographic works. Though her newer work seems to have been considered, ultimately the exhibition became a survey of works from 1976 to 1980, without any of a different direction mixed in. When it came to staging this exhibition, Kinoshita was not just waiting around to be asked. Surviving correspondence includes negotiations with various art-sector individuals over-seas aimed at bringing an exhibition to fruition. While she did have assistance from Uematsu, who was living in Dusseldorf at the time, such efforts by Kinoshita herself must have played a significant role. Kinoshita lamented the situation and reputation of Japanese artists in the West,[62] and seems to have written to people in the art world, around the world, with the idea of opening international doors. In a 1982 missive, while expressing her surprise at the New Painting (Neo-Expressionism) then current, she notes, "I personally do not feel that positive about it." A 1977 visit to documenta 6 [Fig. 11] perhaps indicates she had been in-terested in overseas trends for some time.

In the wake of the exhibition in Heidelberg, there was talk of a show at the

Fig. 9

Fig. 11

Fig. 10

Fig. 9 Leftmost: *Ca-C '81-3*, 1981, Oil on canvas, 130.0 × 97.0 cm
Installation view, Kyoto Independents Exhibition (March, 1981)

Fig. 10 *Ca-C '81-13*, 1981, Oil on canvas, 162.2 × 130.3 cm
Installation view, Kyoto Independents Exhibition (March, 1982)

Fig. 11 At documenta 6, the Fridericianum, 1977

Lenbachhaus Kunstforum in 1983, but for budget reasons this was dropped.[63] Correspondence and photos suggest that for this exhibition Kinoshita was considering new works she had been unable to present in Heidelberg [Figs. 12, 13], endeavoring to take the color and line paintings of 1981—82, and develop them into an installation.[64]

10. 1982—1994 / Return to oils, Los Angeles, final work

With regard to Kinoshita's transition from pastels to oils, the exhibition in Heidelberg, and setback of the failed plans in Munich, came on top of a feeling of having arrived at a dead end of sorts. Finding her thinking around existence becoming less free, and needing to explore other methods, Kinoshita arrived at a new mode of expression that involved changing technique without changing her concept of expressing existence. That landmark work is '82-CA1 (cat. no. 90), an attempt to make the planarity of the canvas, and planarity rendered by the paints, of equal value by wiping the picture plane painted with a brush. 1983's '83-CA74 (cat. no. 94) and '83-CA77 (cat. no. 95) have the painted surface skewed on the surface of the canvas, the kind of deviation seen in Kinoshita's works from around 1978. During 1984 and 1985 this expression with wiping began to create line-like effects, as the relationship between coloring in and wiping started to be reversed.

During this period, the peak of her waterfall-look paintings, Kinoshita worked with Okuda Yoshimi to make her largest-ever work, '86-CA323 (cat. no. 105). This came about as a commission from AD&A in Osaka, which asked the pair to make a work for installation in the Doshisha University Learned Memorial Library. Seen by thousands of students up to renovation of the library around 2017, after being noted in the "Morishita survey" it was moved to another campus of the university for an extended period, and was not on display. Research for this exhibition revealed a new owner, and restoration work was carried out [Fig. 14].[65] Employing blues of varying saturation, and expressing depth with an aerial-type perspective, '86-CA323 recalls the artist's early "Saturation" series.

Fig. 12

Fig. 13

Fig. 14

Fig. 12   Letter to Helmut Friedel, November 25, 1982

Fig. 13   Maquette for Lenbachhaus Kunstforum (1982)

Essay 1

          Oshita Yuji

Fig. 14   Restoration performed by Yokota Masato of Ippudo Inc.

From 1986 to 1987 the color fields "filling in" the picture plane from 1980 onward retreat and are replaced by a gradual emphasis on brushwork, as in *'86-CA350* (cat. no. 107). In terms of coloring, the light and dark of color contrast are reversed, as in *'86-CA358* (cat. no. 108), proving the emergence of different expression. By 1988 "coloring in" expression had changed completely to a style of painting that showed the strokes of the brush. Production gathered pace, and by 1990 Kinoshita had already produced over 600 paintings since *'82-CA1*.

In September 1990, just as she had opened a new door in her career as an artist and the technical evolution of her expression was at its zenith, Kinoshita was diagnosed with breast cancer. By the time of its discovery the cancer was already advanced, and learning that even surgery might not help, Kinoshita visited different hospitals in the hope of finding a non-surgical treatment. In 1991, with the help of an acquaintance she traveled to Los Angeles, visiting a number of hospitals there. The following year, 1992, she spent six months or so in the city, experimenting with alternative remedies as she continued to paint. These are the LA series works such as *LA '92-CA681* (cat. no. 120). Influenced by an environment different to that of Japan, her works took on a lighter, airier feel.[66] She continued painting on her return home, and subsequently divided her time between Japan and Los Angeles before passing away on September 19, 1994 at the age of 55, at the hospice of Kobe Adventist Hospital. *Untitled (Last work, unfinished)* (cat. no. 133), painted on her sickbed, was her 800th work since 1982. If it had been finished and given a title, that title would likely have been *'94-Pa800*.[67]

11. Titles and sizes

The above is a detailed chronological recounting of Kinoshita's artistic career. Yet a number of questions linger around that career. The titles of most of her early works are unknown. "Boundary Thinking" comes from an entry form for an art contest left on the back of a work. The titles "Boundary Consciousness" and "Saturation" that followed are from material Kinoshita assembled and put in order herself. In the photographic works from 1972 onward, we find scattered through the materials left by the artist various iterations of "Untitled" including "untitled," "UNTITLED" and the Japanese equivalent "無題" (*mudai*). Conceptual experiments in themselves are sometimes used instead of titles, and perhaps the artist was not especially concerned with how she named her works. When it comes to year of production, from 1976 onward works are labeled "year of production – order of production." In 1976 this meant in alphabetical order, and in 1977, once A to Z had been exhausted, continuing with numbers, starting from 27. In 1978, numbers were used right from the first work, *'78-1* (cat.no. 57). The same for 1979, except in some cases letters are added after the order of production. This seems to be the order of printing, with letters added to works made in different size variations. In 1979 another rule for titles can be observed, that of "support–process–year of production–order of production" as in *Pa-fold '79-21* (cat. no. 66). "Pa" stands for paper, "Ph" for photograph, and "fold" is self-explanatory. Paintings from 1982 onward are labeled "year of production–support–order of production." From *'82-CA1* onward, even in different years the order of production is not reset but becomes a serial number, reaching 799 by 1994. "CA" appears to stand for canvas, and "LA" for Los Angeles as location of the production. The only titling rule that remains undeciphered is the "C" in pastel works like *Pa-C '80-99* (cat. no. 83). What these works all have in common is the way the borders of the painted section cut across the picture plane in zig-zag fashion, so the "C" may be thought to represent "Cut."

The biggest mystery of all is the titles that start with "Mu." This makes its appearance in the files of works assembled by Kinoshita herself in her final years when she was ill, and is given to works right back to before 1962. "Mu" is possibly the "mu" of *mudai*. However the gap of over 20 numbers between *Beaker* and *Flower Clock*, which were made close together, suggests the existence of some different rule to that of order of production.

In addition, still not fully researched are the watercolors that were produced in parallel with Kinoshita's paintings from 1982 onward. At this exhibition these are confined to *'89-Pa537* (cat. no. 113) and *Untitled (Last work, unfinished)* (cat. no. 133), but when one considers the serial numbers for production from 1984, quite a number of watercolors emerged in the years up to 1994. One can only speculate that Kinoshita did these as she worked to verify that there would be no loss of precision even in a different medium. Because most of the watercolors have titles, it is easy to conclude that they were not sketches or idea drawings for oil paintings, but autonomous works providing practical verification. In actual fact there are only minor differences in composition between works painted in watercolors, oils, and acrylics, and despite the different mediums and supports, the artist has consistently treated works as equally valid irrespective of differences in the plane of the support or differences generated by the medium. This also applies to her verifications of works of varying sizes. Kinoshita made many tiny works such as *'85-CA267* (cat. no. 103) and *'91-CA645* (cat. no.118), which also serve as practical proof that her expression is not a product of sizes.[68] The notes and materials relating to trying out different folding widths in the 1970s also show that sketches and drafts were categorized as such, further evidence that these little paintings are also proper, individual works.[69]

12. In conclusion

Here we have traced the history of Kinoshita Kazuyo's art production, to identify the journey she took in her practice. It has been particularly satisfying to bring to light details of her 1971 "Saturation" series, for example, and video work of 1974, both of which have hitherto tended to be omitted from appraisals of her work. This new knowledge represents a significant advance, and offers vital clues to understanding other early works. In addition, the discovery of a work thought to be an oil painting from 1981, originally believed lost in the fire of 1983, has revealed that Kinoshita's switch from photographs to painting was no abrupt development but arose naturally as a result of her ongoing engagement with questions of cognition.

There is perhaps a need for further research and verification regarding Kinoshita Kazuyo's relationships, and the fact that her definition of the word "existence" changed with each decade. It would be fair to say though that this exhibition has succeeded in piecing together a holistic picture of an oeuvre hitherto only able to be apprehended work by individual work.

*1   Morishita Akihiko, "Kinoshita Kazuyo sakuhin hozon purojekuto" [Kinoshita Kazuyo works preservation project], report (2017). Hereafter referred to as the "Morishita survey."

*2   In addition, *Kazuyo Kinoshita 1939−1994* (AD&A, 1996) and the "Morishita survey" were used as fundamental sources for this essay.

*3   As told in an Interview with Kinoshita's sister Tamada Michiko; the sketches from this period also still exist.

*4   Kinoshita Kazuyo, Ochi Yujiro, Takemura Yoko, "Interview" (1994), in *Kazuyo Kinoshita 1939−1994*, 92.

*5   Kumada Tsukasa, ed., "Chronology," in *Kazuyo Kinoshita 1939−1994*, 96.

*6   Group "Kego" exhibition (Kyoto Shoin Gallery, exhibition dates and other artists unknown).

*7   Kinoshita, Ochi, Takemura, "Interview" (1994), 91.

*8   According to *Kyoto andepandan no 20-nen shuppin mokuroku* [20 years of the Kyoto Independents Exhibition list of works] (Kyoto City Museum of Art, 1978), the titles of the two works shown were *Shokubutsukai* [Plantae] and *Jueki* [Sap].

*9   Formed by Kobe-resident artists Inoue Haruyuki, Okuda Yoshimi, Kawaguchi Tatsuo, Takeuchi Hirokuni, Toyohara Yasuo, Nakata Makoto, Mukai Takeshi, Murakami Masami, Yoshida Tsutomu; active in the 1960s and 1970s. Details about the group appear in the catalogue to the "Group 'i'" exhibition held at the Hyogo Prefectural Museum of Art in 2004.

*10 Kinoshita, Ochi, Takemura, "Interview" (1994), 92.

*11 Ibid. .

*12 An invitational exhibition sponsored by The Mainichi Newspapers. Along with "Trends in Contemporary Japanese Art" launched in 1963 at The Annex Museum of The National Museum of Modern Art (now The National Museum of Modern Art, Kyoto), said to have been a platform for the creative endeavors of young avant-garde artists. For details see Sakagami Shinobu's website (https://shinobusakagami.com, accessed March 21, 2024).

*13 Kinoshita, Ochi, Takemura, "Interview" (1994), 91.

*14 This work is thought to have been renamed *Untitled* by Kinoshita herself in later years. In the pamphlet for the 1971 Kyoto Independents Exhibition, the work appears as *Boundary Consciousness*. There is evidence that Kinoshita renamed the work several times, and in documents compiled in her later years, this work can also be seen under the title *Mu84*.

*15 This series was identified as "Saturation," using an English term, and no Japanese equivalent had been confirmed until research for the current exhibition revealed that the series had been referred to as *Shinshoku* [in Japanese, meaning "permeation" or "blurring encroachment"] in an exhibition review carried in the April 1972 edition of *Sansai*. The artist consistently used the English title, both in the artist's files and in the Interview conducted late in her life.

*16 "Okuda Yoshimi / Kinoshita Kazuyo" (February 7–13, 1972, Shirota Gallery, Tokyo).

*17 Based on the artist's own files relating to works (hereinafter referred to as "artist's files"). The numbers added to titles provide evidence that there were at least 19 works in the series.

*18 Kumada, "Chronology," 96.

*19 "Kinoshita Kazuyo" solo exhibition (July 11–16, 1972, galerie 16, Kyoto).

*20 *The Kyoto Shimbun*, morning edition, July 14, 1972.

*21 Kinoshita, Ochi, Takemura, "Interview" (1994), 92.

*22 One of the six works was restored on the occasion of and shown at this exhibition.

*23 Kinoshita, Ochi, Takemura, "Interview" (1994), 91.

*24 Ibid. Exactly what kind of work it was is unknown, as no photographic record remains.

*25 The title of the work [*Wall*, in English] is as it appears in the artist's files of later years. The title given in the 1973 Kyoto Independents Exhibition pamphlet was *Hekimen* [in Japanese, meaning "wall"].

*26 Kumada, "Chronology," 96.

*27 The name of the shop was Café Moa. The building in Kobe in which it was located still exists. The building is said to contain a mural by Okuda Yoshimi, but this is unconfirmed.

*28 Detailed description in *Kyoto Shimbun*.

*29 Relocated to the south side of Higashi Yuenchi Park in 2019, it no longer exists at the site of the original photoshoot.

*30 A piece in the morning edition of the *Kyoto Shimbun* for August 31, 1973, described the work as "not a 'photography exhibition' of the conventional sort, but a venture into conceptual thinking that compels the viewer to consider a kind of ontology through the visual medium of photographs."

*31 Kinoshita, Ochi, Takemura, "Interview" (1994), 92.

*32 "Signifying: Language / Thing—with the Manifestation of Attitude" (November 6–11, 1974, Kyoto City Museum of Art), planned and organized by Mizukami Jun, former member of the Kansai-based artist collective The Play.

*33 Kinoshita, Ochi, Takemura, "Interview" (1994), 92

*34 Uematsu Keiji Interview (2023), this catalogue, p. 267.

*35 Kinoshita speaks of having shown at the "Signifying: Language / Thing—with the Manifestation of Attitude" exhibition, but never mentions submitting work to the Japan Art Festival. While Kinoshita's participation in "Signifying" can be confirmed from the list of artists, to my knowledge no list of works has been found, preventing verification.

*36 Kinoshita, Ochi, Takemura, "Interview" (1994), 92.

*37 Hirano Shigemitsu makes an important point about *Untitled / Mu38 (Flower Clock)* in his review of the exhibition in the November 1973 issue of *Bijutsu Techo*. Believing that the external can only be rendered a relative entity or object (as opposed to subject) by an ontology in which the external arises solely within ideas as absolute objects or cognition in the aggregate or the greatest common divisor, Hirano was critical of "the kind of conceptual approach that experiments with discourse on cognition or existence solely as part of a methodology," but also argued, with regard to the solo exhibition the following year featuring *Beaker* that "a purer, more intuitive method is preferred when it comes to delving into existence itself, and in that sense, the previous landscape photos were more direct" (*Bijutsu Techo*, April 1974). At the same time he declared approvingly that Kinoshita had "certainly acquired a format worth considering as a way of verifying the condition of existence." Even considering that after this Kinoshita stopped taking photos herself, stopped taking the external as her subject, and by returning to painting moved away from an ontology grounded in the subject-object relationship, this is intriguing when contemplating Kinoshita's methodology. It is also probably related to the way that in contrast to the paintings of her later years, which laid bare equivalence and difference in medium specificity, there was a retreat from the "see-be seen" relationship she dealt with in photographs.

*38 "Photo / Arts—Photography as Method" (January 11–19, 1974) and "Video / Kyoto / 1974" (April 28–May 11, 1974). Video Hiroba cooperated in the planning of the latter.

*39 See Kumada Tsukasa, "Chronology," 96, others.

*40 "'Miru' koto ni tsuite" [On "seeing"] (January 15–20, 1974, galerie 16, Kyoto).

*41 Kinoshita, Ochi, Takemura, "Interview" (1994), 92.

*42 This work is also mentioned in the Morishita survey ("Digitization of existing slides assumed to have been shot by the artist, and a video work, albeit only one, unusual for Kinoshita Kazuyo, has been completed"). The converted miniDV contains extra footage, and it was not certain at that point how much of the footage was the work that was screened. The part that constituted the work was clarified with the help of Amano Kazuo, who organized the exhibition "Video—A New World: Possibilities of the Medium" where the video was shown (1992, O Art Museum, Tokyo).

*43 The work was created and presented as a set of 22 pieces when it was shown at the Muramatsu Gallery, but one piece (the 6th) subsequently went missing, and the work is now in the collection of Nakanoshima Museum of Art, Osaka, as a set of 21 pieces. It is unknown whether the piece was lost during Kinoshita's lifetime or after her death.

*44 Kinoshita Kazuyo solo exhibition (February 25 – March 2, 1975, galerie 16, Kyoto).

*45 Kinoshita Kazuyo solo exhibition (September 8 – 14, 1975, Muramatsu Gallery, Tokyo).

*46 It was Fuji Yoshiyuki who described the work as "filmic" (*Bijutsu Techo*, May 1975). Kinoshita herself meanwhile states that existence does not arise from cognition, but a thing exists as the same thing whether we see it or not, in a 1994 Interview noting with regard to this work, "I colored each part as I saw it, ultimately becoming cognizant of the whole thing…. perceiving and becoming conscious of it, and expanding this also means an increase in entities."

*47 Kinoshita Kazuyo solo exhibition (February 24 – 29, 1976, galerie 16, Kyoto).

*48 In the May 1976 issue of *Bijutsu Techo* art critic Takahashi Toru points out that the element of time is missing from this work, and posits the question of whether it is appropriate to use photographs, assuming memory is an action that goes hand in hand with time.

*49 Art Core Contemporary Art '77 series "Self-Portraits '77" (May 17 – 22, 1977, Art Core Gallery, Kyoto), organized by Takahashi Toru.

*50 According to the artist's files the artwork was produced in March 1976. The fact that the work was not specifically made for Self-Portraits '77" is also made clear in the Interview published in *Kazuyo Kinoshita 1939 – 1994*.

*51 Kinoshita, Ochi, Takemura, "Interview" (1994), 93.

*52 Held from April 28 through May 14 at the Tokyo Metropolitan Art Museum, and from June 1 through 12 at the Kyoto City Museum of Art.

*53 The *Mainichi Shimbun* edition of June 1, 1977, writes that regarding the prize, Kinoshita said she was "used to losing," but that she was probably primed for recognition this time.

*54 In addition to a solo exhibition at Gallery U (1977, Nagoya), mentioned in the 1994 Interview, these shows include a drawing exhibition at Imabashi Gallery (1978, Osaka) organized by Inui Yoshiaki, a solo exhibition at Utsubo Gallery (1979, Osaka), and a group exhibition at Gallery Westbeth (1979, Nagoya).

*55 Kinoshita Kazuyo exhibition (November 1 – 12, 1977, Gallery Kitano Circus).

*56 pp. 102-103 of this catalogue.

*57 In her Interview she notes, "… a French artist was already doing it, so I didn't." Although Kinoshita claims in the Interview that the sheet acrylic installation "still exists in its entirety," its whereabouts is unknown as of 2020.

*58 Based on the photographs that remain in the artist's files, it is believed that the last time she exhibited one of these works was a group show held at Sakabo Bonkura (Kobe) in December 1978.

*59 Based on materials that Kinoshita entrusted to AD&A before her death. See, for instance, p.122 of this catalogue. Stored at Nakanoshima Museum of Art, Osaka.

*60 Kinoshita, Ochi, Takemura, "Interview" (1994), 93.

*61 Ibid., 93. In the draft of a letter addressed to Maeno Toshikuni dated October 9, 1982, she notes that "it is suspected to have been arson."

*62 Her comments include, "When one learns about documenta, the Venice Biennale, Paris Biennale, NY, one also comes to know where Japan ranks in it all." From the draft of letter to Maeno Toshikuni dated October 9, 1982.

*63 A letter addressed to the curator (later director) of the Lenbachhaus Kunstforum (now MaximiliansForum), Helmut Friedel, dated November 25, 1982. The artist seeks to know the exact reason for cancellation, writing "I refuse to relinquish all hope of presenting that project at the Kunstforum next year."

*64 The above-mentioned letter to Friedel also states that she wanted to exhibit not oil paintings, but a site-specific installation.

*65 The Artwork Restoration Project (August 10 – October 31, 2022; Seian University Art and Design, Shiga) was carried out jointly by Nakanoshima Museum of Art, Osaka; Seian University of Art and Design; and the current owner of the work, collector Kitagawa Sadahiro (Kagoya Holdings Inc.).

*66 Kinoshita, Ochi, Takemura, "Interview" (1994), 95.

*67 This work was made into a print by Nomart Editions (Ed. 120), and distributed at a posthumous gathering in the artist's memory.

*68 In the 1990s, Kinoshita also produced large-scale works on No. 300 (approx. 2 × 3 meter) size canvases, prompted apparently by the relocation of AD&A Gallery to a cavernous space in the Port of Osaka area. Up until then her paintings had been mostly on canvases of No. 100 (approx. 160 × 130 cm) in size, but the new AD&A space inspired her to attempt larger works.

*69 As Morishita points out in the Morishita survey, there are works marked with the code "AD." As far as can be ascertained, these do not have Kinoshita's signature on them. In this exhibition they have been treated as resource material.

凡例

· 本書は、大阪中之島美術館 (2024年5月25日−8月18日)、
  埼玉県立近代美術館 (2024年10月12日−2025年1月13日) で
  開催される展覧会「没後30年 木下佳通代」の図録として
  刊行された。
· 各作品について、作品番号、作家名 (木下佳通代の場合は省略)、
  タイトル (和英)、制作年を記載している。
  技法・材質、サイズ、所蔵者名等については、巻末の出品リストを
  参照されたい。
· 作品のタイトルは、所蔵者から提供された情報に基づく。
  ただし一部の作品については、木下佳通代が生前遺した
  作家ファイル等を参照のうえ、展覧会主催者側で変更した。
· 作品番号と会場での展示の順序は必ずしも一致しない。
· 各会場会期中の展示替等により、
  本書掲載の作品が展示されていない場合がある。
  また、都合により大阪中之島美術館のみで展示される作品には、
  作品番号に＊を付記している。
· 章解説は大下裕司 (大阪中之島美術館) と
  佐藤あゆか (埼玉県立近代美術館) が執筆した。
  各章解説末尾に各執筆者の姓を記している。

Notes

· This catalogue accompanies the exhibition
  KAZUYO KINOSHITA: A Retrospective at
  Nakanoshima Museum of Art, Osaka (May 25−August 18, 2024)
  and the Museum of Modern Art, Saitama
  (October 12, 2024−January 13, 2025).
· Plate captions include the following information:
  catalogue number, artist (omitted for works by Kinoshita),
  title of work (in Japanese and English) and year of production.
  Other information (materials and techniques, dimensions, collection, etc.)
  is included in the list of works.
· Titles are normally based on information provided by the collectors,
  with some adjustments made by the organizers according to
  the artist's files and other records.
· Catalogue numbers do not necessarily indicate the order of display
  in the gallery.
· Some exhibits can only be exhibited for a limited period.
  Works exhibited only at Nakanoshima Museum of Art, Osaka
  are marked with ＊.
· Chapter commentaries are written by
  Oshita Yuji (Nakanoshima Museum of Art, Osaka) and
  Sato Ayuka (the Museum of Modern Art, Saitama).
  The author is indicated at the end of each commentary.

1939年4月18日、木下佳通代（きのしたかずよ）は神戸の建具店を営む家に生まれた。幼い頃から絵を描くのが好きだった木下は、親和中学校2年生の時に油絵のセットを買ってもらい美術部へ入部する。誰に教わるでもなく、初めて描いたのは妹の横顔であった。1958年、京都市立美術大学（現・京都市立芸術大学）西洋画科に入学した木下は黒田重太郎、津田周平、今井憲一、須田国太郎に師事するが、彼らよりも彫刻科の教授である辻晋堂、堀内正和に親しむことが多かった。在学時には哲学や教育学も学び、生涯問い続ける「存在」についてもすでに関心を抱きつつあった。

1962年に大学を卒業すると、中学校で美術の教師として勤め始める。1963年には、以降継続して出品をすることになる「京都アンデパンダン展」に初参加し、同年、河口龍夫と結婚。1965年、河口や奥田善巳ら9名によって結成されたグループ〈位〉の活動に協力し始め、行動を共にする。

Chapter 1

1960—1971

Kinoshita Kazuyo was born on April 18, 1939, to a family of joiners in Kobe. A lover of drawing from a young age, in her second year at Shinwa Junior High School she acquired a set of oil paints, and joined the art club. Her first painting, entirely self-taught, was of her sister in profile. In 1958, Kinoshita entered Kyoto City University of Arts, where she studied Western-style oil painting under Kuroda Jutaro, Tsuda Shuhei, Imai Kenichi, and Suda Kunitaro, but generally more acquainted with Tsuji Shindo and Horiuchi Masakazu of the sculpture faculty. She also studied philosophy and education, and was already beginning to develop the interest too in existential matters that would be a persistent theme throughout her life.

After graduating from university in 1962, Kinoshita took up a post as a middle school art teacher. In 1963 she took part for the first time in the Kyoto Independent Exhibition to which she would henceforth be a regular con-

メンバーには加わらなかったが、彼らがテーマとした「存在についての問題」には強く影響を受け、後年振り返ってグループの活動は「自分の一部として考えてやってきた」と語っている*1。

一方、グループ〈位〉との関わり以外に目を向けると、大学在学中の1960年に最初のグループ展を京都書院画廊で開催している。美術教師の仕事やグループ〈位〉への協力と並行して、1966年まで6回のグループ展を大阪、神戸、京都で開催。1966年には、神戸のウィンナ画廊で初の個展を開催した。当初は母や妹、友人など身近な人物をアカデミックなタッチで描いていたが、1962年頃から植物をモチーフとし、「生命体が自在に存在する・出来る」というメッセージを抽象的な絵画として発表するようになる。

奥田善巳と再婚した1970年には「境界の思考」と題したシリーズで、認識や知覚の問題を図形的に表現するようになる。1972年、「滲触」(Saturation)と本人が呼ぶ、グリッド上に輪郭の朧な円や線、滲みのような色の広がりを描いた作品をシロタ画廊で発表。いずれもパウル・クレーの作品等を意識し、絵画における形や線、それらを紐解いたときに現れる「等価に存在する何か」を描き出そうと試みた。理知的に組み立てられた画面上の構成をはじめ、この時期の作品には、彼女の評価を決定づけた、のちの写真作品と共通する要素が、すでに多く見て取れる。(大下)

tributor, and in the same year, married Kawaguchi Tatsuo. In 1965, she began to cooperate with the activities of Group "i" formed by nine artists including Kawaguchi, and Okuda Yoshimi, working alongside. Though never becoming an official member of Group "i" she was heavily influenced by its theme of existence, and reflecting in later years, described the group's activities as something she had always seen as "part of myself." *1

Outside of her involvement with Group "i" meanwhile, Kinoshita took part in her first group exhibition while still at university, in 1960 at the Kyoto Shoin Gallery. While employed as a teacher and working with Group "i" she also managed to take part in six group shows in Osaka, Kobe and Kyoto in the years up to 1966. In 1966, she held her first solo show, at the Wiener Gallery in Kobe. Initially she had painted familiar figures such as her mother, sister, and friends, in academic style, but from around 1962 shifted to botanical motifs, presenting in abstract-style painting a message of "life forms existing / able to exist freely."

In 1970, the year she was married for a second time, to Okuda Yoshimi, in the series titled "Boundary Thinking," Kinoshita began to express questions of perception and understanding in graphical fashion. The following year, 1972, saw her present, at the Shirota Gallery, works featuring what she called "Saturation," ie shapes such as circles and lines with ill-defined contours, and blotting-like expanses of color, painted on grids. Both were attempts to portray shapes and lines in painting, and unidentified "things that exist equally" appearing when these are unfolded, in the manner of artists like Paul Klee. Kinoshita's works of this period already exhibit the intellectually configured picture planes, plus many other elements, found in the later photographic works that would cement her reputation. (Oshita)

---

*1 1994年4月23日 AD&Aギャラリーでのインタビューより。
  (p. 207)

*1 From an interview at the AD&A Gallery,
  (p. 253)

1
題不詳 / む76
Title Unknown / Mu76
1960

2*
題不詳
Title Unknown
1962

植物をモチーフとした油彩作品を
制作した時期の作品。
絵画を通じて、地球上の生命や
私たちの精神に「等価に存在する何か」を
見出そうとしていた。

From Kinoshita's period of oils with
botanical motifs, in which she was trying
to identify through painting
"something existing equally" in life on
the planet, and in our spirits.

3*
題不詳
Title Unknown
1962

4
題不詳 / む80
Title Unknown / Mu80
ca. 1961−62

5
題不詳
Title Unknown
ca. 1961−62

6
無題
Untitled
1962

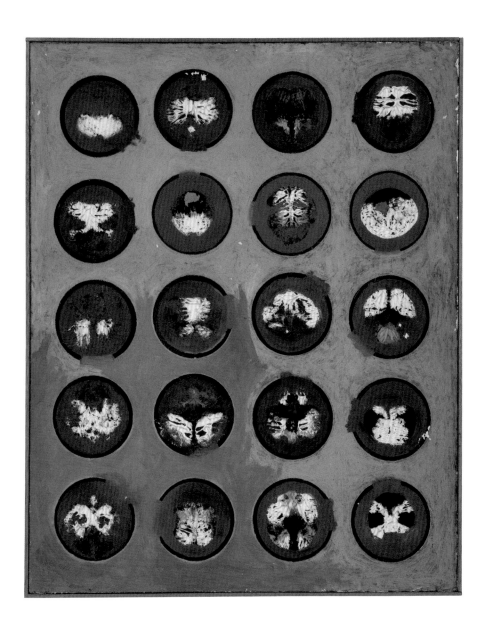

7
無題
Untitled
1962

描かれた立体の一部が、紙のように
めくれている。また別の作品では、
立体の断面が背景と同化し、断面から
立体の外側までつながって見える。
「内側と外側」が等価になることを
意識して描かれたシリーズ。

In one painting, part of the solid
depicted is folding over in the manner
of paper. In others, the cross-sections
of the solid are assimilated into
the background, with the area from
cross-sections to outside the solid

seemingly connected. In this series
Kinoshita consciously aimed for equality
of inside and outside.

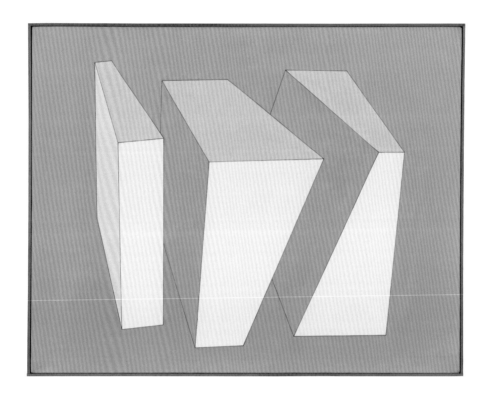

8
境界の思考・A
Boundary Thinking A
1970

9
境界の思考・B
Boundary Thinking B
1970

10*
境界の思考・C
Boundary Thinking C
1970

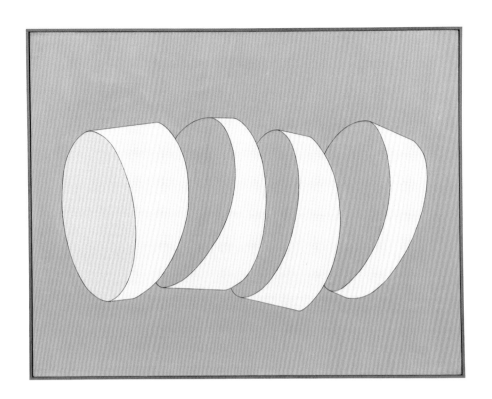

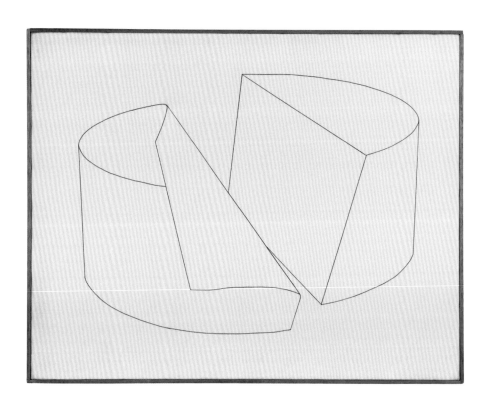

11*
境界の思考・D
Boundary Thinking D
1970

12*
境界の思考・E
Boundary Thinking E
1970

13
境界の思考・F
Boundary Thinking F
1970

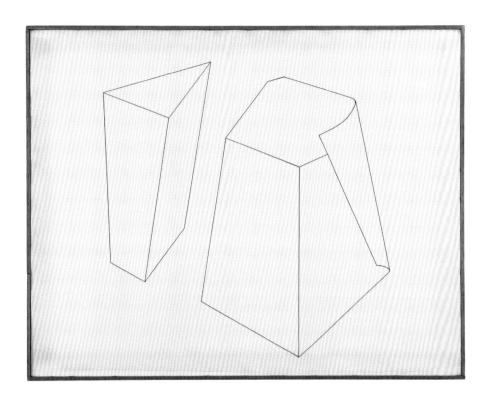

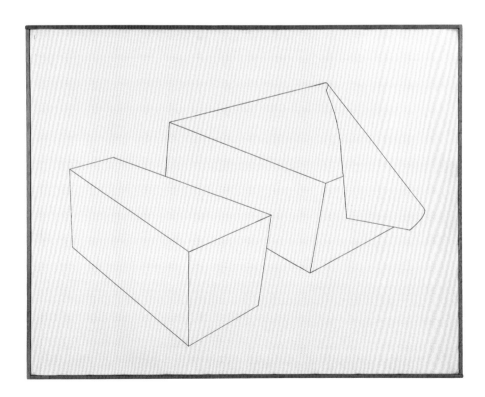

14
[滲触] む95
[Saturation] Mu 95
1971

描かれたグリッドは、カンヴァスに
二次元の広がりを作り出す。
重ねられた色面がグリッドの線上で
「浸蝕」し合うように染み出す表現が、
絵画的な空間の在りかを
示している。

The painted grid forms a two-dimensional expanse across the canvas.
Expression in which the overlaid color
fields permeate the plane, color field and
grid "eroding" each other, showing the
whereabouts of the painterly space.

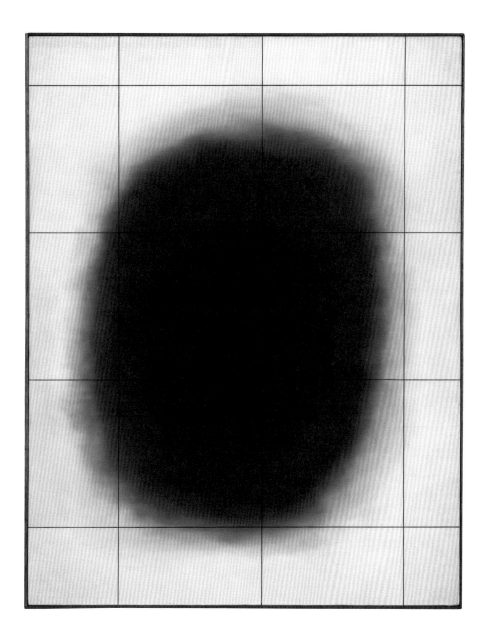

15
[滲触]
[Saturation]
1971

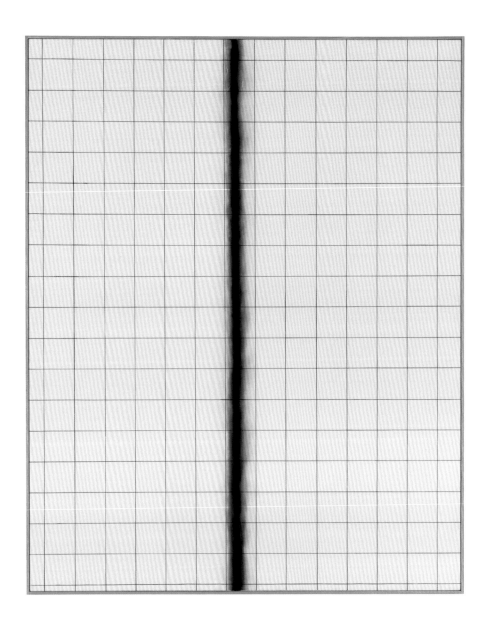

16*
[滲触]
[Saturation]
1971

学生時代から継続して油彩を表現媒体としていた木下で
あったが、1972年から写真作品の制作に着手する。写真
という、対象を客観的に捉えるメディアの使用は、「存在」
や「知覚」、「認識」といった彼女の制作におけるコンセプ
トをより明確に表すことを可能にした。

1972年から1974年にかけては、複数の写真を並べて
構成する組作品を多く手がけた。類似した写真を複数枚
並置したとき、人はそれらのイメージを交互に眺め、イメー
ジ同士の共通点や差異を探そうとする。あるいは、連続す
るイメージに時間の流れを感じ取る者もいる。これら組写
真によって木下は、視線の動きとものの認識システム、イ
メージと時間の関係を改めて鑑賞者に意識させ、ものの
存在と視覚の関係性を鮮やかに提示した。その後、シル
クスクリーンやフォト・コラージュの仕事を経て、1976年
から写真とカラー・フェルトペンのドローイングによるシリー
ズの制作を始める。ここでも問題になっているのは「視覚」

Chapter 2

1972—1981

Oil painting had been Kinoshita's expressive medium of
choice since student days, but in 1972 she started making photographic works. Using a medium like photography that permits an objective grasp of the object, in turn
allowed her to express more clearly concepts in her practice such as existence, perception, and recognition.

From 1972 to 1974 she produced numerous works composed of multiple photographs displayed together. When
similar photographs are placed alongside each other,
people study the images in turn, and look for commonal-
ities and differences. Some sense the flow of time in these
image series. Through these photo sequences Kinoshita
made the viewer newly aware of how the gaze moves,
the system by which we recognize things, and the relationship between image and time, offering a fresh take
on the connection between the existence of things, and
vision. After a subsequent period doing silkscreen and
photo collage work, in 1976 she began a series using

や「認識」である。例えば、真円を紙に描き、その紙を折り曲げたり、少し角度をつけたりして写真を撮る。そこに図像として現れるのは楕円や歪んだ図形だが、私たちは経験上、それが実際には真円であると「認識」する。そして認識した「正しい形」を、写真の上からフェルトペンで描いていく。すると、作品を見る者は、写真が写し出す三次元の場における図像と、ドローイングが示す二次元の場における図像の差異を確認することとなり、人間が視覚を通してものを認識する際の無意識のプロセスが浮かび上がるのである。知的な遊び心に富んだこのシリーズは、やがて線から面の表現へと発展していき、画面上に色が現れ始める。

こうした作品は、ドイツのハイデルベルク・クンストフェラインの館長ハンス・ゲルクによって高く評価され、1981年には、76年以降の写真シリーズを中心とした個展を開催するに至る。しかしながら、制作に細かなプロセスと長い時間を要するうえ、禁欲的でシステマティックなこのシリーズに対し、木下は徐々に抑圧を感じるようになる。変化を求めた木下は、閉鎖的な手法から自身を解放すべく、みずからの手を動かして描くパステルの仕事へと移行する。それは、折り目や直線といった諸要素を写真シリーズから引き継ぎつつも、のちに大きく展開される油彩シリーズの始まりを予兆するものであった。(佐藤)

photos and drawing with colored felt pens. Here again the issues are those of vision and recognition. A perfect circle may be drawn on a piece of paper, then the paper folded, or angled slighty, and photographed. The image that emerges is one of an ellipse, or a distorted figure, but from experience we "recognize" it as a circle. The "correct shape" thus recognized is then drawn on the photo with a felt pen. The person looking at the work notes the difference between the image in the three-dimensional setting shown by the photograph, and in the two-dimensional setting shown by the drawing, highlighting the unconscious process by which humans recognize objects by sight. This series replete with intellectual playfulness eventually progressed from expression in lines to fields, and the appearance of color on the picture plane.

These works by Kinoshita attracted praise from Hans Gercke, a director of the Heidelberg Kunstverein, leading in 1981 to an exhibition of her work there, with a particular focus on the photo series produced from 1976 onward. However little by little, Kinoshita began to find this rather austere, systematic series oppressive, due to the intricate processes and time required to make the works, and seeking a change, switched to work in pastels that involved moving her own hands, in an attempt to free herself from a more inward-looking technique. While retaining various elements from her photo series, such as its folds and straight lines, this pastel work also foreshadowed the major series of oil paintings to come. (Sato)

17
Untitled-a / む102（本数冊）
Untitled-a / Mu 102 (Books)
1972

2枚の並んだ写真は一見同じに見える。
しかし、「本数冊」(cat.no.17) では開かれた
本のページが異なっており、
「壁のシミ（ブロック）」(cat.no.18) では
片方の壁にチョークで印がつけられている。
並列された2枚の写真の違いを
認識したとき、それぞれ別のものとして
意識される。同じ「存在」に対し、
別の認識が在ることを表現した。

At first glance the paired photos in these
works look the same. In *Books* (cat.no.17)
however note that the books are open
on different pages, and in *Stains on
the wall (blocks)* (cat.no.18), one wall has
been marked with chalk.
Recognizing the difference between the
two photos in each work, one becomes
aware of them as different things.

Here the artist expresses the potential
for alternative understandings of the
same something existent.

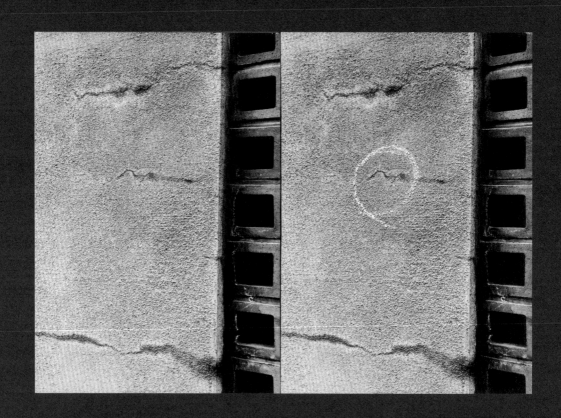

18
Untitled-b / む103（壁のシミ（ブロック））
Untitled-b / Mu103 (Stains on the wall (blocks))
1972

19
Untitled / む38(花時計)
Untitled / Mu38 (Flower Clock)
1973

19
Untitled / む38（花時計）
Untitled / Mu 38 (Flower Clock)
1973

神戸の花時計を撮影した作品。
「花時計の写真」と、
「その花時計を撮影する人を撮影した写真」
の2枚がひと組になっている。
「花時計の写真」には同じ風景が
写されるが、実際には撮影者によって
見えている世界や認識するものが
異なることを示している。
—
Here we have photos of Kobe's Flower
Clock, in pairs consisting of "photo of
the flower clock" and "photo of a person
taking a photo of the flower clock."
The "photos of the flower clock" all feature the same scene, but show the reality
that there are variations in the world as it
appears to each photographer, and what
each photographer perceives.

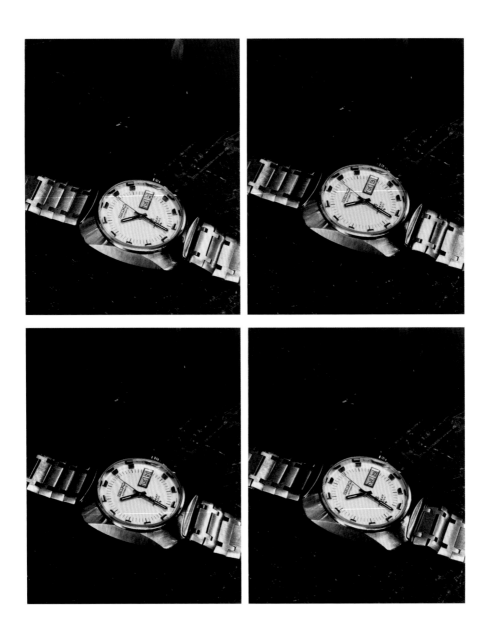

20
Untitled / む59（腕時計）
Untitled / Mu59 (Watch)
1974

すべての時計は同じ時刻を示しているが、
日付が異なっている。

All the watches display the same time,
but the dates are different.

21
Untitled / む60（ビーカー）
Untitled / Mu60（Beaker）
1973

上段には液体が入ったビーカーの写真、
下段にはその液体に温度計が入った
ビーカーの写真が並ぶ。
上段の液体の温度を下段の温度計が
示している、とおのずと認識してしまうが、

その認識は実のところ曖昧で
不確実である。「温度」という目には
見えない差異を視覚化すると同時に、
人間の認識のメカニズムを
提示している。

On top is a photo of a beaker containing liquid, and below, a photo of a beaker
with a thermometer in the liquid.
One automatically perceives the thermometer on the bottom to be showing
the temperature of the water in
the top photo, but in reality this under-

standing is ambiguous and anything
but certain. *Beaker* gives visual
expression to an unseen difference,
that of "temperature," simultaneously
demonstrating the workings of
human cognition.

21
Untitled / む60（ビーカー）
Untitled / Mu60 (Beaker)
1973

22
む61〈物の増加と減少〉
Mu 61 (Increasing and decreasing of things)
1974

何もない空間に、ひとつずつオブジェが
置かれていく。空間が飽和すると、
今度はひとつずつ取り除かれていく。
この経過によって、最初の空の空間と
最後の空の空間は、同じ空間に見えても
違う空間として存在しうる。
本作は映像作品として制作されたのち、
写真作品としても展開された。

Objects are placed one by one in an
empty space. When the space becomes
saturated, the objects are then removed,
again one by one. Due to this process,
the empty space at the start and empty
space at the end may look like the
same space, but potentially exist as different spaces. After the video was made
it was also developed into a photographic work.

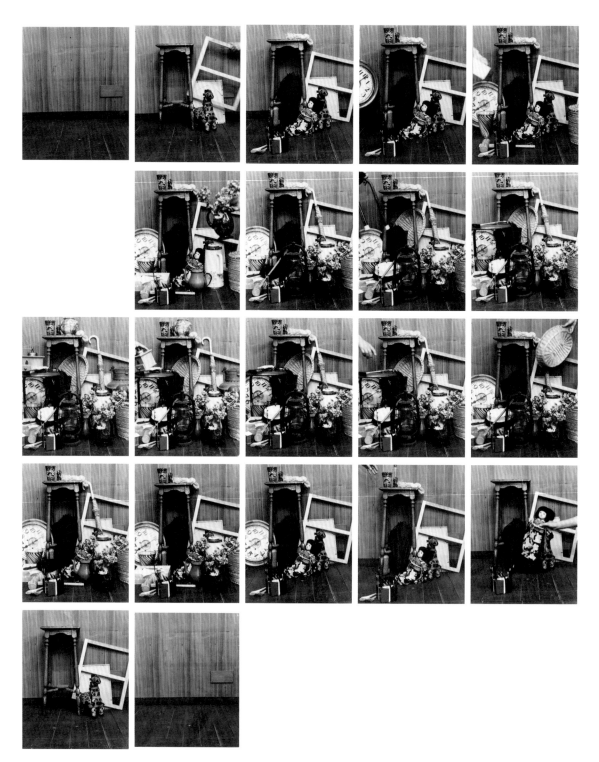

22
む61（物の増加と減少）
Mu61 (Increasing and decreasing of things)
1974

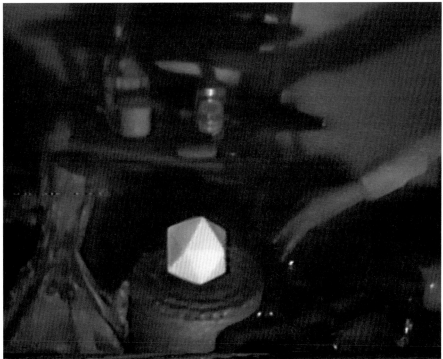

23
題不詳
Title Unknown
1974

同一の風景写真が複数並び、部分的に
着色されている。着色の範囲は徐々に
増えていき、最終的に画面全体が色彩に
覆われる。着色された部分は、人間の
視野と認識を表す。私たちは一度に全体を
見ることはできず、自身の主観に基づいて
見る対象を選択する。そして、見て
認識されることでその「存在」は確かとなる。
—

24
無題
Untitled
1975

  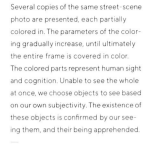

Several copies of the same street-scene photo are presented, each partially colored in. The parameters of the coloring gradually increase, until ultimately the entire frame is covered in color. The colored parts represent human sight and cognition. Unable to see the whole at once, we choose objects to see based on our own subjectivity. The existence of these objects is confirmed by our seeing them, and their being apprehended.

25
無題
Untitled
1975

26
無題 A
Untitled A
1975

untitled C 3/15 1975   Kazuyo Kinoshita

27
無題 C
Untitled C
1975

28
無題 D
Untitled D
1975

KAZUYO KINOSHITA

30

33

30
無題
Untitled
ca.1975

33
無題
Untitled
ca.1975

32
無題
Untitled
1975

—

31
無題
Untitled
1975

32

31

34
Untitled B
Untitled B
1975

35
Untitled
(Some profile or some consciousness)
Untitled
(Some profile or some consciousness)
1976

人間が互いに認識することについて
表現する。自分自身の中にある
客観性と主観性を無限鏡のように
増幅させている。

―

In this expression of the manner in which
humans become cognizant of each other,
the artist takes the objectivity and
subjectivity within the self and amplifies
them in the manner of an infinity mirror.

―

36
む36
Mu36
1976

異なる時期に撮影された作家の
幼少期のポートレートをコラージュした
作品。昨日の「私」と今日の「私」はまったく
同じではあり得ないが、どちらも

「存在」としては同じ「私」である——。
木下はフォト・コラージュの手法により、
こうした同一性と差異の問題に取り組んだ。
——

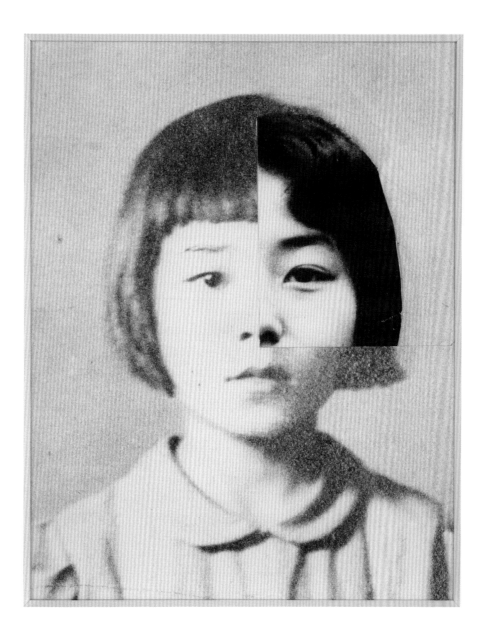

Portraits of the artist shot during different stages of childhood, made into a collage. Yesterday's "me" and the "me" of today cannot be exactly the same, but both are the same "me" as a form of existence. Kinoshita employed the technique of photo collage to address such questions of identity and difference.

37
む37
Mu 37
1976

38
Untitled
Untitled
1976

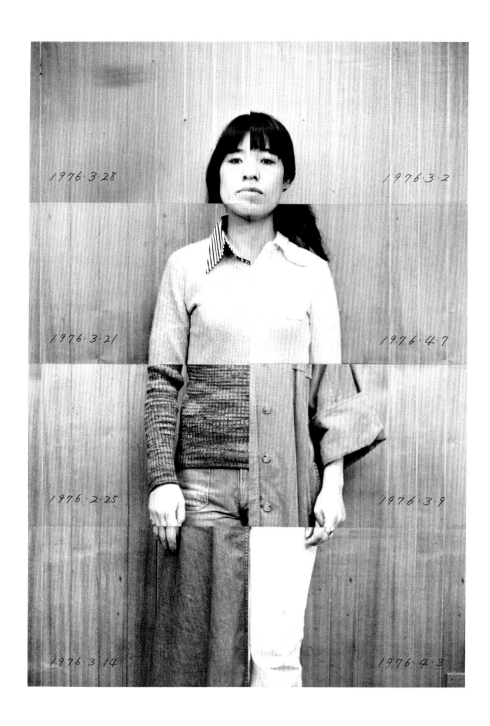

1976·3·28   1976·3·2

1976·3·21   1976·4·7

1976·2·25   1976·3·9

1976·3·14   1976·4·3

39
Untitled
Untitled
1976

40
無題 / む40
Untitled / Mu40
1977

41
無題
Untitled
1977

42
'76-C
'76-C
1976

コンパスで円を描く手が写る。
紙に描かれた真円は、写真上では
楕円となって写し出されるが、
私たちはこれを「真円」として認識する。

同じ図形でも、実際に見えているものと
認識の間では差異があることを示している。
—

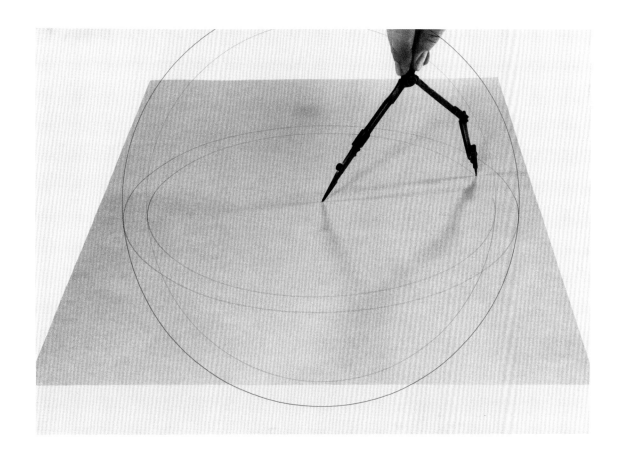

A hand is shown drawing a circle with a compass. The perfect circle described on the paper appears in the photo as an ellipse, yet we perceive it as a perfect circle, demonstrating the disparity between what we see, and what we perceive, even with the same figure.

43
'76-D
'76-D
1976

44

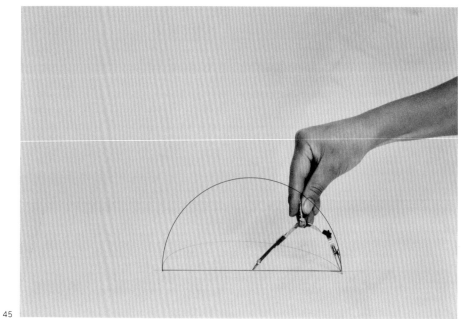

45

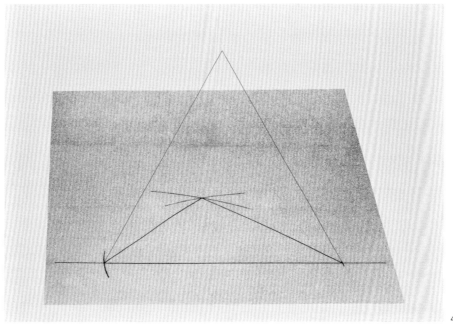

46

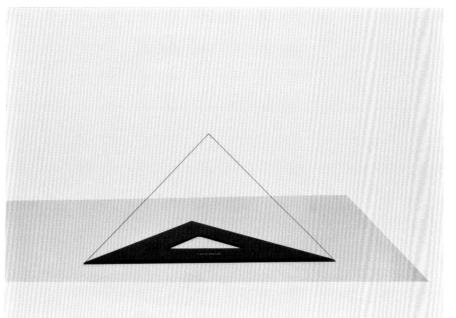

47

46	47
'76-H	'76-I
'76-H	'76-I
1976	1976

48
作品 '77-D
Work '77-D
1977

60年代から何度もコンテストに
応募してきた木下だが、なかなか賞には
恵まれなかった。
本作で第13回現代日本美術展に応募し、
兵庫県立近代美術館賞を受賞した。

Kinoshita entered countless competitions from the 1960s onward,
but was never selected until this work
won her the Hyogo Prefectural Museum
of Modern Art Prize in the 13th Contemporary Art Exhibition of Japan.

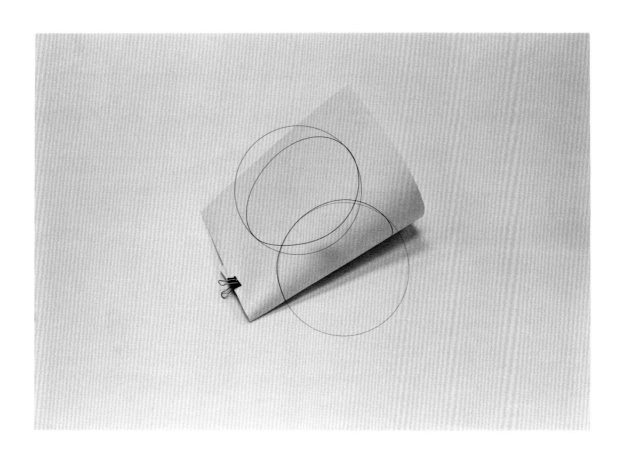

49
'77-E
'77-E
1977

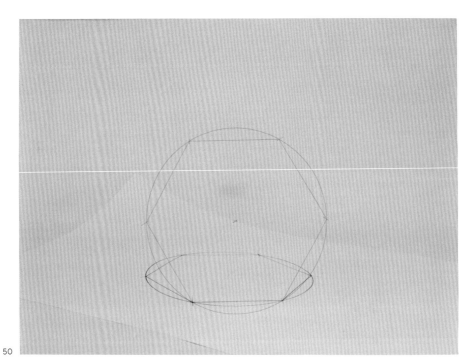

50

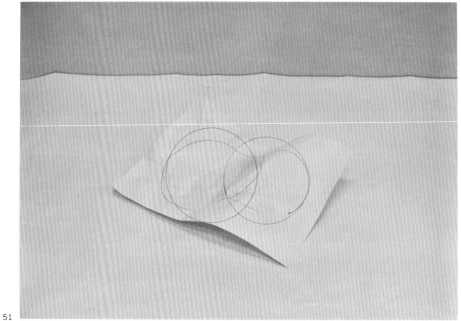

51

50	51
'77-H	'77-J
'77-H	'77-J
1977	1977

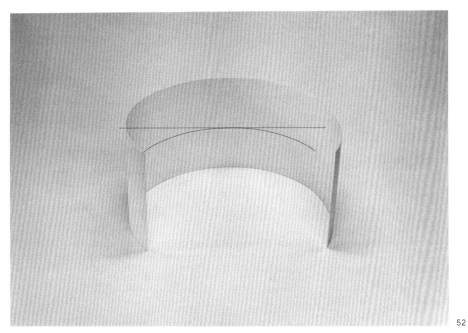

52

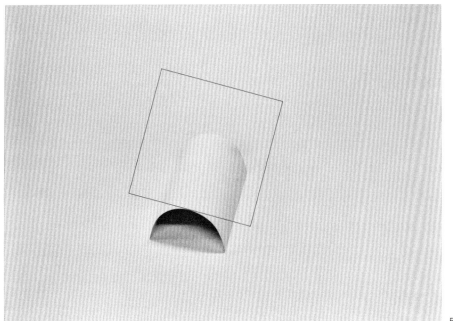

53

52	53
'77-O	'77-R
'77-O	'77-R
1977	1977

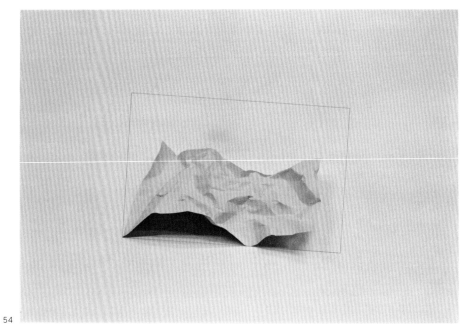

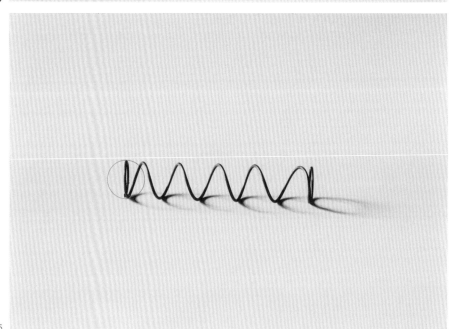

54	55
'77-T	'77-Y
'77-T	'77-Y
1977	1977

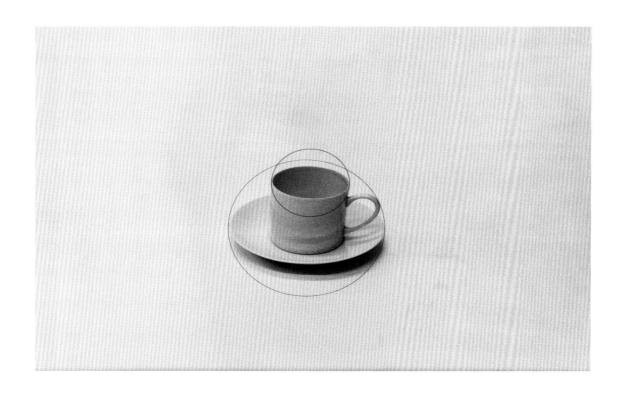

56
'77-27
'77-27
1977

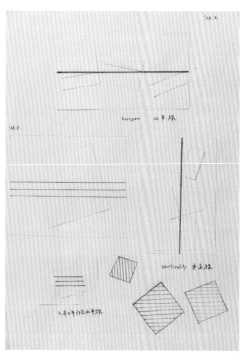

1

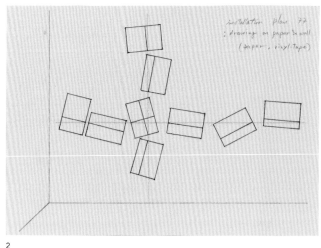

2

3

1
インスタレーションのためのドローイング
Drawing for installation works
1978
—
2
インスタレーションプラン '77
Installation plan '77
1977
—
3
インスタレーションプラン '77
Installation plan '77
1977
—
4
ギャルリーキタノサーカスのための
インスタレーションプラン
Installation plan for
Gallery Kitano Circus
1977

4

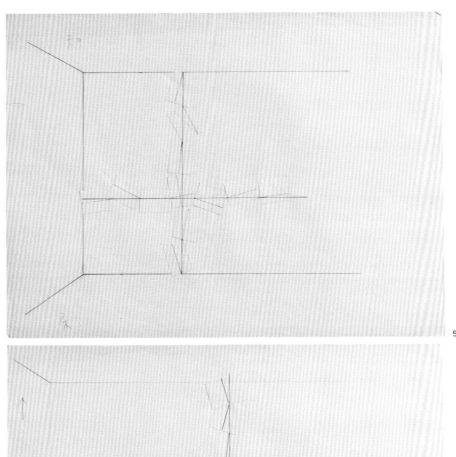

5

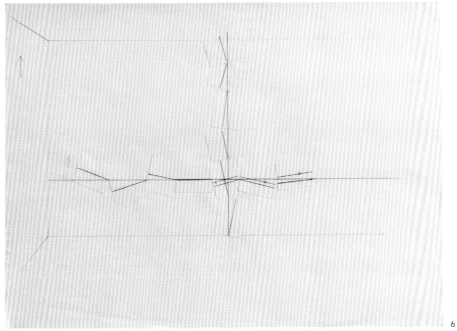

6

5
インスタレーションプラン
Installation plan
ca. 1977

6
インスタレーションプラン
Installation plan
ca. 1977

1

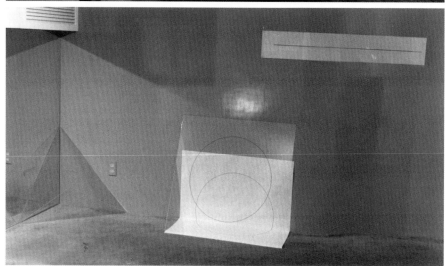

2

1
《Installation D-'77》、ギャラリーキタノサーカスでの展示風景
Installation D-'77, installation view at Gallery Kitano Circus
1977

—

2
（左から）《Installation C-'77》、《Installation A-'77》、《Installation B-'77》、
ギャラリーキタノサーカスでの展示風景
from left to right, *Installation C-'77*, *Installation A-'77*, *Installation B-'77*,
installation view at Gallery Kitano Circus
1977

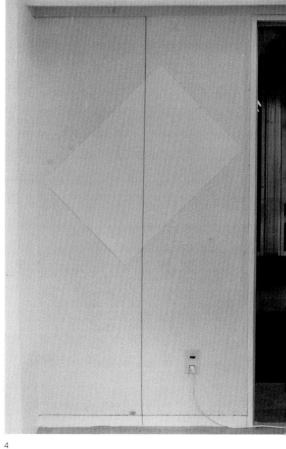

3

4

3
〔左から〕《Installation D-'77》、《Installation F-'77》、
ギャラリーキタノサーカスでの展示風景
from left to right, *Installation D-'77, Installation F-'77,*
installation view at Gallery Kitano Circus
1977

―

4
《Installation F-'77》、ギャラリーキタノサーカスでの展示風景
Installation F-'77, installation view at Gallery Kitano Circus
1977

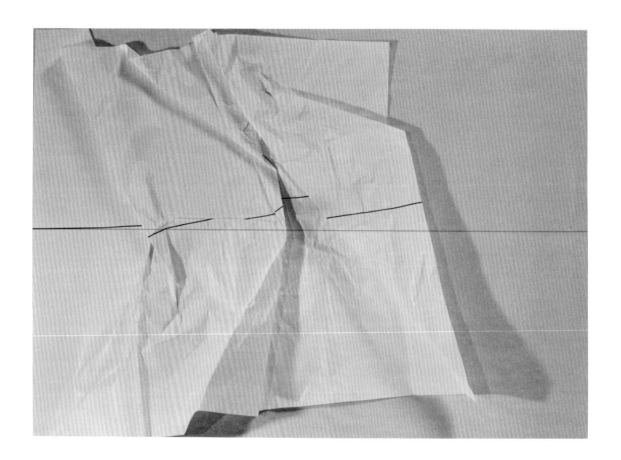

57
'78-1
'78-1
1978

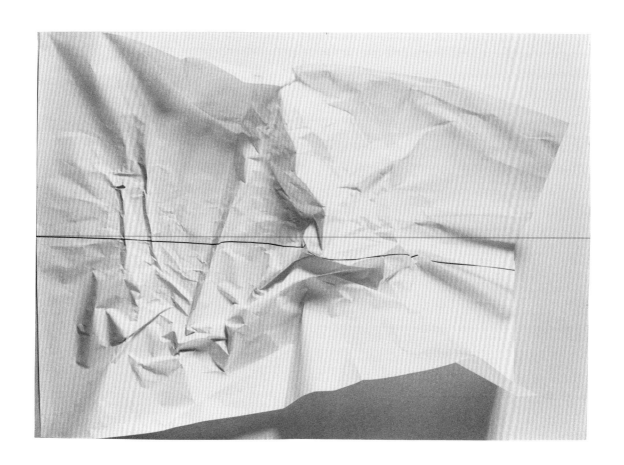

58
'78-4-B
'78-4-B
1978

59
'78-7
'78-7
1978

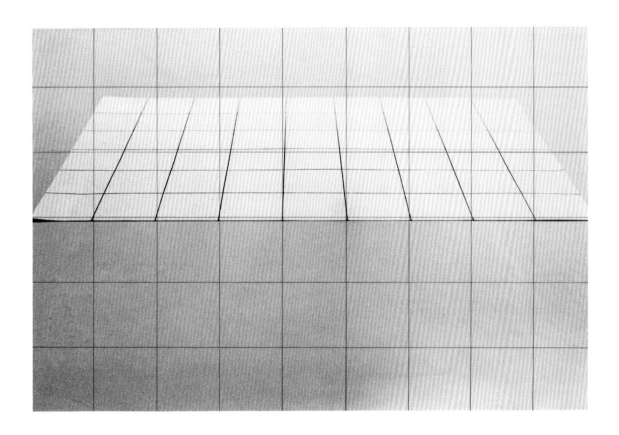

60
'78-11
'78-11
1978

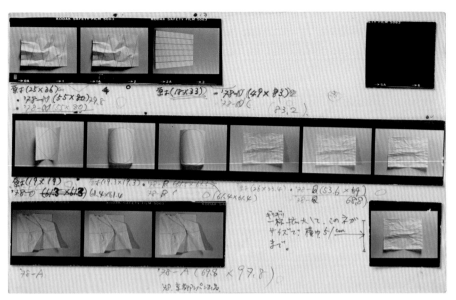

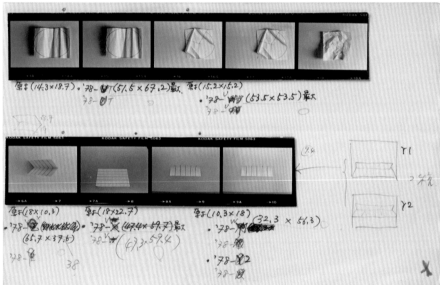

作品プランのためのコンタクトシート
Contact sheet for work plan
1978
—
作品プランのためのコンタクトシート
Contact sheet for work plan
1978

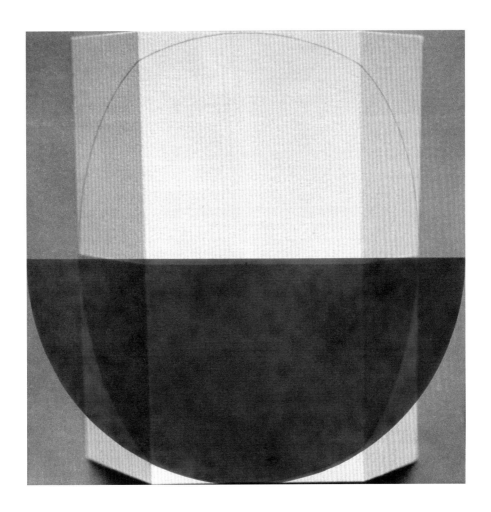

61
'78-35-A
'78-35-A
1978

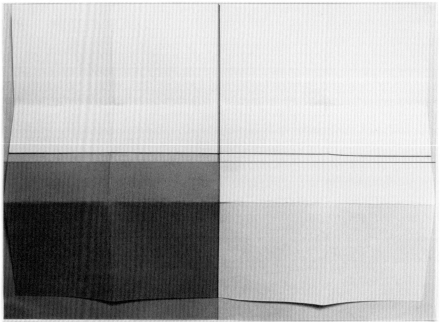

62
'79-1-C
'79-1-C
1979

63
'79-2-A
'79-2-A
1979

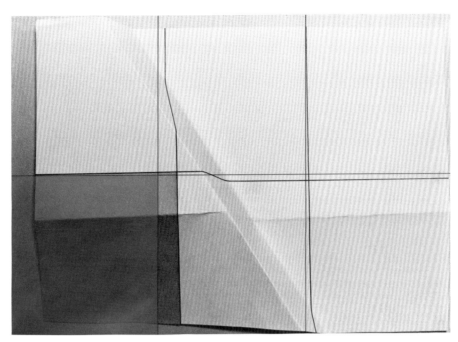

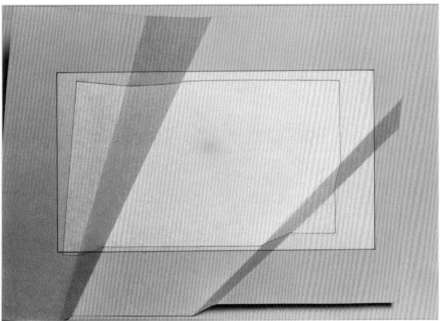

64
'79-5-A
'79-5-A
1979
—
65
'79-7-A
'79-7-A
1979

1978年頃より、撮影され写真に写る紙と
支持体としての印画紙そのものの
差異を示す表現へと展開した。これまで
線で描かれていた「認識した形」が色面で
描かれるようになる。

From about 1978 there is a development
in Kinoshita's expression to showing
the difference between paper
in a photograph, and the actual
photographic paper support. Also from
around this time, the "perceived shapes"
hitherto drawn in lines started to be
rendered as color fields.

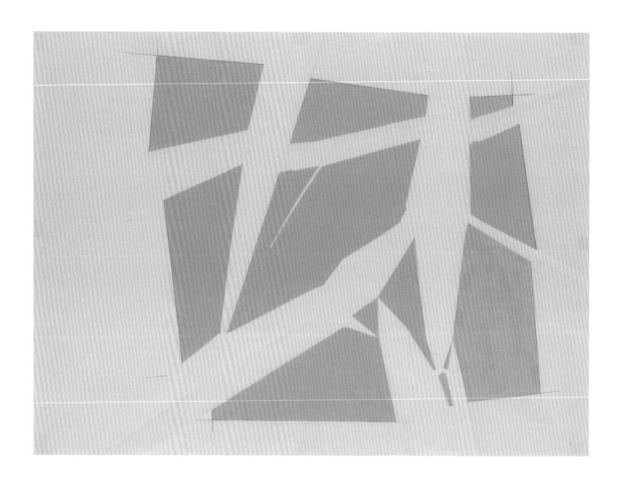

66
Pa-fold '79-21
Pa-fold '79-21
1979

タイトルの「fold」は紙が折られている
ことを示している。紙を折りたたんだ
状態で着色し、再度開いた作品。
この時期より、紙を被写体として写真に
収めることから徐々に離れ、紙そのものを
作品とするようになる。

—

As the title indicates, the paper here
is folded. In this work the paper is
colored after folding, then opened
out again. During this period Kinoshita
began to move away from making paper
the subject of photos, to positioning
paper itself as the work.

—

「Pa-fold」シリーズのためのドローイング
Drawing for the *"Pa-fold"* series
ca. 1979

—

「Pa-fold」シリーズのためのドローイング
Drawing for the *"Pa-fold"* series
ca. 1979

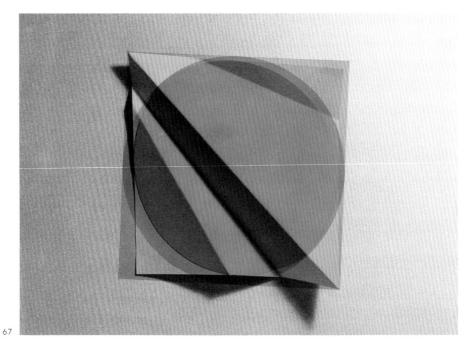

67

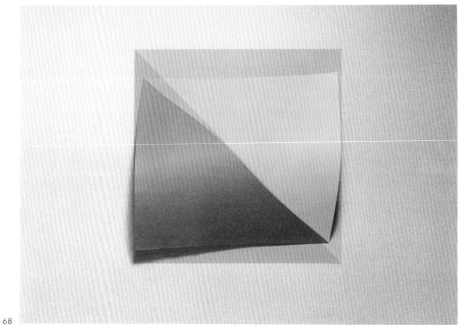

68

67	68
'79-38-A	'79-39-A
'79-38-A	'79-39-A
1979	1979

69
'79-40-A
'79-40-A
1979

作品プランのためのドローイング
Drawing for work plan
ca. 1979

—

作品プランのためのマケット
Maquette for work plan
ca. 1979

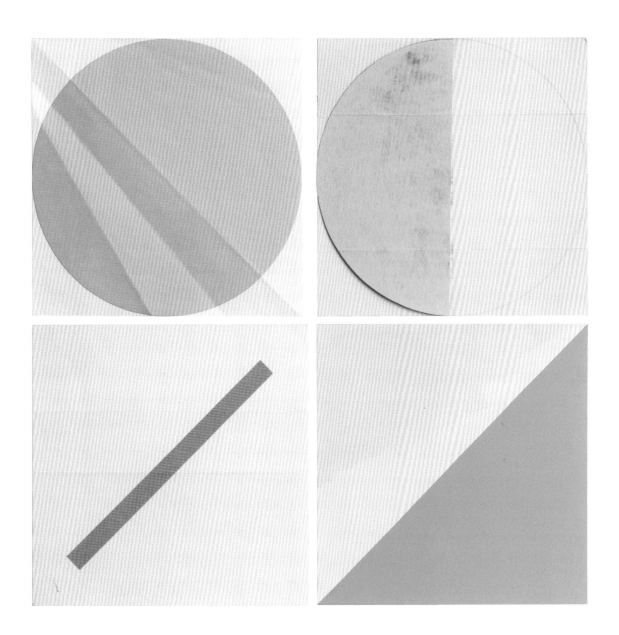

作品プランのためのマケット
Maquette for work plan
ca. 1979

作品プランのためのマケット
Maquette for work plan
ca. 1979

作品プランのためのマケット
Maquette for work plan
ca. 1979

作品プランのためのマケット
Maquette for work plan
ca. 1979

開いた状態の紙に描き込まれていた
線やマス目を、折りたたんだ状態で
認識させることを意図した作品。
不可視の状態から形を認識する本作は、
同時期の「fold」と逆のことを行っている。
ハイデルベルクの個展に出品された
作品のひとつ。

—

This work makes the viewer conscious
of the lines and squares on the paper when
it is open, when the paper is in a
folded state. Here the shape is recognized from an unseen state, making it
opposite to the *fold* series of
the same period. Shown at her
Heidelberg exhibition.

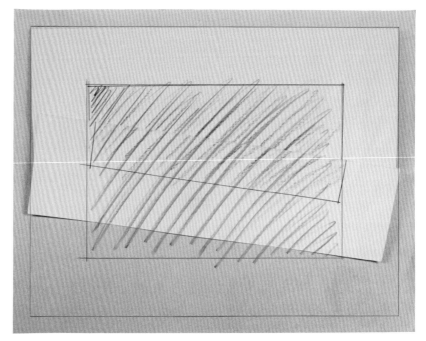

70
Ph '80-5
Ph '80-5
1980

—

71
Ph '80-10
Ph '80-10
1980

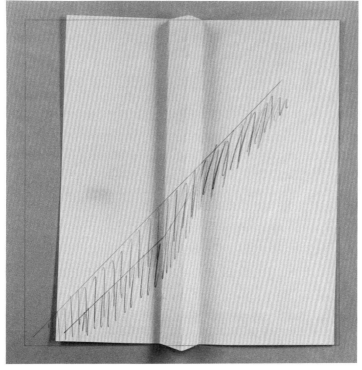

72
Ph '80-11
Ph '80-11
1980

73
Ph '80-14
Ph '80-14
1980

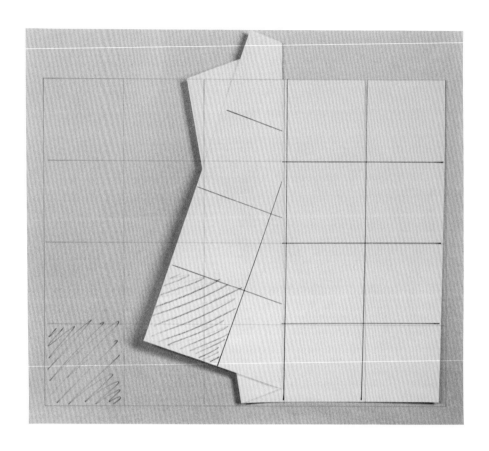

74
Ph '80-21
Ph '80-21
1980

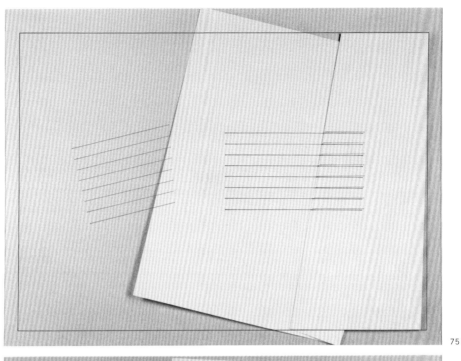

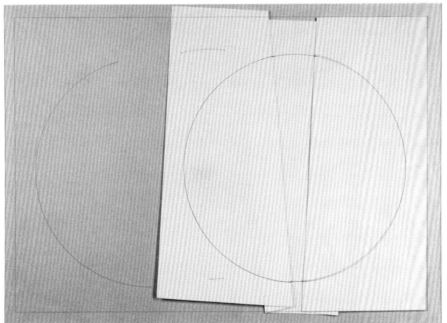

76

75   76
Ph '80-30 Ph '80-44
Ph '80-30 *Ph '80-44*
1980   1980

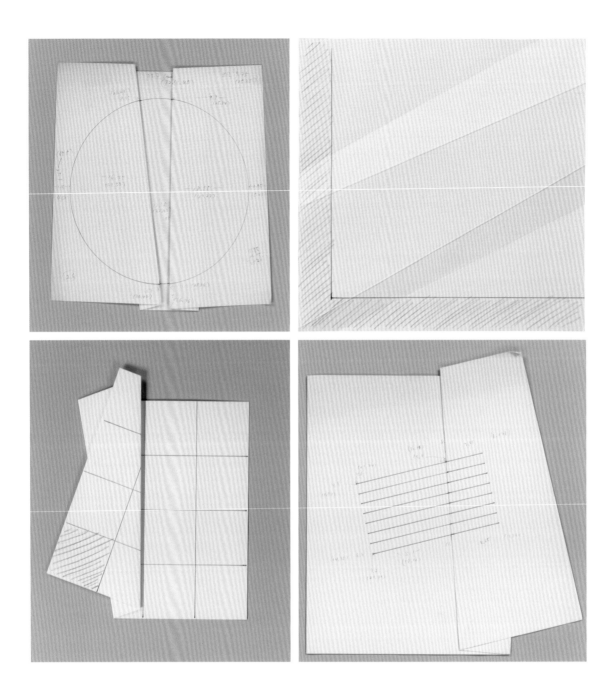

「Ph」シリーズのためのマケット
Maquette for the "Ph" series
ca. 1980

「Ph」シリーズのためのマケット
Maquette for the "Ph" series
ca. 1980

「Ph」シリーズのためのマケット
Maquette for the "Ph" series
ca. 1980

「Ph」シリーズのためのマケット
Maquette for the "Ph" series
ca. 1980

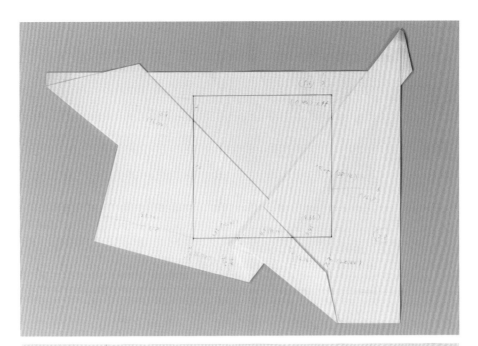

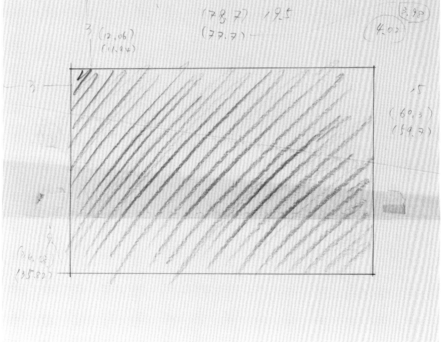

「Ph」シリーズのためのマケット
Maquette for the "Ph" series
ca. 1980

「Ph」シリーズのためのマケット
Maquette for the "Ph" series
ca. 1980

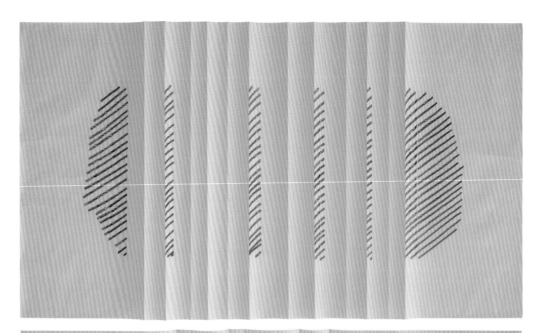

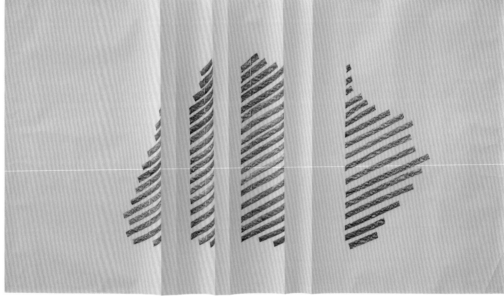

77
Pa-fold '80-35
Pa-fold '80-35
1980

78
Pa-fold '80-36
Pa-fold '80-36
1980

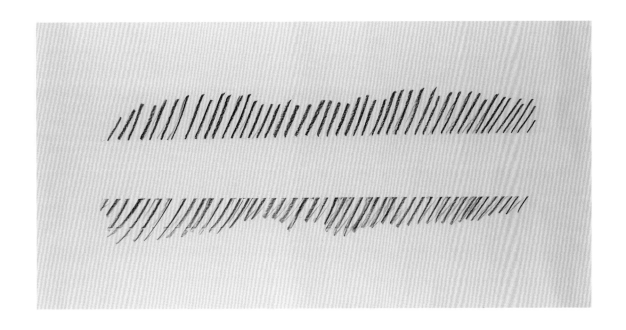

79
Pa-fold '80-37
Pa-fold '80-37
1980

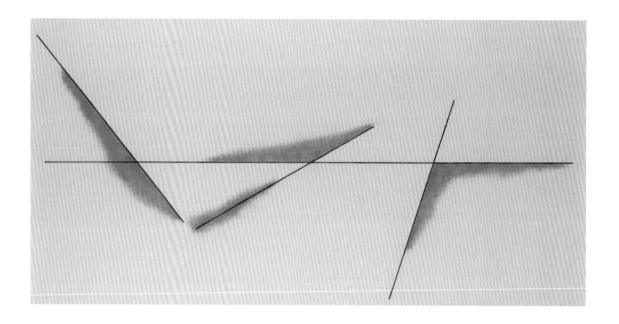

80
Pa '80-74
Pa '80-74
1980

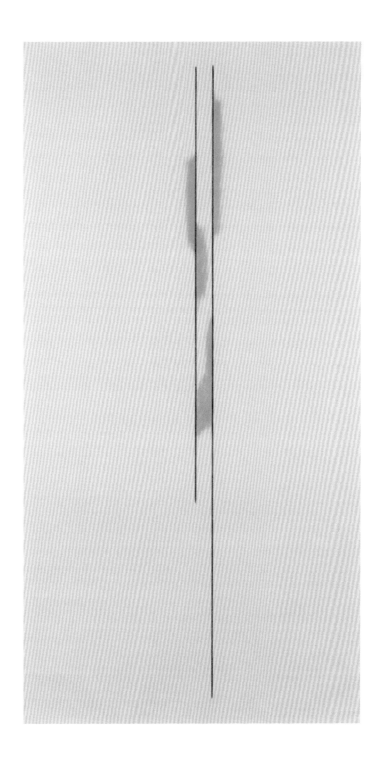

81
Pa '80-86
Pa '80-86
1980

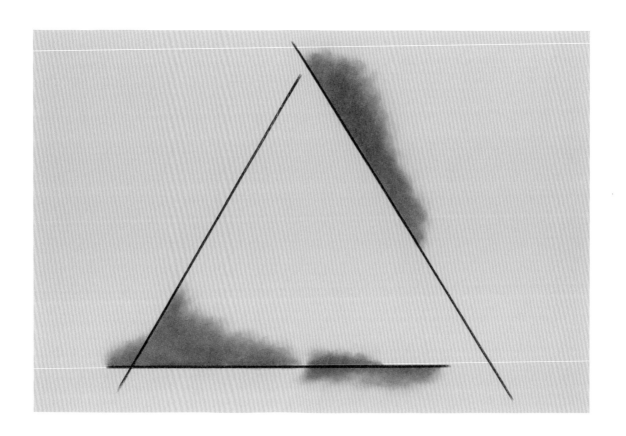

82
Pa '80-105
Pa '80-105
1980

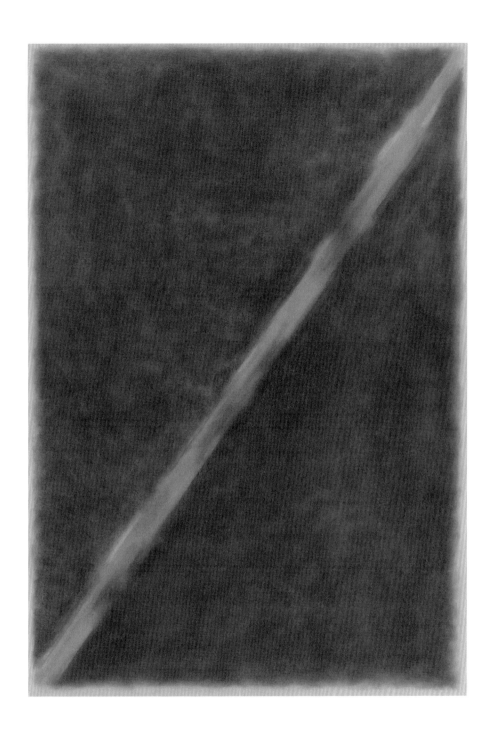

83
Pa-C '80-99
Pa-C '80-99
1980

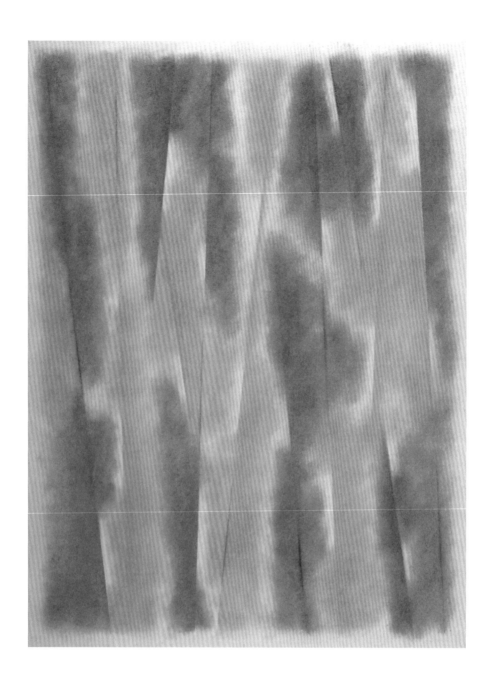

84
Pa-C '80-111
Pa-C '80-111
1980

写真の作品から離れ、1980年より
身体的かつ直接的な表現を求めて
パステルを使用するようになる。
塗り込まれた色面を切り裂くように線が
入っているが、この線は紙の折りや
補助線ではなく、塗分けによるものである。
このパステルでの試行はやがて油彩での
展開につながっていく。

In a move away from photographs,
from 1980 Kinoshita turned to pastels
in a search for more physical and
direct expression. This work has lines
that seem to cut through the painted
color fields, lines that are neither folds in
paper nor guides, but painted on.
This experiment with pastels in due
course led to the artist's next step, in oils.

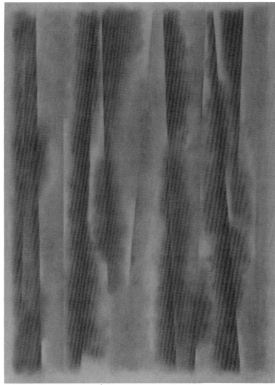

85
Pa-C '80-117
Pa-C '80-117
1980

86
Pa-C '80-120
Pa-C '80-120
1980

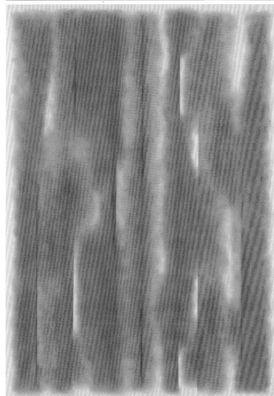

87
Pa-C '81-6
Pa-C '81-6
1981

88
Pa-C '81-8
Pa-C '81-8
1981

89
題不詳
Title Unknown
ca.1981

写真による表現を離れ、1980年から1981年にかけて
パステルを用いた表現を模索した木下。パステルで捉え
ようとした線と色の関係性はやがて、活動初期にも用いた
油彩による表現につながっていく。それまでの制作にお
ける不自由さから抜け出すべく、木下はよりフィジカルな
方法を試行する。そして、描いては塗りつぶすことを繰り
返すうちに、コンセプトを変えることなく新たな表現を見
つけ出した。

「存在」をめぐる概念や理論を理知的に作品に盛り込む
のではなく、「存在そのもの」を画面の上に作ればいい ──
図式的なコンセプトを取り去った木下は、1982年、《'82-
CA1》を発表。表現を模索し悩んだ時期の「描きと潰し」
から発展し、「塗ること」と「拭うこと」が画面上で等しく扱
われるようになる。木下にとって大きなターニングポイン
トになった本作以降、作品タイトルは制作年－支持体－
通番で表記されるようになった。

Chapter 3

1982—1994

During the period from 1980 to '81 Kinoshita moved
away from photographic expression, and explored working in pastels. The relationship of line and color that she
sought to apprehend using pastels in due course led to
the expression in oil colors that had also been a feature
of her early work. Kinoshita experimented with more
physical methods, in an attempt to free herself from previous constraints on her artistic practice. And as she
painted and scrapped, painted and scrapped, she eventually arrived at a new kind of expression, with no change
to her core concept.

Instead of incorporating ideas and theories around existence into works with an intellectual bent, perhaps she
could simply engender existence itself on the picture
plane: having excised all schematic concepts, in 1982
Kinoshita unveiled '82-CA1. In a progression from the
"painting and scrapping" of the period when she was
exploring and struggling with her expression, "applying"

第2章で紹介した写真や紙の作品がそうであったように、絵画においても毎年のように作風がアップデートされていく。1983年から1985年にかけては「線」の積み重ねによって塗面を生み出す表現が現れる。1986年には、AD&Aからのコミッションワークとして、同志社大学の図書館のために幅5メートルを超す自身最大の作品を制作。翌1987年から1989年には徐々に「塗り」は後退し、「線」によって画面に緊張感の凛う空間を認識させる表現がピークを迎える。色の濃淡や塗り重ねによって画面に奥行きを感じさせる描き方は、やがてストロークそのものを見せるアプローチへと昇華していった。

コンスタントに制作と展示を重ね、作家としての新たな頂点を迎えた最中の1990年、木下は乳がんの告知を受ける。手術を拒んだ木下は、制作や展示を続けながらも治療法を求めて国内各地の病院を訪ね、果てはロサンゼルスにまで渡る。1991年から断続的に滞在した現地でも精力的に制作を続け、ストロークを描き重ねて形や空間を生み出す表現は極致に達する。病魔に侵され、残された時間の少なさに「もっと描きたい」と抗う木下は、病床でも制作を続けた。1994年、作風に新たな兆しを見せるなか、木下は55歳でこの世を去った。

絵画へ回帰した1982年以降だけでも700点を超す作品を制作した。表現方法や素材が変わっても、一貫して「存在」についての問いを掲げ、「存在そのもの」を描くことをテーマとしてきた木下の活動は、近年再び国内外から注目され始めている。(大下)

and "wiping" came to be treated as equals on the picture plane. This work, which was to prove a major turning point in her practice, also marked her switch to titles consisting of year of production - support - serial number.

The style of Kinoshita's painting, like that of the photographic and paper works introduced in Chapter 2, was refreshed with almost every passing year. From 1983 to 1985 expression emerged in which cumulative "lines" generated painted fields. In 1986, Kinoshita made her largest-ever work, at over five meters in width, an AD&A commission for the Doshisha University library. The period from 1987 through 1989 saw a gradual retreat in the "painting" of color fields, and a peak in expression making the viewer conscious of tense spaces formed by "lines" on the picture plane. An approach to painting that involved giving a sense of depth to the picture plane through different intensities of color, and applying layers of color, was eventually elevated to an approach that showed the strokes themselves.

In 1990, just as Kinoshita was reaching new artistic heights, and making and exhibiting work continually, she was diagnosed with breast cancer. Rejecting surgery, she continued to work and exhibit while visiting hospitals around Japan in search of treatment, before finally ending up in Los Angeles. From 1991 she spent time sporadically in LA, continuing to throw herself into her work during her stays in the city, and perfecting her technique of producing forms and spaces by the layering of strokes. Besieged by illness, Kinoshita battled to paint as much as she could in the time left to her, even painting on her sickbed. In 1994, just as there were hints of yet another new development in her style, she passed away at the age of fifty-five.

Kinoshita produced over 700 works from 1982 onward, following her return to painting. The practice of this artist, who throughout her career questioned the nature of existence, and made existence itself consistently the dominant theme of her work even while adopting different materials and modes of expression, is now attracting renewed attention both in Japan and internationally. (Oshita)

90
'82-CA1
'82-CA1
1982

自身の表現に行き詰まりを感じた木下は、
存在を認識させるのではなく、
「存在そのもの」を描き出そうと思い至る。
画面に塗り込まれた絵具を布で
拭き取るという手法を通じて、カンヴァスの
持つ平面と、絵具による色面とを等価に
扱う表現に初めてたどり着いた、
記念碑的作品。

Feeling herself to be in an artistic
cul de sac, Kinoshita arrived at the idea
of attempting to depict existence itself,
rather than making the viewer conscious
of existence. This monumental work
marks her arrival for the first time at
expression that makes the planarity of
the canvas, and planarity rendered by
the paints, of equal value, in this case
through the technique of using a cloth
to wipe pigment off the painted
picture plane.

91*
'82-CA7
'82-CA7
1982

92
'82-CA26
'82-CA26
1982

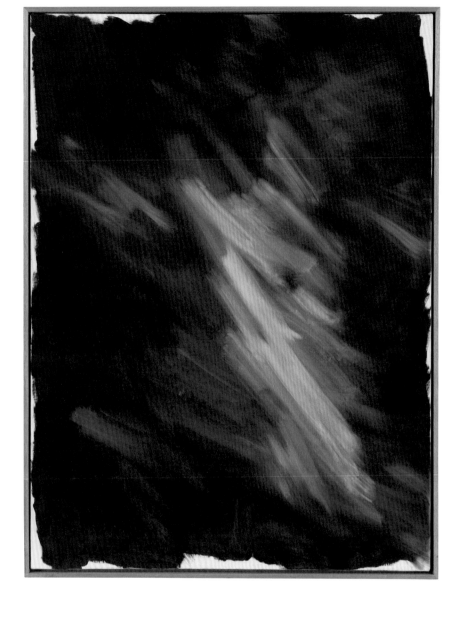

93*
'82-CA62
82-CA62
1982

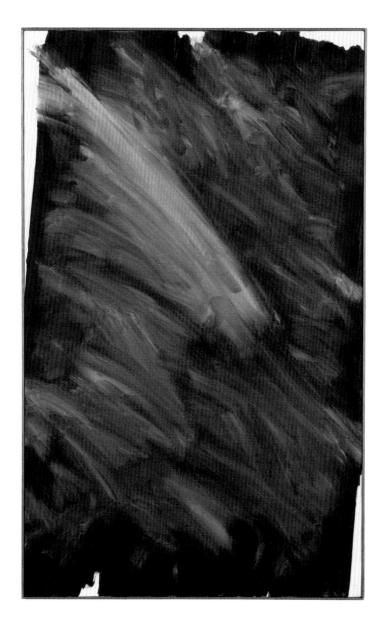

カンヴァスに対し、塗られた面が
傾いて見える。カンヴァスの下地を
残すことで、カンヴァスと色面の「存在」を
同時に出現させようとしている。
まるで筆のストロークを感じさせるかの
ように、布による拭き取りの動きがより
強調される。

The painted plane appears tilted on
the canvas. By leaving part of the
canvas ground, Kinoshita has attempted
to bring about the existence of canvas
and color field simultaneously.
The wiping action is emphasized, as if to
endow a sense of brushstrokes.

94
'83-CA74
'83-CA74
1983

95
'83-CA77
'83-CA77
1983

96
'83-CA88
'83-CA88
1983

97
'83-CA90
'83-CA90
1983

98
'84-CA233
'84-CA233
1984

99
'85-CA251
'85-CA251
1985

100*
'85-CA257
'85-CA257
1985

101
'85-CA261
'85-CA261
1985

102*
'85-CA262
'85-CA262
1985

103
'85-CA267
'85-CA267
1985

AD&Aからの依頼により、
同志社大学のラーネッド記念図書館の
ために制作された。
奥田善巳の《CO-310》(cat.no.106)と
対をなしており、天地の色を指す
《天地玄黄》という別名が付いている。

—

Commissioned by AD&A for the
Doshisha University Learned Memorial
Library, this work forms a pair with
Okuda Yoshimi's *CO-310* (cat.no.106),
and is also known as *Tenchi-Genko*
(Colors of Heaven and Earth).

105
'86-CA323
'86-CA323
1986

104
'85-CA287
'85-CA287
1985

106
奥田善巳 Okuda Yoshimi
CO-310
CO-310
1986

107
'86-CA350
'86-CA350
1986

108
'86-CA358
'86-CA358
1986

109
'86-CA375
'86-CA375
1986

110
'87-CA391
'87-CA391
1987

161   KAZUYO KINOSHITA

111*
'88-CA487
'88-CA487
1988

112
'88-CA517
'88-CA517
1988

113
'89-Pa537
'89-Pa537
1989

大型の油彩作品を制作する一方、
本作のような水彩画の小品も
手がけている。たとえメディウムや支持体、
サイズが異なっても、それらにより作品が
規定されることはない。小さな作品
ながらも、作家のコンセプトが高い強度で
表れている。

As well as making large works in oils,
Kinoshita also produced small
watercolors like this one. A work may be
of a different medium, support, or size,
but is never defined by these differences.
The artist's concept emerges confi-
dently even in this little painting.

114

115

114*   115*
'89-CA554   '89-CA557
'89-CA554   *'89-CA557*
1989   1989

116
'90-CA603
'90-CA603
1990

117
'90-CA605
'90-CA605
1990

118
'91-CA645
'91-CA645
1991

119
'91-CA652
'91-CA652
1991

120*
LA '92-CA681
LA '92-CA681
1992

121

122

121	122
LA '92-CA700	LA '92-CA711
LA '92-CA700	*LA '92-CA711*
1992	1992

123
LA '92-CA712
LA '92-CA712
1992

124
LA '92-CA713
LA '92-CA713
1992

173   KAZUYO KINOSHITA

125
LA '92-CA714
LA'92-CA714
1992

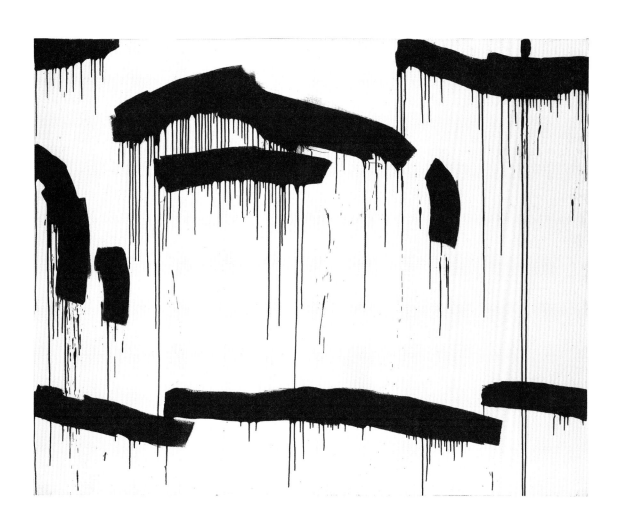

126
LA '92-CA716
LA '92-CA716
1992

127
LA '92-CA717
LA '92-CA717
1992

128
LA '92-CA729
LA '92-CA729
1992

129
'93-CA786
'93-CA786
1993

130*
'93-CA792
'93-CA792
1993

131*
'93-CA793
'93-CA793
1993

132
'93-CA799
'93-CA799
1993

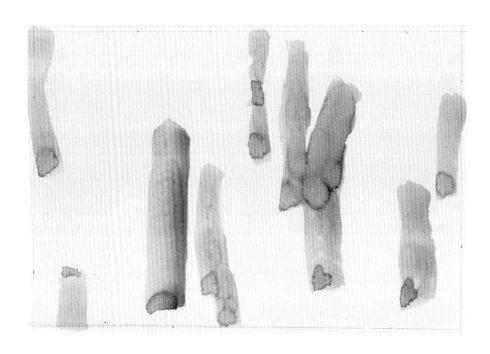

133
無題（絶筆・未完）
Untitled (Last work, unfinished)
1994

亡くなる直前の病床で描かれ、
絶筆となった未完作品。絵画に回帰した
1982年の第1作目から数えると、
本作は800点目となる。完成していれば
《'94 Pa-800》となっていただろうか。

Painted by Kinoshita on her sickbed not
long before her death, this unfinished
work was to be her last. The 800th since
her return to painting in 1982, if finished
one imagines it would have been titled
'94-Pa800.

私論 ── 木下佳通代のこと

熊田司 美術史家

はじまり

職業選択や人間関係の転変激しい10年間を潜り抜けた後、木下佳通代は奥田善巳と再婚して神戸市生田区（現在の中央区）山本通4丁目に落ち着いた。1年半後の1971年10月には同3丁目に移り、住居兼アトリエに美術教室「アートルーム・トーア」を開く。「トーア」の名が示すように、JR三ノ宮駅と元町駅の間を南北に貫く「トア・ロード」を、北に上り詰めて「山本通り」と交差する直前左手の小さな二階家である。そのどんつき西北側には「神戸外国倶楽部（現・神戸倶楽部）」があり、戦前その敷地にあった「トア・ホテル」が通り名の由来で、一時「敵性言語」排斥時代には「東亜道路」と呼ばれたが、今も「トア・ロード」は神戸でひときわ西洋風のおしゃれな通りと認識されているようだ。

　神戸に生まれ育った私は、初夏になると街路樹に植えられた合歓の仄紅い花が彩るこの通りに、ひとかたならぬ愛着があったが、その北端についてはちょっと名の通った西洋骨董店があること以外何の知識も無かった。私が親しんだのはむしろ坂を下りきった南端近く、阪急高架沿いの「サンセット通り」を東に折れて2軒目の、細長いビル地階にあるジャズ喫茶「さりげなく」である。

　木下さんと奥田さんが山本通に落ち着く少し前、すなわち1960年代末から70年代初頭にかけて、「政治の季節」に傷ついて逃げ込むように私は何度も何度もそこに通った。薄暗い階段を降りてそこから二段ほど上るとドアがあり、奥が見通せぬほど紫煙に烟った店にカウンター席が10席程度、JBLのスピーカが耳をつんざく音量でジャズを流していた。テーブル席があったかどうかの記憶が曖昧なのは、カウンター席に陣取って何を話すでもなく身体を揺らし、一杯のコーヒーないしビールで何時間もねばる常客の一人であったからであろう。白いシャツに黒いタイを決めたマスターあるいはスタッフに声を掛けるのは、演奏レコードのリクエスト、もしくは滅多になかったが飲み物の「おかわり」に限られていた。そうしたリクエストの一枚がエリック・ドルフィーの*Last Date*である。

　1964年、死の数週間前にオランダで収録されたこのライブ録音は、痙攣的なメロディーラインを紡ぐ最後の曲"Miss Ann"終了後の拍手や歓声にかぶせて、その直前に採録され

たドルフィーのインタビュー音声を収めている。「音楽を聴いていて、それが終われば空気中に消えてしまう、二度と捕まえることはできません……」という呪文のような語りが耳を離れず、後に木下さんの80年代ペインティング作品を見ていて、そぞろに思い返されたものである。

　しかし、ドルフィーやコルトレーンのリクエストにスタッフは余り乗り気でなかったみたいだ。60年代末の「さりげなく」には村上春樹も通ったそうだが、ウェストコースト・ジャズ贔屓らしい村上の嗜好と通底する趣味がこの店の基調をなしていた。そんなことを思いながら、最近ジェリー・マリガンのアルバム *What is There to Say?*（1959年）を聴いていると、またしても木下さんのペインティングが眼前に現れるような気がして驚いた。ゲストのトランペッター、アート・ファーマーとマリガンのバリトン・サックスが、消えては上書きするようなメロディーラインを交錯させるインタープレイに、ひときわ強くこの幻が現れたのである。

写真を用いた作品とその展開

この時代、木下さんは絵具を用いる初期の絵画試作から脱して、写真を用いた概念的な作品制作に集中しはじめていた。ジャズや、そもそも音楽というものに大きな関心は持たなかったのではないかと思われる。だから上に述べた感慨は、あくまで私の個人記憶の片隅に漣のように生じた観念連合に過ぎない。

　神戸の名物「花時計」は、1950年代後半から市庁舎北側にあって観光名所となっていたが、この「名所」を写真に撮るという陳腐な行為を、時間経過と撮影主体の交換／二重化という操作を加えて、10組20枚の紙焼き写真に構成する《Untitled／む38（花時計）》（1973年、cat.no.19）あたりが、その最初期の成果であろう。これは写真家たちのいわゆる「組写真」、つまり作家が思い描く特定のテーマ、ストーリーを複数のショットで構成する作品とは、似て非なるものである。テーマがあるとすれば、時間の推移と人間の生存ないし行為が切り結ぶ瞬間を定着し、また撮影主体と客体が入れ替わり連環するメビウスの輪のような構造を、写真というメディアを媒介に平面に連続提示する優れてコンセプチュアルな仕事であった。

　この系列の仕事には、シンプルに腕時計の経時変化を捉えた数枚の写真を並べる《Untitled／む59（腕時計）》（1974年、cat.no.20）や、ビーカーの湯の温度変化を温度計を添えて連続撮影した《Untitled／む60（ビーカー）》（1973年、cat.no.21）があるが、やや理に落ちすぎたきらいが無くはない。むしろその前年に制作された《Untitled-b／む103（壁のシミ（ブロック））》（1972年、cat.no.18）の方が、後年のペインティングにつながる契機を秘めて興味深い。壁などの補修のために、亀裂・剥落箇所をチョークで丸囲いしてチェックを入れる準備作業のやり方を、どこかで見たのかも知れない。チェック前後のモルタル壁を同一アングルから撮影して並置する作品で、拡散と集中を往き来する焦点によって変容する視覚のあり方を提起するとともに、経年劣化する物質と、加えられた真新しいチョークによる円のストロークが対照をなして、後年の作品展開を暗示するように思われる。

写真だけをメディアとするこれら70年代前半の仕事を私が知ったのは、大阪中之島美術館(当時の大阪市立近代美術館〔仮称〕建設準備室)が木下作品を継続的に収集しはじめた1990年代以降のことである。同時代的に木下佳通代の作品に注目した最初は、製図用具やそれで引かれた幾何学図形を撮影して焼き付けた大判プリントに、フェルトペンで「像主」たる幾何学図形を「描き起こす」作品群であった。1976年に始まるこのシリーズをどこで知ったのか記憶が定かではないが、はっきり憶えているのは1978年、当時の兵庫県立近代美術館が開催した「アート・ナウ '78」に12点が展示されたことである(p. 211)。

　シリーズ初期の一点に、たとえば木製三角定規を「像主」とする作品《'76-1》(1976年、cat. no.47)があるが、そこから強く想起されるのは古来有名なプラトンの「イデア論」であろう。すなわち[1]道具・家具のイデア、[2]それを模倣して造られた現実の道具・家具、[3]さらにその再現描写たる絵画、という風に「イデア」から遠ざかる三段階の「模倣」の最下位に絵画を置き、その価値を貶めた古典的藝術論であるが、[2]の木製三角定規を[3]撮影して大判印画紙に焼き付け、そして[1]その「イデア」をフェルトペンで直に印画紙の上に作図する、という木下のやり方は通例の画家の仕事とは真逆な、哲学者の純粋思考を図解するがごときものではなかったか。

　どこまで自覚的であったかは措いて、この系列の仕事は丸めたり折り曲げたり、くしゃくしゃにした紙に引かれた幾何学図形の変容を撮して、その原型(イデア)をフェルトペンで描き起こすという風に展開した。加えて当初は斜め上方からのカメラ・アイで線遠近法的に捉えていた紙を、やがて正面から正対直視した撮像へと変化させ、被写体である紙を本来のプロポーションに戻した外郭ぎりぎりに印画紙をカットすることで、より訴求力の強い表現を獲得した。モノクロ印画であるから、線遠近法を捨象して明暗法を際立たせた紙の質感とシャープな線描が映発しあって、魅力的な平面が形成されるのである。これら一連の仕事の最終段階では、「描き起こし」がフェルトペンによる幾何学的な線に留まらず、あるいはフリーハンドのドローイングを加え、またエアブラシによる幾何学図形の「塗り」を施すなど多様化する。いずれにせよ木下の関心事は、1970年代末には「現実」を定着する「写真」から離脱してドローイングや「塗り(ペインティング)」そのものへと移行していったようである。

ペインティング、そして最後の日々へ

私がはじめて木下さんと言葉を交わしたのは、1982年だったと思う。同年9月から10月にかけて、京都のギャラリー16で奥田善巳と木下佳通代は相次いでペインティングによる個展を開催するが、その少し前に案内状を携えた両人が揃って私の勤務先、建て替え前の西宮市大谷記念美術館事務所に訪ねてきたのである。この個展は、油彩によるペインティングに転回してから初の本格的個展であり、やや早く前年頃から油彩作品を制作しはじめた奥田と雁行して、この年木下も油彩ペインティングへと歩を進めた。

突然の訪問は、『美術手帖』(1980年5月号、No.465)に私が書いた1980年京都アンデパンダンの短い展評で、木下佳通代に触れたのを見たからであろう。その文中で、折った紙にパステルの擦り込むような塗りを施し、拡げて見せた木下さんの作を、エアブラシを用いたと私が見誤ったことを注意する意図があったかも知れない。ドローイングからペインティングへと今後仕事を進めようとの抱負を語ったと記憶する。

　こうした過渡期の仕事を経て、木下はいよいよペインティングへと転回(あるいは帰還というべきか)するのであるが、案内状に掲載された第一作《'82-CA 1》(1982年、cat.no.90)は、暗青色の油絵具をたっぷり含んだ平筆で、カンヴァス地を粗く塗り残した色面の中央部を、ぼろ裂や乾いた筆で拭き取ったのがよく解る。制作の中途で唐突に投げ出したような画面は、油絵初学者の試行錯誤を思わせるが、絵画はブラッシュで塗ることで成立するという常識への反問がそこに胚胎している。同様の試作を何十点も重ねた後、画面はより複雑に塗りと拭いを交錯させ、塗り色も暗青色や暗褐色、朱赤などのヴァリエーションを示すようになる。こうした実験は、紙と水彩の小画面でも徹底的に試みられたが、1985年3月神戸新港突堤脇の三菱倉庫にアトリエを借りて大画面の制作が可能となり、ついにはその到達点たる大作《'86-CA 323》(1986年、cat.no.105)が制作されるのである。

　かつて同志社大学京田辺キャンパスを飾ったこの作は、油絵具を滴らせながら全面に暗青色を塗り拡げ、拭き取りまた塗り重ねて、嵐の前兆のような暗雲が画面を覆い尽くす観を呈するが、大画面に挑むひたむきさと苦渋が相半ばして必ずしも成功したとは言いがたい。それが、垂直・水平の要素に整理され、さらに塗りと拭いが重層して空間を内に孕むかのような画面へと展開し、1980年代の末には《'89-CA 554》(1989年、cat.no.114)などの諸作で、風と水蒸気が戯れて雲が湧き、また霧消するがごとき「軽み」の絵画を実現するに至る。比喩的に言えば、モンドリアンが「プラスとマイナスの絵画」で幾何学的絶対抽象に至ったように、木下佳通代は「プラスとマイナスのブラッシュ・ストローク」で自らの「絶対的絵画」を手中にしたのである。

　こうした晴朗清澄で、ある種の諦念が透けて見える「幸福」な絵画世界は、しかし1990年の乳がん宣告によって烈しく乱される。「死」が身近な環境に突然放り出された木下は、底知れぬ不安や生への執着などが心に渦巻き、生き急ぐかのような行動に走る。治療法を求めて国内各地や韓国の病院を行脚し、ロサンゼルスへの度重なる渡航もその延長線上にあった。しかし、一方で残された時間をありったけ自己実現に注ぎ込もうとする、息苦しいばかりの生命力が頭をもたげる。制作においては、乾きの早いアクリル絵具を用い、油絵具を塗っては拭き取る緩やかな時間を端折って性急に作品を産出しようとするが、そこには止みがたい焦慮も垣間見えないではない。それでも、ロスで制作された《LA '92-CA711》(1992年、cat.no.122)など92年の作品は、乾いた風が吹くように爽やかで、そこにウェストコースト・ジャズの暖かいフレーズも混じるかのようだ。

　しかし、1994年4月のAD&Aギャラリー個展には重苦しい雰囲気が漂っていた。垂直

方向が目立つ幅広の刷毛のストロークを重ね、拭き取る余裕もなく白のストロークを分厚く上塗りする作品は力強く、その切迫感に圧倒される大作を煉瓦壁にずらりと並べた会場で、思いのほか元気そうな木下さんと短い会話を交わした。華やいだ装いが少々意外で、5ヶ月後にこの世を去る人とも思えず、壁面に目を転じると作品は消えることなく厳として存在を主張している。ただ、そこかしこに「死」の影がひたひた忍び寄るように見え、暗澹たる思いを禁じ得なかったのである。

　これが、木下さんと私の*Last Date*であった。

Kumada Tsukasa

写真とコンセプチュアリズム

建畠哲 埼玉県立近代美術館館長

木下佳通代は、当初は画家をめざして京都市立芸大の西洋画科に学んだ。在学時の作品の女性像（《題不詳／む76》1960年、cat.no.1）には、教鞭をとっていた黒田重太郎の影響であろうか、キュビスム的と言えなくもない色面分割が見られる。後述するように、それはそれで興味深い事実ではあるが、卒業後は絵画の仕事を継続的に展開することはなかった。彼女ならではの方法を明確にした写真による作品の制作を始めたのは70年代に入ってからであって、その間の制作活動はやや下火になっていたのである。しかし木下自身にとってそれは何ら空白の時期であったわけではなく、むしろ河口龍夫らを中心とする西の前衛美術集団・グループ〈位〉との密接な交流などを通じて、独自のコンセプチュアリズムを形成するための不可欠の準備時期であったに違いない。

　当時の関西の美術を巡る動向はといえば、具体美術協会は集団としてはすでに解散しており、大阪万博（1970年）で盛り上がったメディア・アートも終了後は求心力を失っていて、時代を領導するようなイズムのない状況であった。そうした中で木下と同年代の河口龍夫、少し年下の野村仁、植松奎二、北辻良央らがそれぞれにコンセプチュアルな方向性をもった領域を探求していたことは注目されてよいだろう。木下佳通代は彼らからやや遅れて制作を再開するのだが、1970年代前半から後半にかけての写真を用いた作品は、コンセプチュアリズムの純粋実験ともいうべき純度の高さにおいて際立っていたように思われる。

たとえば1973年の10組からなる写真作品（《Untitled／む38（花時計）》、cat.no.19）は、神戸市にある巨大な花時計を10人の知人に頼んで同じ位置に三脚を立てて撮影してもらったもので、いずれもそれぞれが撮影している情景を背後から木下自身が撮影した写真とセットになっている。写真は同じモチーフの連続撮影が容易であることからシークエンシャルな（順を追って継起的に展開される）組写真をなすことが多いが、木下には時間の推移を対象化する意図はなく、時計の針が示す時刻も（撮影日は異なっているが）どれもほぼ11時前後である。つまり彼女はすべての写真のイメージをサイマルテーニアスに（並置的、同時的に）提示しようとしているのであって、あえて穿った見方をするなら、時計というモチーフは、そのためにこそ（つまり継起的な時間性の排除を"自己証明"するためにこそ）要請されているのである。

それに対してたとえば河口龍夫の《陸と海 (Land and Sea)》(1970年) は海岸の砂浜の波打ち際に4枚の長い板を並べ、潮の満ち引きで板を洗う波の位置が時間の経過とともに変化していく様態を60点の粒子の粗いプリントにしたもので、陸と海の境界としての波という自然現象が極めて即物的な眼差しでシークエンシャルに捉えられている。野村仁の《道路上の日時 (Time on a Curved Line)》(1970年) はカーブする道路を移動しながら、ある程度の間隔を置いて、アスファルト舗装の上にチョークでその場の日付と時刻を記した路面を撮影した組写真で、同じ行為の繰り返しのうちに、まさに直接的にシークエンシャルな時間の経過が対象化されているといえよう。

　彼 (彼女) らは、いずれも無機的、機械的なイメージの記録を可能にする写真というメディアに、それぞれのコンセプチュアリズムの探求を託したのであり、主観的な表現の排除という点では通底しているといえなくはない。しかし河口と野村の組写真がイメージの切断と連続という両義性においていわば微分的な時間軸を宿しているのに対し、木下佳通代の組写真は10組をサイマルテーニアスに、同時的、一望的に提示して見せる。花時計を撮影する人を撮影する視座 (アーティストの視座) はひとつであり、見ている人を見ている人を見ているといった、誰もが思い付きがちな連鎖に陥ることはない。彼女の視座とは本人の言葉を借りれば、造物主であり神ということになるだろう。それは何も傲慢な言葉ではなく、私なりの独断を許してもらうなら、実在の花時計と視覚との相互的な関係を存在論のレベルに桁上げすることなのである。

———

　1976年から77年に制作されたコンパスを使った一連の作品で、こうした同時的な提示の意図はより鮮明にされることになった。《作品'77-D》(1977年、cat. no. 48) は正円を描いた紙を折り曲げて撮影した写真をプリントし、そのいびつになった円のイメージに重ね合わせて、まったく同じ大きさの正円をプリントの上にフェルトペンで描き込んだものである。いうならば多視点の導入によって見え方が変容する円の形を、平面の折り曲げという物理的な操作をほどこしたイメージとして創出し、その歪んだイメージをプリント写真によって再平面化し、その同一平面上にもうひとつの視点としての円を対比的に共存させるという、トリッキーといえばいかにもトリッキーな仕掛けである。

　いささか飛躍した話になるが、考えようによっては、これはセザンヌ的キュビスムにおける多視点のありようと重なっているといえなくもない。セザンヌの静物画では、テーブルの上の果物皿は真上の視点から見た正円だが、同じテーブルに置かれた壺の口の方は斜め上から見た楕円であるという、二つの視点が共存している。木下の作品における写真のイメージと描かれたイメージの同時存在には、どこかでこうしたキュビスムにもつながる絵画空間の問題が意識されていたように思われるのである。

———

　ところでトリッキーであることは、何ら彼女の方法的な実験の純粋性を疑わしめるもので

はないだろう。コンセプチュアリズムの探求は、しばしばトリッキーな発想の転換に結び付くのであって、木下の上記の作品の場合は、三次元の空間を二次元化してしまう写真の機能を逆方向に捉え直し、二次元の空間が発生させる純粋なるイリュージョンとしての三次元のイメージを出現させようとしている。それはつまるところ現実にはありえない二つの視点の同一平面における同時存在の謂いにほかならないのである。

　繰り返しになるが、その点において花時計の作品とコンパスの作品の意図は共有されている。1980年代には再び絵画の仕事へと向かっていくのだが、その前の段階で彼女が一連のこうした緊張感に満ちた作品に取り組んでいたことは改めて高く評価されるべきであろう。それは戦後日本美術におけるもっとも先鋭なコンセプチュアリズムの実験であったが、今見直すなら木下佳通代ならではの極めて知的で端正な美しさを湛えた世界でもあったといわなければなるまい。

思考の結晶 ── 木下佳通代の写真と絵画

光田ゆり　多摩美術大学大学院教授、同校アートアーカイヴセンター所長、ブーアール舎主宰

I 活動期

──

木下佳通代は1939年神戸市生まれ、本格的に作家活動を始めたのを、初めて写真作品を発表した1972年個展からだと仮定すると、そのスタートは決して早くない。高度成長期の1960年代、美術においても廃品芸術、反芸術からポップアートへと注目の動向が熱気を醸していたはずだが、立体も多数作っていたという木下の初期作品は多くは知られていない。

　1972年といえば、木下より7歳年上の田中敦子は具体美術協会をすでに辞して（1965年）危機を乗り越え、南画廊で個展を開いていた。6歳上の菅野聖子は田中と入れ替わるように具体に関わって数学を援用したシステマティックな絵画を制作、グタイピナコテカで個展（1971年）を開いた。京都市立芸術大学で10年後輩の沢居曜子はまさに活動を始めようとしていた。千里丘で大々的に開催された大阪万博（EXPO'70)には関西の作家たちの関わりは薄く、同地に継承すべき成果を残したとも言い難い。京都国立近代美術館の「現代美術の動向」展は1970年で終了した。

　一方1960年代後半から、グループ〈位〉やTHE PLAYらが集団でコンセプトをもった行為の作品を屋外で展開し始めた。京都市美術館では1969年頃から京都アンデパンダン展が活況を呈し、作家グループ主導の映像展など多様な企画が続いていた。さらに兵庫県立近代美術館（当時）では現代作家選抜展「アート・ナウ」が始まる（1975-88年）など、1970年代の関西では先鋭的な試みを発表できる場が形成されていた。作家グループの活動についてはいずれも女性作家の参加はごく限られていたが、木下は本拠地・神戸で写真作品の制作を独自に展開、京都アンデパンダン展に出品し、現代日本美術展等や各種グループ展への参加、東京での個展をはさみながら、ギャラリー16（京都）などでコンスタントに個展を行った。知的で静謐な写真作品世界を築いた木下佳通代は、敬意と信頼を集める作家になった。

　第10回日本国際美術展「人間と物質」展（1970年）前後から、写真製版の版画、ビデオ、組写真、インスタレーションなどの方法を用いた多様な新境地が開かれる一方、「絵画・彫刻」は慣習的なメディアとみなされ根本的に検証し直された。廃品だけでなくFRPやアクリル、鉄、ステンレスなど工業製品、ライトやモーターなどの導入が目立って、「平面・立体」と漸次呼

称が変化していくことにもなった。こうした潮流は、木下の写真作品時代と重なっている。

　1970年代を通して写真作品の制作を継続した木下は、成果と評価を積み上げたのち、1980年頃からは素材と方法を転換させて、パステル画、ついで油彩画に打ち込んだ。これまでどおりの深い思考を厳密に方法化しながら、身体的動的な魅力を加えた油彩画にすぐれた展開を続け、1994年病に没するまで新たな絵画の空間とその評価を獲得していく。木下が絵に打ち込む頃、「平面」は再び「絵画」へと呼び変えられ、あるいはニューペインティングという語が流行のひとつになったものの、木下はこの物語的な表現主義的絵画の潮流とは無関係だった。1980年代に花開く関西ニューウェーブの勢いを見つめ、次世代の作家たちとも交流を楽しみながら、自らの道を進み続けたという。

　木下は、自作について次のように書いたことがある。

　　私は常々、自分の作品が、時と共に風化し、朽ち果てることのない強いものでありたいと考えています。そして作品には美術以外の「こと」を出来る限り持ち込まないよう、表現の問題のみに終始したいと考えています。

「トアロード画廊　木下佳通代展」『画廊プロムナード』1984年10月、p.7

没後30年を迎えて、木下佳通代の仕事の全貌が2つの美術館で紹介される本展は、待望の機会である。わたしもできる限り「表現の問題のみに終始して」木下の仕事について記すことができるよう努めたい。

II 写真とみること (1)

木下は個展などの際に短いステートメントを度々発表してきた。そこでまず課題にしていたのは、「みる」行為の分析と、その先にある「存在」の「認識」についての問いだった。

　「再び、「みる」ことについて・展」(1973年、ギャラリー16)では、知人らの協力を得て神戸駅前の花時計を計10名が撮影した、組写真《Untitled / む(花時計)》(cat.no.19)を発表した。花時計のクローズアップ写真と、各撮影者の後ろ姿遠景の2枚を1セットとする、10組20点のシリーズになる。どれも似たような花時計の写真だが、撮影者の遠景と組み合わされて初めて、撮影者がすべて異なることがわかり、同時刻に撮影された2点の写真が呼応する。ただ、花時計も後ろ姿も、それぞれほぼ同じ位置から撮影されているので、時計の指し示す時刻と撮影者の姿以外に、各組の写真にこれといった差異はない。

　同展展評で平野重光はこれを「事物の客観的存在 ── すなわち見ることの以前に物の存在があること」の実験だととらえた。「主体がもつさまざまな観念や意識や気分」のもとで見るという行為は、「事物の先在性」とは「別物であるはずだ」との考えのもと、「事物を客観的存在」だと問おうとしている、と平野は書いている[*1]。花時計という事物は、撮影者たちの入

れ替わりにも超然として存在する客体だ、ということなのだろうか。平野の解釈は、次の作家自身のステートメントとも符合する。

> 再び、「みる」ことについて・展
> 人が或る「存在する」事物を「みる」時 ── その存在する事物は、一般的な概念、個人的な観念、日常的かつ状況的要素、個人的嗜好あるいは認識の差異による種々の意識、等によって、普遍的性格と共に、個別的な性格を持つものとして、より強く変化に富んだ在り方を呈しているかにみえる。しかしそのすべての意思のかかわりを断ち切る時、それは、それ自体として、たゞ「在る」ことだけが認識される。
>
> 同展リーフレット、1973年

ただ「在る」、「存在する」「事物」を認識するため、「意思のかかわり」を断ち切るのは、ここでは撮影者と被写体を写した遠景写真であり、遠景を撮影したもう一人の「みる」人（作者である木下だろうか）の役割になる。「事物」と、カメラを使って「みる」撮影者たちを、周囲の空間ごと、もう一人の「みる」人が撮影している。花時計の写真だけなら、私たちには撮影者の差異はわからず、周囲に広がる光景も知ることはなかった。遠景の写真は、見る行為をとらえたメタ的な視点なのだと言ってよい。

　ただ気になるのは、遠景撮影者の背後に、より遠景からの撮影者はもう置かれないことである。遠景10点が同一人物の撮影によるかどうかわからないまま、この撮影者の個人性は問われないのはなぜか。これを、木下は本作で写真の2種類の役割を、1組2点にそれぞれ振り分けたからだ、と考えてみたい。その役割とは、「みる」行為を明らかにする「視覚・視野の再現」としての「写真」と、レンズの「客観性」による「記録」としての「写真」とでも記せるだろう。花時計の写真は前者「視野」を、遠景写真は後者「記録」を、と作家は写真の2種の役割を振り分けて、ひと組にしている。

III 写真とみること（2）

もし遠景からの撮影者をさらに置くなら、撮影者の撮影者を無限につなげざるをえず、別の実験になってしまうだろう。ここで思い浮かぶのは、3年後の作品《Untitled (Some profile or some consciousness)》（1976年、cat.no.35）である。二人の人物を撮影した写真をその人物が一人で見る、それを撮影し、その写真をさらに見る……これを繰り返すことで、見られた自分を見る行為が、層状に重ねられた作品である。

　同作の対象が、対面する二人の人物（カップル）であるのは、木下作品には稀な例で、興味深い。はじめに、彼らは互いを見ていた。観察者であり見られる対象でもあった。向かい合う自分たちが写真として示され、それを見る、見ている自分自身が見られる（撮影される）、その写真を見る

……この循環が示される。互いはお互いをどう見ているのか、確かめる術はない(ここに「視野」としての写真はない)。本作は見る行為を「記録」する客観性の写真の層である。逆説的に写真画面で示されるのは、見続けても見切れることなく循環する、二人の人物の視野の不一致になる。

木下の自画像でもある《Untitled》(1976年、cat.no.39)も気になる作品だ。自分自身の正面立像の定点観測である。定点からの機械的な時間差撮影で、全身を8つに分割し、写真の各部分をつなぎあわせて、多時刻の自分を編み上げている。各パーツに記された撮影日時の幅は小さく、定点観測というよりは複数時間の像のコラージュというべきかもしれない。つまり衣服を替え髪型が多少違っていても、彼女自身はほぼ変わらずに同じ場所に立つ、存在の確かさを証明するかのように。ここで写真は客観的「記録」として使われている、と言ってよいだろう。

そうではあっても、対象が自分自身であるからこそ、本作は2種類の写真のゆらぎを内包していて、それが魅力にもなっている。つまり自分自身を見る視野を、人は持てず、鏡か写真を使うしかない。自動シャッターの自写像は、「記録」であるだけでなく、見えない自分を自ら見ようとして設定する「視野」代行でもあった。

IV 写真とみること(3)

美術評論家・中原佑介の主著『見ることの神話』(フィルムアート社、1972年)にも、「見ること」と課題がタイトルされている。第10回日本国際美術展「人間と物質」展コミッショナーを務めた中原は、「見る」をキーワードにした1965-71年のエッセイから本書を編んだ。批評家としての全盛期を迎えていた中原は、コンセプチュアル・アート、映像、パフォーマンス、インスタレーションなど最新潮流を、「見る」ことを問い直す営為として捉える軸を示した。宮川淳、石子順造ら同時代の評論家もこのテーマを共有し、「見る」主体に無意識に含まれる先入観や慣習、個人的あるいは時代的な志向を分析しようとした。それらを可視化し意識化しようとする態度が、制作と鑑賞の根本的な検証のために必要だとする考えは、同時代にかなり共有されていたようだ。石子がグループ「幻触」の理論的支柱となって錯視効果を採り上げたのも、中原と「トリックス・アンド・ヴィジョン」展(1968年、東京画廊及び村松画廊)を企画したのも、美術の描写技術が生み出してきた錯視空間(イリュージョン)を考察し直すことが、美術そのものの検証につながると考えたからだった。「見ること」の分析と検証は、現代美術の転換のために求められた同時代的な課題だった。

しかも国際的な課題だった。1960年代後半から、オランダのヤン・ディベッツ[Fig. 1]、イタリアのジュゼッペ・ペノーネ[Fig. 2]、アメリカのヴィト・アコンチ[Fig. 3]、エドワード・ルッシェ[Fig. 4]らが代表する動向があり、組写真を使って空間の認識、時間の経過における対象の変化、行為と空間の関わり、などを可視化し分析する作品が繰り広げられた。木下の身近にも、野村仁[Fig. 5]、河口龍夫らの組写真の仕事もあった。

木下も自身のやり方でこうしたパラダイムを共有していただろう。彼女が追求するのは、存在そのものの純粋な認識。そのために妨げになる諸々を指摘し、意識化するための設定を設けるとき、カメラが必要になり、写真作品を手がけた。

木下はすべての存在するものを等価に認識する状態を、高校時代から思い描いてきたという。

> 意識が霧のようになって宇宙に漂えるなら全てを確認できる。最小単位の意識だけは残っていたいという願望が心情的に10代の頃からありました。(…)
> 私が本当に見ようとしているのは、"等価に存在する何か"。生命体でも精神でも。
>
> 「インタビュー」『木下佳通代 1939−1994』AD&A、1996年、p.91 (本書p.206に再録掲載)

> 意識を空間に浮遊させること
>
> 『神戸っ子』212号、1978年12月、p.60

彼女はすべてをくまなく見通せる、超越的な、神の視点に憧れていたのだろうか。そうなれば得られるはずの、「存在は等価」という信念が木下の制作の基点になっていた。偏りのない認識の下では、存在も存在しないものも、すべては等価である、と。

この考えを伝えようと、透明の立体を作るなど、試行していたらしい。1970年の「境界の思考」シリーズの3点 (cat. nos. 8-10)も、そうした例だったに違いない。立方体、円錐、円柱という、セザンヌの有名な言葉「自然を円筒形と球体と円錐形で捉えなさい」を思い出させるような、幾何学立体が輪切りにされている。その内部は、立体を包む空間と同じ色。「存在」の内部と外部は同質、等価だというメッセージだろうか。

Fig. 1

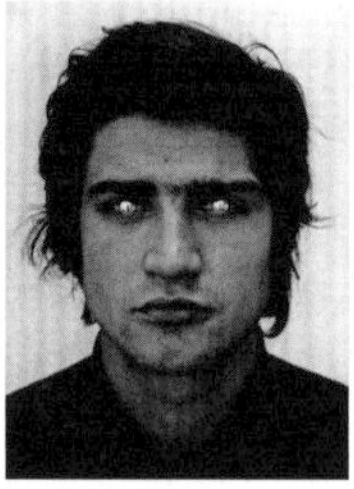
Fig. 2

Fig. 3

Fig. 4

Fig. 1 ヤン・ディベッツ《Perspective correction − My studio 1, 2: square》1969年
出典:『ヤン・ディベッツ展カタログ』鎌倉画廊、1982年、頁数無

Fig. 2 ジュゼッペ・ペノーネ《自分の目を裏返す》1970年
出典:『ジュゼッペ・ペノーネ − 石の欠陥』豊田市美術館、1997年、p. 114

Fig. 3 ヴィト・アコンチ《Following Piece》1969年
出典: *Vito Acconci*, PHAIDON, 2002, p. 38

Fig. 4 エドワード・ルッシェ《Phillips 66, Flagstaff, Arizona, 1962, from Twentysix Gasoline Stations》1963年
出典: *Ed Rucha and photography*, Whitney Museum of American Art, 2004, p. 113

Fig. 5 野村仁《Photobook 又は視覚のブラウン運動》写真製本、1972−1974年、豊田市美術館蔵
出典:『見る 野村仁: 偶然と必然のフェノメナ』赤々舎、2006年、p. 19

Fig. 5

存在すべてが同質、等価であるとは、日常のわたしたちは認識しない。特定の何かを、何らかの意識で見ることになる。木下がシルクスクリーンでひとつの写真を連続して刷り、時間差における「視野」として使って、手彩色を加えていったシリーズ (1975年、cat. nos. 24-34) には、等価に対象を見ようとする困難、あるいはそのための段階が示されている。

　観察者と対象の関係をテーマにした、写真や写真製版の版画作品は、ほぼ同時代に少なからず見受けられる。吉田克朗は《Work》シリーズの一部 (1969-74年頃) [Fig. 6] で観察者の視点を色彩や像のずれで示そうした。植松奎二は《見ること・風景》(1974年) [Fig. 7] の組写真で自分の視点を都度変えながら、ほぼ同じ風景を連写した。彼らの作品は、時間のなかで視点が対象との関係を結んでいく過程を示している点で、木下作品と通じ合う。三者は見る主体と対象との関係性を可視化しようとした。異なるのは、木下作品が、一種の結論を用意した点ではないだろうか。写真が時間を止めるとき、視点が順次移動しながら、最終的には全景を見渡せる、と示唆されている。「存在」の「等価」をめざすという、明確な基本姿勢を持つゆえに、木下は主体の諸条件を解消すべきだと考えていた。

V 写真とみること (4)

ついで木下が手がけたのは、紙上の幾何学図形を撮影するシリーズである。このシリーズが最も多くの点数を発表したはずで、木下の代表作のひとつというべきだろう。

　幾何学図形はまずコンパスを使って描かれる円から始まった。対角線、平行線、正方形、三角形、グリッド。様々なヴァリエーションがある。

　あらかじめ基本幾何学図形が紙に手描きされ、その紙を撮影する。撮影角度によって、または紙の反りや折れによって、幾何学形体はゆがむ。このシリーズの写真は「視野」の役割を担う。わたしたちは経験上、視野内の図形のゆがみを無意識に修正し、これが正円であるという情報を加味して認識するのを常とするが、もちろん木下の厳密さはそんな曖昧を許さない。日常的なものに縛られた視野を美的に摘発し、認識の別の地平に導くのだ。

　彼女は、もともと紙に描かれていたものと同図形を写真面に手描きして、再現する。このとき、撮影された紙に描かれた図形と、写真面に描かれた図形が同寸になるよう設定される。

Fig. 6
吉田克朗《Work 13》1971年
画像提供：Yumiko Chiba Associates

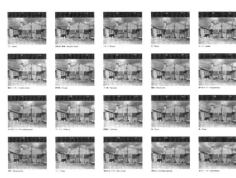

Fig. 7
植松奎二《見ること・風景》1974年
画像提供：Yumiko Chiba Associates

そうすれば写真の表面と、その向こう側の存在 ── 近過去に撮影された紙 ── が、別時空間の層を貫いて、重ね合わされる。フェルトペンで写真面に描かれた図形は、写真の撮影情報には含まれない、時空を隔てた外部、手前側にある。写真面という、視野像の表面に後に加えられた線である。(紙上に描かれた)三次元空間内の図形と、(フェルトペンで最後に描かれた)二次元の写真面上の図形と、同寸同形図が重ね合わされるとき、両者のずれと相違が、視野のゆがみを可視化する。あるいは、対象を「みる」わたしたちに、正解(?)が示される。

　元の紙が距離をもって撮影され周囲に余白空間が生じる場合と、写真面の全面が元の紙とほぼ同一面積になる場合がある。おおまかには、木下は前者から後者へと展開していったようだ。前者では、写真面は紙を客観視する「記録」に近づく。後者では写真の「視野」は、紙面そのものに近づくだろう。

　制作作業は緻密である。よく選ばれたシンプルな色彩のペン描線をモノクローム写真面に加え、緻密さの基盤の上で、静謐さとともに、ほのかな楽しさを伝えてくれる。これは知的なゲームなのだ。作家は念入りに準備を行う。

　　この作品の制作は観念やイメージや恣意性を可能な限り抑制した上で、選んだ紙にまず、折る、或いは線を描くなどして手を加え、そこから新たな次元に出発出来る状態を作ることから始まります。
　　あとはその状態の設定と同様の方法で、行為或いは関わりを拡げていきますが、丁度際限なく装置を設けていくように押し進め、紙の表面と手を加えた状態とが等価にみえる段階で、完結ではなく、打ち切ります。私が意図すると云えるのは、作品が非常にリアルに、みるという体験を可能にするものとなることなのです。

『Viewかんざき』36号、1981年、p.23

木下は撮影前の紙に対してまず「状態の設定」を行い、「紙の表面と手を加えた状態とが等価にみえる段階」を作ることで、みるという体験をリアルにする、という。

　紙は、机上に置かれている。紙という物質としての面、机上という場としての面、それを見る「視野」の代替としての写真面。3つの平面がそれぞれの「設定」上に重なることで、幾何学図形の元来の状態と、みる体験とのあいだのずれを示すことができる。このずれは、正確さを追求する態度ゆえに静謐になり、無駄な情報を注意深くとり除いているために、美しい。「観念やイメージや恣意性を可能な限り抑制した」作業が生み出す、すみずみを満たすほどの均衡が、抒情的にさえ見える逆説がある。

　初めに行う「状況の設定」を変えると、様々な見え方のヴァリエーションパターンを生み出せる。この蓄積のあと、木下は同様の「状況の設定」を、写真で撮影せず、画廊空間の中に設置するインスタレーションの試みを行っている(1977年、pp.102-103)。画廊には描画する紙、机、そして写真面の代替として置かれたであろう透明アクリル板が使われた。記録写

真からだけでは、三次元の構成がどう実現できたのか、わたしは十分には理解できないでいるが、紙、机面、アクリル面（写真面の代替）という3つの面が実空間で破綻なく重なるには困難が生じる可能性はある。インスタレーション化はその後展開しなかったようだが、木下が閉じた写真面の均衡から脱出しようと考えていたことがうかがわれる。

1981年、木下はハイデルベルク・クンストフェラインで個展を行った。当時西ドイツにも住んでいた植松奎二の紹介もあって、木下の写真作品が高く評価されたひとつの成果だろう。ただ、この時はもう、作家は別の方向に踏み出していた。国際的な美術の動向も、別の方向に動き出していたように思われる。

VI 絵の空間(1)

写真を使って見ることの検証を行ってきた作家は、次の扉を開く。

> 写真の使用によって、観念が先行し、表現が手段となる恐れが出てきたために、直接描くことを始めたのですが、この表現方法の変化によって、より大きな展開を得られたように思います。色彩は紙の表面とまったく等価に色面として在り、線は形としての意味を持たず、境界でもなく、ただ色面の中での深みとなり、なおかつ種々の表現要素の総てが、一つの作品としての平面を成立し得ればと考えています。
>
> 「木下佳通代展」『美術手帖』2月号、No. 477、1981年、p. 251

描画はまず、紙にパステルで描くことから始まった。紙に折り目をつけ、直線を置き、線の一部に沿ってパステルを部分的に擦り込んだ《Pa′80-74》(cat.no.80)、《Pa′80-105》(cat. no.82)。こうしたペーパーワークには、写真作品の「状況の設定」からの自然な連続性がある。

木下はパステル着彩を、「色彩は紙の表面とまったく等価」に「色面として在」るよう、意図したという。パステルを擦り込んだ色面が、塗られていないそれ以外の紙面と等価である、と。黒で引かれた直線は、「形としての意味を持たず」、なんらかの「境界でもな」い。形の輪郭にならず、ただ線としてのみ紙面に置かれる線が、「色面の中での深み」を生む、と書く。

やや難解な言葉づかいで、木下は絵画空間のことを語っているのだ。遠近法が描き出す三次元的なイリュージョンとは異質な、絵画にだけが持ちうる空間について語っている。みることの根本を検討してきた木下が、錯視効果で三次元の疑似空間を表す遠近法を試みるはずはない。もちろんキュビスム的なファセットの浅浮彫、触知的な空間イリュージョンも求めはしない。視覚上にのみ存在する、絵画面（ピクチャープラン）独自の、特別な「深み」について語っていたはずである。

ここで木下の意図を掘り下げるために、ほぼ同時期に高松次郎が試みていた「平面上の空間（Space in Two Dimensions)」(1973−86年) シリーズ [Fig. 8] と比較してみたい。高松は「影」

Fig. 8
高松次郎《平面上の空間》1973年
画像提供:
Yumiko Chiba Associates

の絵画シリーズを1964年から継続して発表しながら、影と絵画の関係の考察から始まった彼自身の探求を、投影、遠近法へと進めて、平面と立体の両方でその成果を発表してきた。そして1970年前後から、おそらく遠近法とは全く異なる、絵画独自の空間を探求しようとし始め、その試みを彼は「平面上の空間」と名づけたのだとわたしは考えている[*2]。

　　三次元イリュージョンの錯視効果を排除するために、高松はこのシリーズをまず、非具象の絵にする必要があった。画面の中の形体は互いに空間的関係のイリュージョンを生じさせやすい。ここでの描線は、形を囲む輪郭線としては使わず、あくまで線として画面に置くことにした。高松は「平面上の空間」をまず紙・鉛筆画として発表(1974年)し、初めてカンヴァス絵画として発表した個展(1977年、東京画廊)まで色彩は使っていない。形にならない開いた状態の線に、寄り添いながらも接触せず、地の部分を十分残して、色面を作らない色彩の使い方を採った。カンヴァスのままの白い部分が色彩部分に対して、後退しあるいは逆に前進するような前後関係を生じさせないよう、高松は細心の注意を払っていた。さて、こうして記してみると「平面上の空間」の特徴は、木下の初期パステル画および上記の彼女の文章と深く通じ合っている。

　　木下はまもなくペーパーワークからカンヴァスへと移行して、色数を絞り、筆触のせめぎあいで作られる画面を探求していく。一方、高松次郎の「平面上の空間」はこの後、色面が並列し、細い色面が幅のある線でもあるような余白のない画面へと進んだ。続いて1980年から「形」シリーズを始め、高松は様々な色彩のうねる線で画面全面を埋め尽くした。両者の展開は並行してはいないが、自らの方法で絵画独自の空間を表そうとする課題を、二人の作家が共有していたと考えてみたい。

VII 絵の空間(2)

木下が最後まで取り組んだ白と赤、白と青、などほぼ2色に色を絞った1993−94年の絵画シリーズを見るとき、筆触と筆触のあいだに凝らされた熟慮とデリケート極まる筆致に、ひきつけられずにはいられない。そこには多様な方向に引き裂かれるようにたゆたう、複雑な動きによる絵画空間が描き出されている。

　　マーク・ロスコが自身の大画面に、単純化した大きな色面を塗っていくとき、色面の境界部分に細心の注意を込めていたことが想起される。1950年代−60年代半ば頃の代表的なロスコの絵には、カンヴァスへのマットな塗り込みに筆のかすれ、絵の具の滴りが加わって、微妙な浮遊感が現出していた。ことに色面の外縁部分は、「羽毛のよう」と言い表される繊細な揺らぎを生み出して、後退的とも前進的とも言い難い、ロスコ作品独特の絵画空間を現出していた。木下がロスコのカンヴァスを見たかどうかはわからない。彼女が描いたの

は一見、ストロークと呼べそうなペインタリーな描線だが、実際には単純な単層ではない。ひとつの方向に進む単線ではなく、たゆたうように複数の方向に向かおうとする、色面のようなストロークのような、何ものかなのだ。しかもそれは、前進色の白色に交錯しながら浮かび上がる。ロスコの筆致と比較したい要素が、木下の後期絵画には含まれている。

　1991-92年頃の、一度描いた筆致を拭い取って沈め、影のようにした上からさらに描いていくシリーズにも、それがあてはまる。初めに描かれる筆致の動きと互いの関係性は、拭い取られる前のまま保存されながら、白色の背景に影のように沈められることで、透明度を獲得して浮遊力を備える。その上層にあえて前進色の白ともうひとつの色による筆致が重ねられることで、前後関係を超えた、いくつかの質を備えた重層的な動きが生み出されている。現実の三次元世界では見ることのできない、絵画にしか生み出せない空間だと云えないだろうか。木下の各筆致はのびやかに身体的な運動を感じさせながらも、それぞれの長さ、互いの近さ、方向、繊細な重なり、それぞれの関係性がきわめて緻密にコントロールされ熟慮されていることに、気づかされる。

　画家は、描いたものを浮遊させ、絵画空間を限定させないまま深めていこうとしたはずである。どこからともなく差してくる光が、画面全体をくまなく満たしている。これらの絵を見ていると、大木の樹下から木漏れ陽を見上げる時に似た、湧き差してくる光を、絵の中にどうにかしてつかみ入れようとする画家の存在が、身近に感じられる。

爽やかなほど、厳密でまっすぐな態度、木下の美術に対してぶれることのない作家的決意がどの作品からも伝わってくる。美術以外のことを呼び入れないのは、個人的な思いにとらわれず美術思想を純化させたいという意思。表現の問題に制作を限定することによって、作品を自立させ得ると考える態度。存在そのものに迫りたいと願った彼女の初心が貫かれていることを教えられる。かつて確かにあった日本の「現代美術」において、木下が立っていた地点をわたしたちはさらに知る必要がある。

*1　平野重光「展評」『美術手帖』11月号、No. 373、1973年、pp. 291-293
*2　光田ゆり「どこにもない場所－画家・高松次郎の実験」ダラス美術館、高松次郎展カタログ掲載予定、2025年

木下佳通代 インタビュー (再録)
(編：鳴原 悠)

——

本インタビューは『木下佳通代 1939–1994』(AD&A、1996年) に収録された木下
佳通代の最晩年のインタビューを再録したものである。インタビューは1994年4月23
日、AD&Aギャラリーにて越智裕二郎、竹村楊子を聞き手に行われ、越智が責任編集
を務めた。

再録にあたり、越智による付記も併せて所収した。なお、文中の誤字や脱字は改め、最
低限の表記統一を行うとともに、編者により [　] 内に註や本展出品番号を補った。

K: 木下　　O: 越智 (静岡県立美術館・当時)　　T: 竹村 (AD&A)

O　1939年 (昭和14年) 生まれということですが、神戸はどちらのお生まれで
　　すか？

K　長田区です。家、店、工場、全て戦火でなくなりました。終戦が、幼稚園の
　　時です [Fig. 1]。

O　それじゃ、教科書を墨で塗った世代でしょうか？

K　いいえ。

O　ヤミ市など覚えている世代ですか？

K　いいえ。小学校から慰問で元町の進駐軍に歌って、お菓子をもらったこ
　　とは覚えています。

O　「飢え」とかの思い出は？

K　そんな事は、無かったです。親がよくしてくれました。幼稚園の時、三木市
　　方面に疎開していまして、そこでは、お米の少ないおかゆでした。ひもじ
　　い思いはしていません。

O　神戸に戻って、まわりに何もない気はしませんでしたか？

K　あまり無いですね。須磨区の滝川高校に避難していて、照明弾が、とてもき
　　れいでした。爆弾が落ちたことなどをよく聞かされました。校舎づたいに避
　　難していた人たちが、全員亡くなられたとか。私は、幸い生き延びましたが。

O　京都市立美術大学 (現・京都市立芸術大学) に進まれましたが、いつ頃アート
　　に目覚められたのでしょうか？

K　はっきり意識したのは、中学生です。小さい頃から描くのが好きで、よく
　　誉められました。中学2年生の時、油絵のセットを買ってもらい、美術部へ
　　入部しました。誰に教わるでもなく、その道具で初めて描いた絵をよく覚
　　えています。妹の横顔です。中・高と美術部、バレーボール部、コーラス部
　　に在籍していて、スポーツでクタクタになる事が多かったのですが、美術
　　方面に行くつもりでいました。美大へ行く勉強をする意識が無くて、高校

3年生の時、美術の先生に「本当に美大に行くつもり?」と聞かれて、「はい」と。デッサンも何も勉強していなくて、入れないと困るので、石膏像のたくさんある学校に放課後一人で描きに行きました。

O　中学・高校は?

K　親和学園。

O　京都市立美術大学は、ストレートで入られたのですか?

K　私の年から、学科試験で落としてから実技試験のシステムを取り入れました。私の学年は、優等生が多かったです。新しいやり方だから入れたのかも。

O　入学した年は?

K　1958年(昭和33年)。

O　京都市立美術大学の授業はどんなものでしたか?

K　午前中、学科・一般教養。午後4時頃まで実技。1回生は石膏デッサン。2回生はヌード。先生は、黒田重太郎・津田周平・今井憲一・須田国太郎。須田さんの作品は好きでした。あまり先生の影響は、無かったです。彫刻科の辻［晋堂］先生・堀内［正和］先生にかわいがってもらって、洋画の先生とは、あまり交流ありませんでした。

O　大学時代は、いい学生でしたか?

K　本当に良い学生というのは、大学にいながらアカデミックでないのでしょうね。自分はそうではなく、もっとはみだしたりどん欲に学んだりすれば良かったと卒業してから後悔しました。

O　卒業後は?

K　神戸のマンモス中学校に。暴力問題のあった時期で、3年余りで教育者として挫折を感じて辞めました。その後、親和学園で美術を教えていました[Fig. 2][Fig. 3]。

O　その頃から、作家活動を?

K　発表は、大学の2回生からグループ展、京都市美術館などに出品しています。

O　どんな作品を描いていらっしゃいましたか?

K　学校では、アカデミックな具象しか評価されませんでした。その頃の作品は、静物・植物などの形を借りた抽象的なもの。再現的な具象は、一度も発表していません。

　　私は、いつも言い続けているんですが、人って10代に感じた事・考えた事がずっと尾を引いて、自分の一生のテーマになる事が多いと思います。この年になって振り返ってみると、自覚は無かったんですが、人に何か聞かれると、いつも同じ事を答えていました。私も10代の頃に、関心を持って考えたことがテーマになって、そこから一歩もでられないままでいるんだなって。

　　15-16才の頃に友達と夜空を眺めていて、もし、ずっといって最後があるのだろうか?宇宙の果てに壁や境界があるとすれば、その向こう側はどうなっているんだろうか?[ということを語り合っていました。]宇宙の無限となると、人間の思考が止まってしまうでしょ。もしかしたら境界があるかもしれない。見つけたと思っても、他にあるかもしれない。そうすると、その宇宙の存在全てが希薄になってしまい、リアリティーを失う。物の存在は、相対的

Fig. 1
木下佳通代生家（木下建具店）

Fig. 2
神戸市立丸山中学校教師時代（1962年撮影）

Fig. 3
神戸市立丸山中学校教師時代（1962年撮影）

なものとしての存在が希薄になると、自分の存在も希薄になり、恐怖感を
味わう。ずっと持ち続けていた不安を取り除くには、自分の存在を確認す
る事で埋めることが出来ました。意識が霧のようになって宇宙に漂えるな
ら全てを確認できる。最小単位の[霧のような存在として]意識だけは残って
いたいという願望が心情的に10代の頃からありました。

　自覚はしていなかったんですが、何故か、最初から抽象風な絵を描い
ていました。最初の頃は、地面・地球の中へどんどん関心をよせていっ
てその中にある生命体を描こうとしていた。次に、植物の形を借りて、そ
の生命体が自由に存在する・出来るというメッセージを絵にし始めました
[《題不詳》1962年、cat.no.2などを参照のこと]。形はあるけれども囲われたもの
ものではない、自在に動けて開放されている世界。ポール[パウル]・クレー
の精神的自由さ、"見えないものを見えるようにする"から私は、見えないも
のの世界に存在するなら、自在に存在することが、出来ると思った。ポー
ル[パウル]・クレーの絵は形も線もあって、線を解くと、全てが等価な面に
なる。視覚的に、豊かな感性を表現するために、色彩や形を使っているが、
私が本当に見ようとしているのは、"等価に存在する何か"。生命体でも精
神でも。そういう見方でクレーは、好きだったし、影響も受けました。

O　補足をしながら1971年頃までの事を。

K　ずっと同じ思いを持ち続けていて、一番身近な[一緒に暮らしている]人と話
していて、はじめの人もクレーに興味を持っていて、私と同じ所もあり、違っ
た所もあった。奥田[善巳]には、ヴァージニア・ウルフが同じ事を言ってい
ると言われました。(参考: 木下佳通代「五十対の眼」『美術情宣』7月号、no.3、美術情
宣編集委員会、1974年、pp. 24-25)

　"存在"に関わるあらゆる事を考えたり、メッセージとして表現したりし
てきた。存在のあり方について内側と外側を等価にしてしまう。空気中の
塵(最小単位の物質)から始まり、我々も創造されたものの一部でありながら、
強い欲望を持っている。人間は、欲望のために存在を確認したり、神と同
じように存在物を創造することで、欲望を得ようとする生物だと思う。どん
どん欲望が強くなって自分自身の存在をより強く確認しようという思いが、
存在そのものを生み出そうとした。傲慢に言えば、神になろうとした。それ[何
か存在するものを生み出すこと]が、私の生きる方法・生き方になったと思います。

　内と外、右と左、上と下。例えばバックに空が描いてあって、平面的に
描かれた人間をめくると中に空が描いてあるとか、幾何学的な球とか立
方体を平面的に描いてそれをめくると外と同じ色彩で同じ空間があるも
のをカットしてそれが見えていると、外側と等価な空間になるというような
絵[「境界の思考」シリーズ、1970年、cat.nos.8-13]を描いていました。

　20代の頃は、立体もたくさん作っていました。物の形はあるんだけど、
その存在を空間と等価にするためにガラスで作ってたり、皮膚に石膏をじ
かにつけて、雌型が出来るとひっくり返して並べて見せて、内側と外側を
等価に表現しました。その頃、お金がなかったので画廊を借りられず、あ
らゆるコンクールに出しましたが、ほとんど落選しました。だから、立体の
作品は残ってません。

セロハン3000枚を使って存在を表現した作品がありました。無色透明で形はあるんだけど、透過していて見えるのは、壁と床だけ。存在ということは、どういう事なのか？そういう事をやり続けてきて、その頃に少しキューブ風な絵を描いていた。立体を分割して、開放して、平面にすることが自分の思いとうまくつながった。人間を面で分割して一つ一つの面が、外側の空間の二次元の面とつながって等価になっている。だから、全て等価にしてしまおうと。碁盤の目の線［「滲触」シリーズ、1971年、cat.nos.14-16］は、二次元の広がりを表していて、平面の存在と広がりのために線を描いているんですけれども、線が途切れているでしょ。それは、括られてはいけないし、括られていないという私の思い。全てが、流通している、浸蝕し合ってる。それが、存在なんだ［Fig.4］。

Fig. 4
「奥田善巳・木下佳通代作品展」
(1972年、シロタ画廊) にて

O　木下さんの周辺でのグループ〈位〉の活動は？

K　グループ〈位〉の存在は、私には影響が強かったですね。あるグループが神戸にあって、その人たちが具体と反具体とに分かれたんです。その頃、河口［龍夫］が美術手帖によく載っていて、その人たちから呼びかけがあり、そのグループに私の同級生が2人いて、グループに加わる事になりました。何故か、女の人は、入れたくないという感じがあって、私もその頃は、生活するのが大変で、どうしても入りたいというわけじゃなかったんですが、グループの意図は、存在についての問題で、私自身肯定できるものでした。ほとんど毎日、私の家に集まり9人［グループ〈位〉のメンバー、井上治幸、奥田善巳、河口龍夫、武内博州、豊原康雄、中田誠、向井孟、村上雅美、良田務］で討論していました。グループの活動は、自分の一部として考えてやってきました。短期間ではありましたが、9人［の考え］が一致した所で発表して、それが終わるか終わらないうちに次に移ったりして、何カ月かごとに発表してました。それらの全てに協力してきました。

O　河口さんとは、いつ頃ご結婚されたのですか？

K　1963年頃かな。大学を出て2–3年目です。彼も私も高校の美術部の部長で、文化祭のとき出会いました。毎日のように会ってました。結婚して暮らした時間は、短いんですが、10代の終わりからいろんな意味で、私自身が出来上がっていく10年間を共に過ごしました。存在に関する関心は、共通したものがあったと思います。

O　1972年のギャラリー16の仕事は？

K　71年のシリーズだったかもしれない。その頃までは油彩をやっていて、自分自身の思考の中では、存在についてのメッセージが尾を引いていました。その時期に、京都の若い男性の作家が何人か集まってグループで仕事をしないかと、誘われたから、［奥田と］二人で話し合って、何かプランを考えてそれを持って人を集めようかという事にしました。私は、自分で自分のコンセプトで写真のプランを作ったんですが、7–8人集めた中でひとり、女性は入れたくないという事が私のところに伝わって、それなら結構ですと断りました。それで、作家ではなくて、自分の友人を10人集めて、協力してもらいました。グループで協力して出来るプランだったので、とにかく10人必要で、その方法として写真を使うことを考え付いたんです［《Untitled／む

38（花時計）》1973年、cat. no. 19]。それをやってみると、自分が伝えたいメッセージが平面の油彩画よりもイージーに伝わりました。

O　その伝えたいメッセージの解説を。

K　物の存在というのは、例えば、花時計なんですけど、地球上の人類が亡びてもしばらくは、存在するでしょう。宇宙も。それは、絶対的存在と考えています。それ以外の存在のあり方は相対的存在なもので、この2つは、別々の物ではなくて、存在ひとつの証であると考えました。まず、ひとりの人がカメラを設定して写真をとる。又、次の人が同じ事をしていて、ひとりひとりが写している。それは、全て時間も違うし、その人が見た風景も相対的なものだから違うはず。全部違うはずなんですけど、同じ存在にしか見えてない。絶対的存在と相対的存在はあって、しかし存在は、ひとつでしかないというメッセージを視覚的に表そうとしている。自分自身のコンセプトがイージーに伝わるのが面白くて、写真の仕事が続きます。

　　Saturation[滲触]のシリーズは、好きだったんですが、叙情的にとられる事が多くて、本当は、私はよかったと思うんですがその頃はそれに我慢できなくて、もっと自分のメッセージを伝えたかった。

O　ビーカーの作品 [《Untitled／む60（ビーカー）》1973年、cat. no. 21](1974年1月[ギャラリー16の個展にて発表])は？

K　上下2枚ずつ10組。違うのは、目盛りが違うだけで、一見すると全部同じ水に見えるけど、現実は全部温度が違うんだという、シンプルな作品です。見る事と、認識する事と、存在する事のずれを表しています。

　　ギャラリーシグナムで、フォト・アート展 [「PHOTO／ARTS－方法としての写真－」(1974年)] に呼ばれて、同じ写真で、時間が同じで日が違う [《Untitled／む59（腕時計）》1974年、cat. no. 20]。存在の中に時間も入ってくるし、時間そのものが存在である [Fig. 5]。

O　1974年9月。村松画廊での発表。この作品はたしか、部屋に一つひとつ物を置いていって、一つひとつ取っていくという作品 [《む61（物の増加と減少）》1974年、cat. no. 22] ですね。

K　最初の空間と最後の空間は、同一の存在であるように見えますが、ただ、この時間の間には、これだけの存在があり、消えていった。ひとつの存在、空間の存在にしても、認識の違い、方法によっては、存在に関する概念を変化させる事が出来る。

O　場所は、トアロードのアートルームですか？

K　そうです。ギャラリーシグナムで一緒に発表した人たちが、手伝ってくれました。8ミリで撮ってそれをプリントして画廊に並べたんですが。それを1992年、○美術館でビデオに作り替えました [「ヴィデオ／京都／1974」(ギャラリーシグナム)で発表された映像作品(cat. no. 23)をVHSに変換し、「ビデオ・新たな世界－そのメディアの可能性」(○美術館、東京)において展示した]。

O　この壁の作品 [《Untitled-b／む103（壁のシミ（ブロック））》1972年、cat. no. 18] は？

K　2枚で1点の作品です。全く同じ写真・存在なんですが、壁に、チョークで印をすることによって、それを見たという認識を持った瞬間、同じ壁の存在は、違うものになってしまいます。本当は同じ存在でしかないんですが、

10人が認識することで、10の存在の表れ方をするし、変化が起こるというこうことをいろんな例で見せていきたかった。シグニファイングに出した時の作品。名古屋の水上 [旬] さんたちが企画されたグループ展 [「シグニファイング－言語・事物／態度の表明とともに」(1974年、京都市美術館)] に参加しました。

O　1975年の作品で、バス観光の写真に色を塗っていくもの [《無題》、cat. no. 25] ですね。

K　一箇所見ることによって色を着けていく、最終的には、全て認識する。認識のあり方による存在。物を見るということは、知覚して認識するということで、それを広げていけば存在が増えていくことでもあるんです。人間は、考えるんだけど、でも存在は、見ようと見まいと、認識しようがしまいが、同じ物であるということに最初と最後はしたかった。

O　全て、写真製版して、シルクスクリーンで、手彩色ですね。

T　すごく新鮮なんですが、この作品は、受け入れ易かったのでしょうか？その頃はどういう時代でしたか？

K　1970年代は、写真を使った作品が多かったです。世界の関心が強かったコンセプトとか方法論とかが、それぞれの作家に影響を与えたし、私自身も影響を得ていると思います。グループ展の話がなければ、写真を使わなかったと思います。私は、この仕事をやって良かったと思っていて、自分のコンセプトを再確認できたし、存在に対するメッセージを送るのではなく、存在そのものを創り出そうとそれから変わっていったというか、表現の方法を少しずつ強めていったのは、この仕事をやったから出来たという気もします。この仕事が自分の中で終わってなければ、時間がもっとかかったと思います。

O　1976年2月。ギャラリー16での作品は、ちょっと違った傾向になっていますね。

K　見せ方が少し違います。視覚と、知覚して認識する事を写真のピントにもってきた。いちばん、ピントが合っているものが見えているもので、合っていないものが、見えないもので、こういう方法でいろんなものを撮っていきました。これ [《Untitled (Some profile or some consciousness)》1976年、cat. no. 35] は、また少し違う作品ですが、人が人を見て認識するということを自分の中にある客観性と主体性とだぶらせていって、それを写真に撮っていってます。これを見るこの人自身、この写真を見る人自身、自分を見ている本人、もうひとりの人を見ている本人という風に全部見えるようにしていきました。人間の存在も相対的な見る人の認識でいろいろな存在になり得るんだけどひとつでしかない。写真を撮って、とにかく毎日創り続けました。ところがこの頃になりますと、写真を使う若い作家が増えてきて、新鮮な何か人を引き付けるものを出すには、難しい表現媒体になってきました。なんとか写真の一般性から抜けられないかを考えていて、紙にドローイングしたものに移りました。新しい事をやり始めたら、この仕事に興味が失せたのです。新しいものに興味が湧いて、どんどん創り出したために、この頃の作品は発表しなかったんです。たまたま1977年に高橋享さん企画の自画像展 [アート・コア現代美術77シリーズ「自画像'77」(アートコア・ギャラ

Fig. 6
アート・コア現代美術77シリーズ「自画像 '77」
(1977年、アートコア・ギャラリー) 展示風景

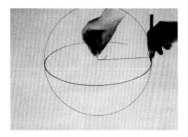

Fig. 7
《'76-A》1976年
出典:『美術手帖』3月号、No. 462、1980年

リー、京都)]に声をかけて頂いて、そういえば、自分の顔を使ったものがあっ
たと思い出して出しました[《Untitled》1976年、cat.no.39ほか][**Fig.6**]。

O　そして新しい仕事に移られたわけですね。作品「A」[**Fig.7**]については?

K　自分で、糸と鉛筆を使って円を描いて、それを誰かに撮ってもらう。その円
　は、視覚的には楕円ですけれど、見たと同時に知覚しますから真円と認識
　されているわけです。見えている形が楕円であるということで、何かに置
　き換えていけば、楕円としか存在を認識しないこともありますが、でも本当
　は、真円なんだ。認識のずれを表示することで、存在に近づこうとしたも
　のです。

O　たくさんのバリエーションがあって、とてもきれいですね。

K　平面の存在物として、魅力的でなければ駄目だと思う。普通の写真の様に
　一見して、「ああ、写真だ」と見過ごしてしまうようでは困る。それをより表現
　物として、平面をつくるためにレイアウトを考えます。小さな紙に描いて
　それを写して、拡大すると粒子が荒れて、フィルムもASA-400を使うと
　さらに荒れるでしょ。そうすると表面が砂目の様になって写真に、ドロー
　イングの様な肌合が生まれるんですね。そういう肌合の空間にしたかっ
　たんです。

T　写真をやり始めたときは、魅力的でなくてもよかったんですか?

K　その時に自分自身がいちばん伝えたかったのは、存在に対するメッセー
　ジだったからそこまで考えていませんでした。[次第に写真を使う作家が増え
　てきて、同じような]風景写真がでてきたころは、写真そのものが面白くなかっ
　た。誰が撮っても、上手に撮ってもあまり変化もないし。もっと視覚的に
　違ったものにしたかった。
　　作品は、カラーフェルトペンを使っていて、知覚・認識した形には、色を
　使っています。印画紙は、普通のものではなくCH印画紙を使っています。

T　これは、自分の手を自分でシャッターを押されたんですか?

K　自分の手の場合は、他の人に頼みます。手があらわれているのは、全て私
　の手です。最初のうちは、説明過多になりすぎて、コンパスは無いほうが
　いいのですけどね。

O　1977年2月にアンデパンダンの仕事をされますが、ちょっと違う傾向の
　仕事では?

K　神戸の仲間たちと"塗る"というタイトルで作品をつくるんです。作家同士
　の懇親展のようなものですね。

O　ギャラリーUというのは?

K　今は、ないんですけどね。国島[征二]さんという彫刻をやっている方が
　やってました。

O　スタイルが洗練されてきましたね。

K　今やっているペインティングは、依存するものが表面に託さないというこ
　とで、例えば、この作品は[インタビューで木下は、1977年頃の写真作品を指しなが
　ら、「このシルクスクリーンの作品は」と発言している]、存在に対する考え方・あり方
　というのがよりどころで表現が出来ているから、よりどころとするものがあ
　るんですね。だから、今より精神的に楽ですね。

T　ある種、デザイン的・構築的というか。

K　ひとつのコンセプトがあって、それに基づいて表現していくのは、楽なんですけどね。

　　神戸の「キタノサーカス」でのインスタレーション［「木下佳通代展」（1977年、ギャラリーキタノサーカス、神戸）］。これは、厚いアクリルを使っていて、全て残っています。水平線を存在させた作品。普通は、紙に描かれた線と考えるから、紙を主体に考えるとこれは、水平線ではないんです。だから、存在なんて認識の違いであいまいなものになります。それを1枚の紙と物質としての線を使うことでインスタレーションとして壁にたくさんやりたかった。ところが、フランス人が同じ事をしていたのでやめました。

O　1978年のアート・ナウは現在の仕事につながっていく作品を出品されていますね［《'77-O》1977年、cat.no.52ほか］[Fig.8]。

Fig.8
「アート・ナウ'78」（1978年、兵庫県立近代美術館）
展示風景

K　線から面へ。だんだん欲がでてきて色が使いたくなってきたんです。最初は、空間を含めて作品にしていたんですが、空間を除いて、空間面のサイズそのものの大きさの作品にしていこうとしました。1979年ぐらいになると、どんどんいろんな表現がしたいという欲がでてきて、吹き付けるのではなく、実際にドローイングを写真の上に色鉛筆でやりだしました［cat.nos. 70-76］。この後すぐにドローイングを始めたのでこの時期の作品は、発表していません。

　　1979年頃からカメラを使わなくなってきました。

O　ドローイングへいく、まさに変換期の作品ですね。

K　作品や表現に人間の手垢とか、個人の情感を重要と考えないんです。

　　写真の仕事をしている時に、砂目をきれいにするのにとても時間がかかりまして、最高1枚5−6時間かかったものがあるんです。毎日それだから、表現することの抑圧があった。フィジカルに表現したいというのがありました。

O　1980年の京都のアンデパンダン展はドローイングに移られているんですか？

K　ドローイングですけども、まだ紙を折っています。それは襖に使う紙で、折曲げて出来る線と描いている線を等価に使って面をつくっていって、色面をパステルで。この紙を使った大きな作品は、たくさんあるんです。存在に関するコンセプトをよりどころに形をつくっています。

O　どこかで発表されたんですか？

K　シティ・ギャラリー（元町）で一度だけ。

O　だんだん私たちの知っている木下さんに近づいていきますね。

K　こうして今見てみると、クレーの考えている世界と違うものなんですが、表現の見え方が私の中で尾を引いているみたいですね。線によって囲まれた面の内と外を見せているんですけれども、結局は、等価の二次元の平面であることを伝えたいんです。1980年まで写真をつくっておいて、それをしまい込んで、ドローイングを始めて、ドローイングも結局しまい込んで発表の機会がなかったです。

T　パステルになられた素材的な理由というのは？

K　出来るだけ面に確固たる形として存在させるんじゃなくて、紙の平面と色

を置いた面とが、それほど違った次元にならない為に、柔らかい浸透した平面が欲しかったんです。そのためにパステルは、効果的でした。黒い線は、ダーマトグラフという何にでも描ける鉛筆を使っています。

T ぼかしているというよりは、しっかり描いている感じですが。

K パステルは定着が弱いから紙の中に必死に擦り込んでいます。だから、色は、しっかりと定着してます。どんどん描きたくなって、色を使いたくなって。これをやっている間、ずっと気になっていることがあって、線を引くことによって表現があからさまに自分のコンセプトに依存しているから私にとっては、安易なんです。この安易というのは、作品の強さに結びつかない思いがあって、なんとか、コンセプトを隠して表現できないだろうかと思いながらつくりました。

O 1981年からまた、少し違った展開が見られますね。岡山県総合文化センターで発表された作品は？[Fig. 9]

K 水性用のカンヴァスを使っています。その頃に、パステルからオイルを使ってカンヴァスに、同じような仕事をやってましたが、その分が火事で焼けてしまいました。

O 1981年−1983年は、どの様なことを？

K パステルからカンヴァスに変わって同じシリーズで作っていたんですが、その頃は、煮詰まっていました。存在に対する考え方に自由さをなくしていっていると考えていました。燃えた作品からここに移るまですごく時間がかかっていて、しんどかった時期です。描いては、潰した時期があって、あるとき具体的に描いたものを潰したんです。そうすることで、ひとつの事が見えてきて、そこで表現に対する方法を変えることが出来ました。表現に対するコンセプトとか、作品そのもののコンセプトを変えるのではなくて、表現に対する自分の方法をやっと変えることが出来た。自分の存在論、概念的なものを全て表現にもってくるのではなく、存在そのものを自分が画面の上に作ればいいんだと。自分が表現したものを存在させればいいんだと。ある意味では、図式的なコンセプトを取り去ることが出来たんです。よりどころをはずすことは、不安でしたから慣れるまでに時間は、かかりました。《'82-CA1》[cat. no. 90]。シリーズの最初の作品で、私にとって大事で、あるものを取り除けた作品です。

O 1982年10月。《'82-CA1》。ギャラリー16での発表ですね。

K この頃から通し番号をつけました。

O 現在、700まであるということは、700枚描いてこられた？!

K この作品は、最初、筆で描いてそれから布で、拭って。この拭っているのは、カンヴァスの平面と絵具を置いた面とが、等価であること。自分の中では、今までどおりだから、二次元の面を等価にしたいという思いがあるから、これをやっているわけです。そういう方法をとりながら、作品そのものが存在となるように。宇宙の星などの全ての存在が神様に創られて、ランダムに見えるんだけど、一定の相対的な秩序で、存在しているんですね。でも、我々から見れば、自然に存在していて、その存在は、物凄く強いんです。そのような存在のひとつにしたい。要するに、創造神になりたい。

T　後ろの世界とか、別世界を感じるのですが。

K　私には表現の方法であって、限られた平面をいかに自立させ、積極的に存在させるか。そのために、このコントラストが必要なんです。小さな面の存在する力と色面の存在する力は、私の中では、等価に考えている。それで、限定された二次元の存在物になっています。存在させたものが、それが発する何かは、私が全て言葉で説明できるものであれば、今までと同じ事で、全て言葉で説明できてしまうんだけど、言葉によって説明できてしまうものでは、存在としては、非常に弱いと思います。創造物と呼べるものにするには言葉を越えた存在、働きかけてくる何かがないと創造物には、なり得ない。その部分が必要な為に自分の概念的なものをとりはずした。それまでの作品も言葉を越えて存在を感じさせる表現でありたいとしてたことは確かだから、それがないと思わないんだけど、よりその部分が大きくなければ、創造物でありえない。

O　1981年にドイツに行かれていますね.

T　ドイツでの、この時点でのコンセプトはどうでしたか？

K　ドイツの美術館の館長［クンストフェラインン館長ハンス・ゲルク］が写真を使った作品が好きで、最初から写真の仕事でやっていくということでしたから、この時点では、あまり見せていませんでした。でも作家は、その都度、今やっていることを見せたいんですけどね。強く働きかけることが必要でした。具体的に、色面が強く見える方法をとってきていると思います。作品の前を通って記憶に残らないとか、違いが分からないような存在では、困りますよね。平和な、安定した作品を与える事も重要なことかもしれないですが、私の場合は、違和感を感じさせるとか、人の意識を立ち止まらせるとか、少し改めてもう一度考えるという意識の刺激が欲しかった。自由でありたい。それまでは、ひとつのコンセプトに基づいてやっていたから、ある意味では、拘束されていたでしょ。

O　1983年は、82年と違った感じで。

K　画面に"斜め"をもってくるということは、表現の必然性で、強さだとかを。

O　1986年の拭うところから今度は？

K　ところどころ、拭うこともあるんですが、どんどん描き込んでます。この頃の仕事は、私も好きなんです。

T　色が、紺とか。

K　単色が多いですね。色と色の調和によってできる平面よりも、自分の描く［事で出来上がる］空間に興味があるので、たくさんの色を使うのは、必要じゃありませんでした。自由に描いていたとしても、何かイメージが出来てきて、見る側も何かイメージを求めようとして見てしまうと思う。だけど、私には、ひとつのイメージとして成り立たないことが必要でした。見えかけたと思ってもすぐなくなってしまう、それでいて、存在する。私の場合は、描き込んだ部分と、そうでない部分が、等価なひとつの平面でつくらなければいけない。何にも見えなくて、どんなイメージにもならない、描かれた線とか色とか形が、空間の緊張感をつくっていって、それぞれが必然的にそこに必要になれば、作品が完成します。イメージが絵になるのではな

く、絵として存在する。

O 一見、東洋的な空間構成にも見えますが。

K 東洋的な考え方とかは、意識していません。油絵を使っていますが、伝統的なヨーロッパの絵に則ったものは、やりたくない。どういう材料を使っていても、その作品を見たときに、その作家の生きた時代の文化とか民族性がどこかに、にじみ出てくるものでなければならないということはあるんです。例えば、線を引いたとしても東洋人とヨーロッパ人では違うんですね。私は、筆のストロークが表れないように、もっと人間が筆を使って表現するということで見えてくる〝自由なものにしたい〟という思いがあるので、筆を使って描いているうちに手慣れて、筆勢とか精神的なものまでも表現できるようになると思うんです。そういうものは危険なので、できるだけ初めて筆を持つ、ぎこちなさを大事にしたい。一筆で、心地よく精神的に修練された線を引くことは、決してしなかったです。

O これだけたくさんの仕事をされながら、一作、一作非常に高い緊張感を作品がたたえていて、敬服するわけですが。

K 色も、違う色を使っても自分の同じものをつくれないかという思いがあるので、違った色も挑戦してみるんですが、自分がつくっていく画面によって自分自身が、拘束されていくことがあるんです。それはその都度、避けていかないといけないんです。

T 1989年AD&Aで展覧会をされたんですが [Fig.10]、89年は、ある種のピークだったと思うんですが。

K いちばん最初にパステルから抜け出た時の油彩の仕事の次に、自分では少し気持ちが安らぎました。

O 1988年。《'88-CA487》 [cat.no.111] 辺りは、過渡期ですか。抜け出すのは、《'88-CA488》、《'88-CA489》ですね。

K 存在と同じくらい、自然な必然性のある形とか線を自分で決めるわけにはいかなくて、ひとつ置かれたものに対応して、自分が突き動かされて次を見つけていくということの繰り返しで、出来上がっていくんですけどね。

O 1989年は、抜けられた頃ですか？

K そうですね。しんどさから少し抜け出た頃です。

O 1枚描くのにどれくらいの時間が？

K だいたい、80％描くのに1日だったり1週間だったりします。あとの20％ぐらいが1週間だったり2ヵ月だったりします。

O 作家の中に煮詰まったものが、溢れ出てくる感じがしますが。

K できるだけ画面に頼ってしまって、ひとつ置いたら描くものから自分が突き動かされていくという風になっていったので、わりと自由に描けたんですね。

T 例えば、この時代の作品がいいから、もう一度描いてくださいと言われれば、描けませんよね？ たまに、こういう話は持ちこまれるのですが。

K ある程度まで類似したものは描けますが、その時の必然的に起こっていた感覚は、戻ってこない場合もあります。

T 1991年のAD&Aでの展覧会は、赤が印象的ですね。

K 赤を青と同じように使えた。画面が、生き生きと動いてないといけないし、

Interview 1
—
An interview with Kinoshita Kazuyo

緊張感がなければと思うし、だからといって、描かれている面とそうでない面で、形をつくるのではなく、それぞれがあるだけで、ひとつの緊張した平面の空間になっているという絵がつくりたい。

T　1992年のLAシリーズについて。

K　私は、自分自身、我が強い人間で、アメリカに行ったから何か影響を受けて作品が変わるということは、考えていなかった。でも1年間暮らしてみて、カリフォルニアの環境がやっぱり私に影響を与えたみたいで、日本では、はじめて画面に筆を下ろすまで、メディテーションをする時間がもっと必要で、精神的にある程度、鎮静してから筆を動かすんですが、LAでは、あまりその必要はなかったんです。気軽に筆運びができたし、筆をおいていってできる空間の緊張感とか、存在の重さとかを気にしないで描いていけるというか。全てが、軽やかに考えたり、描いたりできました。ある意味からすると、深刻さが抜けているのかもしれない。空間のあり方も少し違います。ちょっとした事にも環境の影響があって、日本から持っていった服が着られなかったんです。むこうの風景に馴染まないというか [Fig.11]。

O　今回も新たな展開がありまして、私たちを驚かせました。非常に力強いというか、見るものを引き付ける強さを持った仕事を1994年4月にAD&Aの個展 [Fig.12] で見せてくださったんですが。これについて。

K　いわゆるストロークと呼ばれているものをできるだけ自由にしたい。描き重ねることで、形や色が出来上がっているんです。ストロークによって絵をつくっているのではなくて、必然性を求めて描き重ねて、形とか空間が出来上がっていくように努力していたんですけどね。できるだけ自分の意図的なものが入り込まないように、より画面に自分を委ねていく努力をしました。LAでつくった作品を完成しきれなくて、それを捨てきれなくて持って帰ってきてずっと置いていたんです。それを描き続ける事ができなくて、潰そうと思って眺めているうちに、今やっていることをその上にダブらせようと思って、新しい仕事をやる方法に重ねたんです。中間的な感じになっているし、また違った感じですね。最初に意図したものも壊されているし、この時の考え方も完成できない。自分の意図から離れた自由な空間が出来てしまったというか、恣意的なものが、取り外されたというか。

T　この作品のグリーンは？

K　この作品は、出すのをやめようか最後まで迷っていました。画面に身を委ねて、画面の方から自分自身が必然的なものを求められてやっていくという風に画面全体に気遣いをして完成させてるのですが、この作品は、細かい気遣いをある程度、無視をしてやってみました。ゆっくり考えてやってみると、もう少し描き込んだ方がいいところもでてくるんですが、それをしないで自分の体のリズムに合わせて描いた部分が多いんです。だから、自分で「完成した」というものが、ないまま終わっているので、出そうかどうしようか迷ったんです。

　今、やっている仕事は、自分自身でも言葉にするのは難しいです。言葉で掴めないものを作りたいという思いが強いから、なおさらそうなっていくのですが。もし、画面を理論的・構造的に説明をしろといわれたら、難し

Fig. 11
ロサンゼルスにて（1992年頃）

Fig. 12
「木下佳通代展」（1994年、AD&Aギャラリー）展示風景
画像提供：AD&A
撮影：柄松稔

くて出来ないかもしれない。もしも、いえるとすれば、自分の本当に必然的な表現なんですとしかいえないですね。何故、こうしたのか？何故、この色があるのか？といわれれば、表現の為に必要だったからそうなったとしかいえないし、自分でそう見えるように描いたのではないんだから。表現として、画面の方から自分自身が求められた。今は、自分の作品をそんな風にしか話せないんですが。ただ、今までよりは、自由になれたと思います。

T　世の中の評価というようなものからもですか？

K　そうではなくて、画面の上で表現していく事に関しての自由。以前は、パターンみたいなものが秩序になってきて、それに拘束されて自由を失うから、表現が豊かでなくなることもありました。そのためには、それを壊さなくては、いけない。そういう意味からすると、今の仕事は、画面の上で拘束されるものが今までより非常に少ない。そういう意味で自由になれたと思います。

（1994年4月23日 AD&A Galleryにて）

付記

このインタビューは体力を、すでにかなりなくしていた木下佳通代氏に、彼女の最後の個展の折り、その会場となったAD&Aにおいて、その協力のもとに行われました。その頃、がんが彼女を不帰の人にするであろうということが誰の目にも明らかであり、彼女の仕事に対する自身のコメントを、この最後のチャンスに記録しておかなくては、ということでなされたものであり、彼女自身が作成した時系列による作品ファイルを前に会話が行われています。4時間以上かけたでしょうか、それが限界でした。木下佳通代氏もすでに充分な体力、またがんに対抗する薬により以前の思考力を充分に残していたわけではないので、このインタビューに出てくる時期や関係者に対する彼女の思い違い、記憶違いがあるかも知れません。彼女の仕事に対する自身のコメントを記録しておく本旨に鑑み、そういったことがあれば関係者には御寛恕いただければ幸いです。またそういう事実があれば編集責任である越智、もしくはAD&Aまでお知らせいただければ幸いです。

越智裕二郎 [1996年]

（左から）越智裕二郎氏、木下（インタビュー記録映像より、1994年）

植松奎二インタビュー
（編：佐藤あゆか）

—

2023年10月17日、国内外で活躍するアーティスト・植松奎二氏に、大阪府箕面市の植松氏のアトリエでインタビューを行った。本展の担当学芸員3名（大下裕司、中村史子、佐藤あゆか）が、木下佳通代との交流や作品制作の裏側などについて、木下と深い親交を結んでいた植松氏にお話をうかがった。

木下佳通代との出会い
木下佳通代さんとはどういった経緯でお知り合いになられたのですか。

—

僕は大学生の時から知っていました。1967年、後に木下佳通代さんのパートナーになる奥田善巳さんが国際青年美術家展 *1 で日本文化フォーラム賞をもらいました。作品は《容器（ネガへの挑発 I）》と題されたもので、画面の中央に白色のネガのドラム缶を、まわりをローラーで青色と赤色に塗っていました。その賞を獲った後に、神戸のトアロード画廊でグループ展 *2 をしていたんですよ。奥田さんと具体の向井修二ともう1人、東山明って、僕の大学の先輩なんですけどね。それを見に行った時に会場に奥田さんがおられました。奥田さんはよく話される人でね。本当に論理的にね、初対面なのに自分の作品のこと、現代美術のことをものすごく一生懸命話してくれるわけです。なぜこんなに話し続けなければならないのかと思ったものでした。そこには熱気とエネルギーがあった。作品から来る観念的でクールな精神的な思考とは、対照的なものでした。それが奥田さんとの最初の出会いです。しばらくして、1967年に神戸の東遊園地で池水慶一さんとかいろんな人がやった野外でのハプニングの展覧会（第1回PLAY展）*3 があってそれ見に行ったら、善巳さんも見に来ていて。その時に初めて木下佳通代さんと会ったんですよ。付き合いはそれからですね。

　1969年に彫刻の森美術館（箱根）の第1回現代国際彫刻展に僕が出した時に、奥田さんも出しておられた。その頃、カズさん［木下佳通代の愛称］と奥田さんは神戸の山本通で喫茶店をやっておられたんですよ [Fig. 1]。そこにはしょっちゅう行っていました。善巳さんがコーヒー入れたりいろいろして、カズさんも手伝ってたのかな。僕も神戸に住んでいて、歩いて行ける距離にいたから。その辺からずっと知り合いです。

—

An interview
with Uematsu Keiji

Fig. 1
喫茶店にて

Fig. 2
絵画教室で静物画を描く木下

Fig. 3
「木下佳通代展－実在と認識…
そしてもう一つのリアリティーへ・1979－1991」
(1991年、ギャラリー16) DM

その喫茶店は作家の仲間たちが集まるような空間だったのでしょうか。

—

喫茶店では他の作家の人と会った記憶はないです。その何年か後にカズさんと善巳さんがトアロードに家を買って、1階が板の間のスタジオで、2階、3階は住居になってる住居兼アトリエだったんですが、そこへ移ってからですね、善巳さんのところに神戸の作家たちがよく集まり始めたのは。善巳さんとカズさんはすごく信頼されてたから、しょっちゅう作家が出入りしてたね。2人はアトリエでアートルーム・トーアという絵画教室をし始めて、そこでは生徒さんは静物画を描いたりして、別に抽象画を描いてるわけじゃなかったですね [Fig. 2]。カズさんはどっちかっていうと着物の染色、帯とか反物の絵付けをずっと家でやったりして。それでできたものを2人で京都へ運んだり。その絵画教室へ来ていた人たち、最初はみんな具象の絵を習いに来てたけど、2人の影響を受けてその後抽象的な作品を描く画家や立体を作る作家になった人、たくさんいますね。皆さん信濃橋画廊などで個展をしていました。生徒さんでも同じ作家としての付き合いでしたね。生徒ではなく作家友達として辰野登恵子さんとか、よく来られてた。着物の絵付けとか染色をしたと聞きました。あと児玉靖枝さん。児玉さんも、ある意味カズさんを尊敬していたと思います。そんな感じで、いろんな若い作家にものすごく慕われてた。カズさん、善巳さんの美術に対する姿勢と熱意、作家としての生き方に影響を受けた人はいっぱいいたと思います。

植松氏所蔵の木下作品について
植松さんは木下さんの作品を所蔵されてもいらっしゃいますね。
本展にも3点出品いただきますが、これらはどのような経緯で
所蔵することになったのでしょうか。

—

《'91-CA645》(cat. no. 118) は購入したものです。1991年、僕がちょうどドイツから一時帰国しているときにカズさんが京都のギャラリー16で個展 **4** をしていて見に行きました。案内状には「実在と認識…そしてもう一つのリアリティーへ」と書かれていました [Fig. 3]。個展会場には何年間もの油彩が展示されていて、その中で一番新しい作品にすごく惹かれました。空間と筆のストローク、伸び伸びと描かれている画面に新しい展開が感じられ、コレクションしたいなと強く思ったんです。もちろん大きな作品がすごく良かったのですが、お金もそんなにないので小さな作品を分けてもらいました。画面は小さいですが、いろいろなものが凝縮されたカズさんの世界がありました。コレクションできて嬉しかったこと覚えています。

《'78-4-B》(cat. no. 58) と《'79-5-A》(cat. no. 64) は、カズさんが1981年のハイデルベルクの個展で展示して、それが終わって日本に帰るときにもらったものです。作品は日本からいっぱい持ってきて、その中から選定して展示したからね。展示した作品と他の作品の中から「奎ちゃん作品あげるわ」と言って、僕が2点選んだんです。いい作品なんですよ。この頃の写真とフェルトペンで描かれたシリーズ作品は見ることと認識することを的確に表現した作品で、すごくいい作品を2点ももらえて幸せでした。

西宮市大谷記念美術館には、植松さんが旧蔵していた木下作品が
収蔵されています。

—

あれ（《'85-CA287》(cat.no.104)）は僕の作品と交換したものです。カズさんと善
巳さんとは、彼らのペインティングと僕の立体や写真の作品とを交換したりし
ていました。西宮市大谷記念美術館の新収蔵品展*5に、僕が持ってた善巳さ
んとカズさんの作品が出てて、僕が彼らにプレゼントした作品も一緒に展示さ
れたんだけど。僕があげたものには「善巳さんへ」とか「カズさんへ」とかサイン
が入ってる。あるとき、もう僕が持っている彼らの作品を全部寄贈しようと思っ
てね。自分とこの家で置いていても、僕もいっぱい持ってるから。いろいろな人
に見てもらいたいし、カズさんと善巳さんの作品は1箇所同じとこの方がいい
なと思って、西宮に寄贈したんですよ。
　　《'86-CA358》(cat.no.108)もカズさんの作品と交換したものです。1986年、
僕が日本にも家を借り始めた頃にもらったもので、自宅では、ひと部屋にカズ
さんと善巳さんの作品を2点ずつ展示してました。部屋には2人の作品から迫
り来る熱気と息づかいがありました。

—

木下との交流
木下さんとの作品のやり取りは、いつ頃からされていたのでしょうか。
木下さんが生前、「私の作品をゴミにしないでほしい」と
AD&Aに託した資料ボックス*6の中には、
植松さんからもらったと思われるプランドローイングや写真などが
多数含まれていました。

—

1975年の9月からドイツに行ったでしょ、僕。いつも日本に帰ってきたら必ず
カズさんと善巳さんのところに行ってたんです。そこで「次こんなんしよう思て
んねん」とか言ってプランを描いて、2人にアイデア見せたりしていました。しょっ
ちゅう作品の相談をしてましたね。僕は他の人に相談することは滅多にない
んだけど、「次はどうしようかな」って、すごく悩む時もあるわけですね。そんな
ときに、僕が唯一信頼して作品のことを相談できるのが、彼らでした。描いた
ドローイングを2人の家に置いて帰ったりしてた。だからカズさんのところにいっ
ぱいあるんですよ、きっと。だからそれは、作品の交換とかそんなのではなく、あ
げたものです。僕の資料がそんなにあると聞いて本当に嬉しいです。大事に
してくれてたんだなーと感慨無量です。

—

本展に出品する写真作品《Untitled-a / む102 (本数冊)》(cat.no.17)と
《Untitled-b / む103 (壁のシミ (ブロック))》(cat.no.18)は、木下さんが
写真を使い始めた最初の時期に制作されたものですが、
この写真を現像するラボを紹介したのが、植松さんだったと聞きました。

—

いや、その2点は僕が写真焼き付けしたんです。僕は立体、インスタレーショ
ンと並行して、写真とビデオと、フィルムとか、いろいろやってました。1972年

ぐらいから写真始めてたからね。それでカズさんから「写真を現像して作品を作りたい」と相談されて。当時、僕は兵庫県立工業高校のデザイン科に勤めていて、学校が立派な写真室と現像の部屋を持ってたわけですよ。僕もそこで自分の作品の写真焼き付けをしたりいろいろしていてね。「現像してくれへん？」って聞かれたから、「そんなんうちでやったるわ」と言って。これ、結構大きいパネル2枚でしょ。それで合計4枚作った。カズさんもその場にいて、パネル貼りまで一緒にやりました。

　このあいだ、西宮市大谷記念美術館で「72年展」*7 あったでしょ。もう忘れてたんだけど、見に行ったらカズさんの作品が展示されてて、「あれ、これ僕が焼いたやつや」って。この作品はカズさんがジャパン・アート・フェスティバル*8 に応募したんです。それが落ちて返ってきて、その後どこにも発表しなかった作品だったと思います。すごく懐かしかったですよ。記憶が蘇ってきました。見ることの意味を問うような作品で、後の写真とフェルトペンでのドローイングが一緒になる作品につながっていく、最初の頃の重要な作品だと思います。この後の写真を焼くラボは僕が紹介しました。

ドイツでの個展

1981年、木下さんはドイツのハイデルベルク・クンストフェラインで個展を開催しました。ちょうどそこが紙の作品を制作した最後の時期だと思われます。ドイツでの交流についてお聞かせいただけますか。

—

僕は1981年の10月頃に日本に帰ってきて、大阪府立現代美術センターの「今日の作家シリーズ」というので個展をしたわけね。その後ドイツへ戻るときに、カズさんと一緒に飛行機で帰ったんです。作品もロールで巻いて持っていって、その中から展示する作品を選んでね。個展のタイトルは「Kazuyo Kinoshita 1976–1980」。作家を招待して個展をするシリーズの展覧会「Angebote zur Wahrnehmung」の一部として行われたものでした。Wahrnehmungはドイツ語で「知覚」の意味。だから「知覚への提案」とか「知覚への提示」とかそういうタイトルです。ハイデルベルク・クンストフェラインの館長のハンス・ゲルクが1年に3人作家を選んで、会期は別々ですが、3人の作家全員が「知覚への提案」というテーマで個展をするんです。館長は写真の仕事も好きで、コンセプチュアル・アートのヤン・ディベッツの写真とか、ドイツで早くからいろんな写真の作家の作品を紹介してて、ちょうどそういう企画を思いついたんですね。作品は写真だけでなく、立体の作家もいた。いちばん初め、僕がやったのは1979年かな。ドイツの作家とスイスの作家と僕と3人でやって。そのときに日本人の作家をいろいろ紹介したわけですよ。翌年に展示をしたのが竹岡雄二さん。彼はデュッセルドルフに住んでいたから。その次の年にカズさんが個展をした。面白いのはその館長、日本が好きでね。日本人の作家を毎年1人ずつ入れていったんです。すごいでしょ。カズさんに注目したのはもう早かったですね。展示したスペースは、今は全く新しくなってるけど、あの頃のカズさんの展示のドキュメンテーションみたいな写真があるでしょ。あれを見れば個展会場がよくわかります [Fig. 4]。自然光が入っていて、整然と作品が展示されて

いて理知的ないい個展でしたね。あの写真は僕が全部撮りました。デュッセルドルフの僕のスタジオの暗室で焼いたんです。

タイトルにある通り、ドイツの個展では76年から80年までの写真作品を中心に展示されたようですね。

—

このときはペインティングに移る少し前の頃か。やっぱりアーティストだから、本当は作家の現在を展示したかったわけですよ。パステルやペインティングの作品も、本当は見せたかったんだと思う。でも、海外で展示するときは作品を絞った方が観客も納得するし、現地のディレクターも写真作品の方が好きだったし。それで、中原佑介さんにもあの文章*9頼んだんですね[Fig.5]。中原さんも、写真とかちゃんと作品絞って、時代を限定してやった方がいいよと木下さんに言ったんです。やっぱり前の作品ではなくて今の作品の展示をやりたいけど、ドイツでは作家として全然知られていなかったから、それなら写真でやるかということになって、一応本人も納得してやったんですよ。だけど本当にいい展覧会でしたよ。

　ハイデルベルクの展示の後も、カズさん、ドイツに1ヶ月いる間にミュンヘンのレンバッハハウス美術館とコンタクトを取ってたんです。レンバッハハウスのクンストフォルムといって、街の中心地の地下に大きな企画展示場があって、そこでインスタレーションで個展をしませんかという話になったんですが、それは流れてしまいました。本当に残念でした。

レンバッハハウス美術館での展示プランを考えるために制作された小さな模型を撮影した写真が、資料として残っています。

—

その写真、僕が撮ってます。僕のスタジオでそのモデルを作りました。アイデアを考えて、打ち合わせに行って、こういうプランでやりたいってモデルを作って、それを持って行ったりしてたんだけど、どういうわけか日本に帰ってから話が途切れてしまって。ほかにもパリ市立近代美術館のキュレーターにも会いに行ってました。フランスのどこかで紙作品による展覧会に招待されたりもしてたね。それからドイツのビーレフェルトの「写真誕生150周年」*10という展覧会にも呼ばれてた。僕とか若江漢字さんも出してるけどね。DuMont出版社の『Bildgebende Fotografie』という本に大きく取り上げられたりもした。

写真からペインティングへ
ドイツの個展の前後、木下さんは写真からペインティングへと移行していきますが、この時期の作品について植松さんはどのように見ていましたか。

—

カズさんと善巳さんとはものすごく親しかったけど、2人の作品のことについてあんまり喋った覚えはないんです。僕はよく相談していましたけど、カズさんから相談されたことも、善巳さんから相談されたこともなかったです。2人が何

Fig. 4
「Kazuyo Kinoshita 1976–1980」
(1981年、ハイデルベルク・クンストフェライン) 展示風景
撮影：植松奎二

Fig. 5
(左から)植松奎二氏、中原佑介氏、木下(1987年)

か共有してたかはわからないけど、善巳さんの仕事を最初の頃から見ていって、木下さんの仕事もずっと追って見ていくと、同じような時期に2人ともペインティングに変わっていくでしょ。やっぱりこれはお互いに話してると思う。カズさんの仕事にはずっと一貫性があるでしょ。写真からドローイング、ペインティングに変わっていく過程に、全部一貫性がある。自分自身の仕事と一緒に考えてみると、僕は1972年ぐらいからインスタレーションの仕事、立体の仕事、写真の仕事、フィルム… 若いからいろんなことやりたいんですよ。カズさんもいろんなことやりたかったと思います。それで写真をやって、カズさんと善巳さんの考え方も合ってたと思う。カズさんはメンバーではなかったけど、河口龍夫さんたちのグループ〈位〉といつも一緒にいて、善巳さんはメンバーだったでしょ。グループ〈位〉の人たちは「存在」とかそういうことをしょっちゅう話してるわけですよ。だから、「存在」とかそういう言葉を展覧会のタイトルに使ったりとか、いろいろしてくる。そういうなかで72年に写真をやり始めるけど、それまでカズさんはペインティングやってたでしょ、生物みたいな、幾何学的な。それよりも写真の方が自分の考え方をいちばん的確に出せたんだと僕は思うんです。例えばこの円の作品(《'76-C》(cat. no. 42)、《作品 '77-D》(cat. no. 48))でも、「見ること」はどういうことかというのが示されている。その空間、1つの平面に円を描いて、それをちょっと曲げて、写真に撮って、そこに同じ円を描く。すると、空間の二重性が出てくる。「見ること」とは何か、実際に円を認識するのはどういうことか、そういうのは結構写真で表現しやすかったと思います。写真は1980年まで、結構長いことやっておられたんですね。

1980年には、パステルを使った制作を始めています。

—

僕も自分の仕事で、72年から写真を始めて、76年ぐらいにやめたんだけど。なぜ僕が写真をやめたかというと、自分が本当に何をやりたいかってことを考えたわけですよ。僕は彫刻から始まってるから、やっぱり立体をやりたかった。だから、アイデアもまだいっぱいあったんだけど、「もうこれはええわ」とぴたっとやめて。いろんなことやるよりもやりたいことだけをやろうと。カズさんの仕事を見てると、写真というのは表現しやすいですよ、見ていて分かりやすいし。ここを折り曲げて、線を描いて、開いて… コンセプトがすぐにわかる。そういうなかで、やっぱり善巳さんも元々ペインティングから始まって、写真の仕事やったり立体の仕事をやったりしてたからね。それで、カズさんと同じような時期にペインティングに変わるでしょ。80年あたりで、自分が本当にやりたいのは何かというのを2人で話し合ったと思うんです。ある意味、写真による表現みたいなのはもういいと、もう十分やった気がしたと思ったんじゃないですかね。

—

Interview 2

—

An interview with Uematsu Keiji

木下さんご本人も、抑圧された写真表現から離れて
80年、81年とパステルの表現で模索し、カンヴァスでの表現に
たどり着いたとき「表現に対する自分の方法をやっと変えることができた」
とインタビューで語っています。

———

僕もそれはわかるような気がします。あるとき、日本に帰ってきてカズさんに
会ったら写真からパステル（《Pa-C '80-117》(cat.no.85)）になっていて、それは
もうびっくりしました。つながりとしてはわかるんだけど、僕はそんなに良いと
思ってなくて。それでこの後、油彩の絵具を拭き取る仕事になっていったで
しょ。この空間の捉え方というのは面白いなと思ってきてね。あと、86年頃の
色を重ねた《'86-CA362》[Fig. 6]、《'86-CA363》あたりの仕事は僕はあん
まり好きではないんです。だけど、ここから色の線を減らす方に移っていった
のはよくわかります。この辺の展開、素晴らしいと思います。

　　紙を折ったりする写真の仕事にしたって、境界をパステルでぼかしたりす
る仕事にしたって、ある意味システマティックなんですよ。自分で作品の出来
上がりが見えてるわけです。そのうえで、それをいかにどれほどの作品にする
かという感じでやってるから、やっぱり自分のなかで飽きてくると思う。だから
もう写真の仕事をやり遂げたというのはわかるような気がするんですよ。それ
で、ここまでこなしてペインティングになってくると、これはもうspontaneous
（自発的）でしょ。

　　自分で拭いたり消したり、どの辺を拭こうか、どの辺でやめるかって。この
後の線の仕事になってきたら、ここに線を入れて、ここに線を入れて … 線を
入れるだけで空間も全部変わってくるでしょ、絵画って。そうすると新しい絵
画をどのように作るかという仕事になってくる。そこにはものすごい自由があ
るわけです。

　　カズさんがすごく大きい絵を描いてる時、ちょうど日本に帰ってきていてア
トリエに行って、「あ、すごいええわ」と言ったことがあります。カズさんも自分
でもいいと思ってるんだけど、どこで止めるか、どこまで描くかにものすごく悩
んでましたね。こういう作品はどこで止めるかというのはとても大事だし、難
しい。1週間もずっと同じように制作途中の作品を見てることもあった。でも、
やっぱりそこには自由があったと思うんです。そうしたら、どんどん開けていけ
るでしょう、自分のなかで。だから、最後の方にペインティングに向かっていっ
たのはよかったと思います。94年にカズさん亡くなったけど、もし生きておら
れたらどうなってたかというのはすごい楽しみでしたね。

———

がんとの闘い、最後まで描き続けた晩年

木下さんは晩年、がんの治療のためにたびたびロサンゼルスに
滞在しながら、制作を続けられました。
最後に、この時期のことについてお話しいただけますか。

———

カズさんががんになったのがわかったのは、1990年の秋かな。そのときのこ
とよく覚えています。がんになったと言って、カズさんも気さくな人だったし「奎

Fig. 6
《'86-CA362》1986年
出典：『木下佳通代 1939–1994』AD＆A、1996年、
p.46

ちゃんしこりを触ってみる?」とか言って。そのときいろいろ話してたんだけど、がんが見つかったときステージが結構進んでいたと思うんですよ。それで、「今手術をしても助かるかどうかはわからへん、このままほっといても、あかんかわからへん、そしたらどっちにしようかな」と、すごく悩んだ。「手術してもあかんのやったら、手術しなくてももう一緒や」と。それなら手術しないでいこうかなという感じで。善巳さんともいろいろ喋ったなかで、結局、カズさんが好きなように生きたらいいということになったと思うんですよ。それで最後まで絵を描き続けて、1994年に神戸アドベンチスト病院のホスピスに入ったわけですよ。その頃、僕は1週間に1回ぐらいお見舞いに行っていたんですよね。病院では資料の整理をずっとやってましたね。よくやっていた。あとは水彩画を描いたりして。最後に描いた水彩《無題(絶筆・未完)》(cat. no.133)を版画にして、お葬式のときみんなに配ったんですよね。それは僕も持ってて、西宮(市大谷記念美術館)に寄贈しました。だけど本当に「生きること」にはすごく執念を持ってましたね。やっぱりもっともっと仕事したいという感じで、ずっと。がんの治療をしてるときも。もし手術して、うまいこといかなかったら、もう絵は描けないわけ。そういう意味では、手術しないで最後まで絵を描いていけたから、よかったんだと思います。最後まで現役の作家だった。今回、回顧展ができて本当によかった。本人もすごく喜んでいると思います。

*1 「第4回国際青年美術家展 日本・アメリカ展」(1967年3月4日−14日、西武百貨店SSSホール、主催:社団法人日本文化フォーラム)
*2 「向井修二・奥田善巳・東山明3人展」(1967年4月4日(?)−16日、トアロード画廊、企画:神戸新聞社)
*3 「第1回PLAY展」。1967年から関西を拠点に活動する、池水慶一を中心とした美術家集団THE PLAYによる展覧会。神戸市三宮の東遊園地にて3日間1時間ずつ、参加者それぞれがハプニングを繰り広げた。
*4 「木下佳通代展−実在と認識…そしてもう一つのリアリティーへ・1979−1991」(1991年7月23日−8月4日、ギャラリー16)
*5 「コレクション・五題」(2022年1月22日−3月13日)
*6 現在は大阪中之島美術館が「木下佳通代アーカイブ」として所蔵。
*7 「Back to 1972−50年前の現代美術へ」(2022年10月8日−12月11日、西宮市大谷記念美術館)
*8 日本の現代美術を海外に紹介することを目的として、1966年から1977年にかけて開催された展覧会。主催団体は社団法人国際芸術見本市協会(現・社団法人国際芸術文化振興会)。
*9 ドイツでの個展に際し、美術評論家・中原佑介が展覧会図録に寄稿した文章のこと。
*10 「自律的イメージとしての写真−実験的デザイン1839−1989」(1989年9月3日−1989年11月12日、ビーレフェルト・クンストハレ/1989年12月15日−1990年1月28日、ミュンヘン・ヴァイヤリッシュ・クンスト・アカデミー)

Kinoshita Kazuyo: A Remembrance

Kumada Tsukasa Art Historian

Beginnings

After a tumultuous decade of career decisions and changes in personal relationships, Kinoshita Kazuyo remarried and settled in the district of Yamamoto-dori 4-chome, Ikuta-ku, Kobe (today part of Chuo-ku, Kobe) with fellow contemporary artist Okuda Yoshimi. A year and a half later, in October 1971, they moved to nearby Yamamoto-dori 3-chome and opened the art classroom Art Room Tor in their combined home and studio. As the "Tor" in the name alludes, it was located close to the northern end of Tor Road, in a small two-story house on the left as you head up the hill, just before the intersection with Yamamoto-Street. Tor Road begins further south, passing between JR Sannomiya and Motomachi train stations before extending north. At its northern end stood the Kobe Foreign Club (known today as the Kobe Club), in grounds that before World War II had been occupied by the Tor Hotel, the source of the road's name. In years when "enemy languages" were shunned, "Tor" was written "To-A," changing the meaning to "East Asia Road." It remains one of Kobe's most stylish Western-style streets to this day.

As someone born and raised in Kobe, I always had immense affection for this street, particularly in early summer when the mimosa trees lining it burst into pink bloom. However, I knew little of Tor Road's northern end except that there was a well-known Western antique shop there. I was more acquainted with the southern end at the bottom of the hill, specifically the jazz café Sarigenaku (lit. "in a casual manner"), nestled in the basement of a long, narrow building two doors east of Tor Road on Sunset Street, which runs alongside the elevated section of the Hankyu railway line.

In the late 1960s and early 1970s, just before Kinoshita and Okuda settled in the Yamamoto-dori district, I often found myself drawn to Sarigenaku as if seeking refuge from the political upheaval of the times. Descending a dim staircase, and then going up a couple of steps, I would find the entrance of the small bar, so shrouded with a haze of cigarette smoke that I could not see to the back of the room. There was a counter with about ten seats, and jazz was blasting through JBL speakers at ear-splitting volume. I cannot remember clearly whether there were tables or not, probably because I was a regular at the counter, silently nodding to the music for hours for the cost of just a coffee or a beer. I exchanged few words with anyone, and interaction with the owner or staff, always dressed in a white shirt and black tie, was confined to record requests or, on very rare occasions, ordering another drink. One of my requests was for Eric Dolphy's *Last Date*.

Recorded in the Netherlands just weeks before Dolphy's death in 1964, the live recording ends with the frenetic melody line of the final track, "Miss Ann," followed by applause and then a clip from an interview with Dolphy recorded just before the concert. His haunting words lingered with me: "When you hear music after it's over, it's gone, in the air, you can never capture it again..." Later, looking at Kinoshita's paintings from the 1980s, the words resurfaced in my mind.

The staff at Sarigenaku seemed unenthused about playing Dolphy or, for example, John Coltrane. I have heard that that Murakami Haruki also frequented the café in the late 1960s, and the vibe of the place seemed more in line with the cool West Coast jazz he favored. I was recently reflecting on this as I listened to the Gerry Mulligan album *What is There to Say?* (1959), and I was surprised to find Kinoshita's paintings springing into my mind's eye. It was the dialogue between Art Farmer, sitting in on trumpet, and Mulligan on baritone sax, with their intertwining and overlapping melody lines, that conjured up these vivid images.

Kinoshita's photo based works

In the early 1970s, Kinoshita was shifting away from her early experiments with paint and focusing on conceptual photographic works. I get the sense that she was not terribly interested in jazz, or in music in general for that matter. The associations I described are simply my own personal impressions, fleeting thoughts from the recesses of my memory.

Kobe's Flower Clock, on the north side of City Hall, has been a tourist attraction since the late 1950s. Photographing this landmark is a cliché, but Kinoshita turned it into one of her earliest works of conceptual art, capturing the passage of time and the interchange and overlapping of subjects in a set of twenty photographs (ten pairs) titled *Untitled/ Mu 38 (Flower Clock)* (1973, cat. no. 19). This work is superficially similar but essentially diverges from the approach typical of sets of photos, in which a photographer constructs a thematic narrative with multiple shots. If there is a theme here, it is that of the remarkable conceptual work of capturing moments in which the flow of time intersects with human existence or activity, composed in a continuous planar sequence through the medium of photography, and creating a structure akin to a Möbius strip in which the roles of subject and object alternate.

Related works include *Untitled / Mu 59 (Watch)* (1974, cat. no. 20), featuring a sequence of photographs depicting the passing time on a wristwatch, and *Untitled / Mu 60 (Beaker)* (1973, cat. no. 21), which documents temperature changes in the water in a beaker as indicated by a thermometer. While these may come across as overly methodical, *Untitled-b / Mu 103 (Stains on the wall (blocks))* (1972, cat. no. 18), made the year before, is far more compelling, foreshadowing the direction her future paintings would take. It may have been inspired by the common practice, during repairs, of using chalk to circle and mark cracks and peeling areas on walls. This piece, juxtaposing shots of a mortar wall before and after marking, taken from an identical angle, presents a visual state that alternates between dispersal and concentration while also contrasting the aging material with the fresh chalk outlines, prefiguring the evolution of her subsequent explorations.

I first became aware of these early 1970s works, composed solely of photographs, in the 1990s when Nakanoshima Museum of Art, Osaka (then known as the Osaka City Museum of Modern Art Planning Office) began actively acquiring Kinoshita. Among her early work that drew my attention around the same time was a series in which she photographed drafting tools and geometric shapes drawn with them, then made large-format prints and drew on them with a felt pen to accentuate the shapes of the subjects in each image. I do not remember exactly where I first encountered this series, initiated in 1976, but I clearly recall that twelve works were featured in *Art Now '78* at the Hyogo Prefectural Museum of Modern Art (predecessor of the Hyogo Prefectural Museum of Art) in 1978 (p. 258).

Early works in the series such as *'76-1* (1976, cat. no. 47), with a wooden set square as its subject, are strongly reminiscent of Plato's famous theory of forms from ancient times. This classical art theory positions painting as the lowest step in a hierarchy of imitation: (1) the ideal forms of things as ideas, (2) the actual things made as imitations of these ideas, and (3) paintings that imitate these imitations. Kinoshita's method of photographing a wooden set square (an example of category 2) and printing it on large-format photo paper (category 3), then outlining the "idea" (category 1) directly on the print's surface with a felt-tip pen, could be likened to illustrating a philosopher's abstract contemplation, quite the opposite of the conventional painterly approach.

Setting aside the question of how intentional this was, this series evolved as she photographed transformations of geometric shapes on crumpled, folded, or wrinkled paper and then restored their original shapes (ideal forms) by drawing with a felt-tip pen. Initially, she shot the paper from a vantage point diagonally overhead, causing it to recede into the distance in linear perspective, but as the series developed, she began photographing the pieces of paper head-on. By trimming the photo paper, reinstating its true proportions, to the very borders of the subject, she achieved a more arresting effect. Elimination of linear perspective accentuated the chiaroscuro of the black-and-white prints, enhancing the interplay between the texture of the paper and the crisp lines and producing an engaging flat surface. Towards the end of the series, the act of restoring shapes by drawing extended beyond felt-tip pen line drawings to include freehand drawings and airbrushed "paintings" of geometric shapes. In any case, by the late 1970s Kinoshita's emphasis had transitioned from capturing reality in photographs to the practices of drawing and painting themselves.

Painting, and final days

I believe I first spoke with Kinoshita in 1982. In September and October of that year, she and Okuda Yoshimi had back-to-back solo shows of their paintings at galerie 16 in Kyoto. Just before the exhibitions, the two of them visited me at my place of employment (the Otani Memorial Art Museum, Nishinomiya City, before it was rebuilt) bearing invitations. For both of them, these were the first substantial shows after they shifted their focus to oil painting. Okuda had begun working in oils a bit earlier, around the previous year, while Kinoshita had taken up oils that same year.

Their unexpected visit was probably prompted by their seeing my brief review in *Bijutsu Techo* (no. 465) of the 1980 Kyoto Independent Exhibition, in which I mentioned Kinoshita. In the review I had erroneously described Kinoshita's technique of rubbing pastel into folded-up paper and then unfolding it, mistaking the medium for airbrush. They may have intended to correct this misunderstanding. I remember discussing their intention to transition from drawing to painting moving forward.

After this transitional period, Kinoshita decisively shifted, or perhaps I should say returned, to painting. The first work, appearing on the exhibition invitation and titled *'82-CA1* (1982, cat. no. 90), was clearly made by roughly and liberally applying dark blue oil paint with a flat brush, then partially wiping it off with rags or dry brushes to reveal the coarse texture of the canvas in the center. The seemingly incomplete state of the painting suggests the trial-and-error explorations of a novice oil painter, but it also challenges the traditional notion that paintings are solely defined by brushwork. After dozens of similar studies, her canvases evolved to show more intricate interplay of paint application and removal, with a palette extending to shades of dark blue, dark brown, and vermilion. She also applied such experimentation rigorously in smaller works on paper and watercolors, but in March 1985 she was able to rent a studio in the Mitsubishi Warehouse next to Shinko Pier at the Port of Kobe, enabling her to work at larger sizes and leading to production of the landmark '86-CA323 (1986, cat. no. 105).

This painting, formerly on view at Doshisha University's Kyotanabe Campus, featured dripping strokes of dark blue oil across the entire surface, which she subsequently wiped before reapplying further layers of paint. The impression is of looming storm clouds enveloping the canvas. The artist's dedication and frustrations in tackling such a large canvas are evident, and the work cannot be called a complete success. However, this approach evolved into works where vertical and horizontal elements were systematically arranged, and further paint application and removal generated a sense of internal space with depth and dimensionality. By the late 1980s, this led to paintings such as '89-CA554 (1989, cat. no. 114), imbued with *karumi* (lit. "lightness") reminiscent of clouds playfully tossed by the wind and dispersing. To draw an art-historical analogy, much as Piet Mondrian achieved absolute geometric abstraction with his "plus and minus paintings," Kinoshita found her own form of absolute painting by adding and subtracting brushstrokes.

It was a clear, tranquil, and joyous realm of painting, in which a kind of resignation could also be seen at some deep level. However, the joy was abruptly shattered by a breast cancer diagnosis in 1990. Suddenly faced with looming death, Kinoshita was plunged into anxiety and seized by a desperate desire to live, spurring her to act as if racing against time. Seeking treatment, she traveled to clinics throughout Japan and in Korea. Her repeated trips to Los Angeles were also connected with this quest. During this period, an overwhelming vitality emerged as she endeavored to devote her remaining time to self-realization. In her art, she switched to fast-drying acrylics so as to bypass the slow process of layering and removing oil paint in a fervent effort to produce more work. In this there was an unmistakable sense of urgency. Nonetheless, works made in Los Angeles, such as *LA '92-CA711* (1992, cat. no. 122), exude a refreshing clarity, as if harmonizing with the balmy sounds of West Coast jazz.

However, a sense of gloom pervaded her April 1994 solo show at AD&A Gallery. The works on view were characterized by bold vertical strokes, which were applied repeatedly with a broad flat brush. Lacking the time to wipe away paint, she overpainted instead, with heavy white brushwork. The gallery's brick walls were lined with these large, intense works, radiating a sense of urgency. During the exhibition I spoke briefly with Kinoshita, who seemed in much better health than I had expected. Her vibrant clothing and demean-

or betrayed no sign that she had just five months to live, and as I turned back to the works on the wall, their powerful and determined presence remained undimmed. Nonetheless, the mood was undeniably somber, overshadowed by the creeping specter of death.

For Kinoshita Kazuyo and me, this was the *"Last Date."*

Photography and Conceptualism

Tatehata Akira Director, the Museum of Modern Art, Saitama

Kinoshita Kazuyo initially studied at the Department of Western Painting at Kyoto City University of Arts, with aspirations of becoming a painter. In the portrait of a female figure (*Title Unknown / Mu 76*, 1960, cat. no. 1) which she painted while a student, it is possible to observe a division of color planes in a manner almost reminiscent of cubism, perhaps due to the influence of artist Kuroda Jutaro who was her teacher at the time. This in itself is an interesting fact, and is discussed briefly below, but Kinoshita did not continue painting on a regular basis after graduating from university. It was not until the 1970s that she began producing photographic works that clearly defined her unique approach, with her artistic practice having somewhat slowed down up to that point. However, this was by no means a blank period for Kinoshita. Rather, it was likely an essential preparatory period for her to devise her own form of conceptualism through close interactions with the avant-garde art collective Group " i," founded by Kawaguchi Tatsuo and other artists in Western Japan.

As for trends surrounding art in the Kansai region at the time, the Gutai Art Association had already disbanded, and media art, which had gained momentum at Expo '70 Osaka, was no longer drawing attention following the event's closing. The situation was such that there were no 'isms' acting as a driving force in art. In this context, it is worth noting that Kawaguchi Tatsuo, who was Kinoshita's contemporary, as well as slightly younger artists such as Nomura Hitoshi, Uematsu Keiji, and Kitatsuji Yoshihisa, were each exploring areas with a sense of conceptual direction. Although Kinoshita Kazuyo resumed her practice a little later than these artists, her photographic works from the early to late 1970s seem to stand out for their sheer purity, as if they themselves could be described as genuine experiments in conceptualism.

For example, in her 1973 work (*Untitled / Mu 38 (Flower Clock)*, cat. no. 19), consisting of a series of ten photographs, Kinoshita asked ten acquaintances to each take a photograph of a giant flower clock in Kobe by setting up a tripod in the same position. Each of these photographs is paired with a photograph taken by Kinoshita herself from behind each person while they were in the process of taking the above photograph. Photographs are often presented in the form of a sequential series since it is easy to take consecutive photographs of the same motif, yet Kinoshita here has no intention of making the transition of time the subject of the work. As such, the time indicated by the hands of the clock (although the dates of the photographs differ) is consistently in the vicinity of 11 o'clock. In other words, she attempts to present all the photographic images simultaneously (in juxtaposition and concurrently), and it is reasonable to point out that the motif of the clock is required precisely for this purpose (i.e., as a means to 'self-certify' the elimination of sequential temporality).

In contrast, Kawaguchi Tatsuo's *Land and Sea* (1970), for example, is a series of sixty coarse-grained prints that are a photographic record of a site-specific installation in which the artist placed four long wooden planks along the seashore and methodically charted the way the position of the waves washing the planks changed over time in correspondence to the ebb and flow of the tide. Here, the natural phenomenon of waves serving as the boundary between land and sea is captured in a sequential manner from an extremely pragmatic perspective. Nomura Hitoshi's *Time on a Curved Line* (1970) is a series of photographs documenting an asphalt pavement with chalk markings indicating the current date and time that the artist had made at certain intervals while walking along a curving road. One could say that in this work the sequential passage of time is directly objectified through the repetition of the same action.

All of these artists entrusted their quest for conceptualism to photography, which by nature of its medium, enables the insensate, mechanical recording of images. It indeed would not be unreasonable to say that they are consistent in their elimination of subjective expression. However, while Kawaguchi and Nomura's series of photographs have what could be considered a fractionally-differentiated time axis in their images that are ambiguous between discreteness and continuity, Kinoshita Kazuyo's photographs present the ten pairs in a simultaneous and comprehensive manner. There is precisely a single perspective (the artist's point of view) from which she photographs the people photographing the flower clock, and the work does not succumb to the mere chain that tends to cross everyone's mind—that is, looking at a person looking at another person looking at something. Her perspective, as she describes in her own words, is that of God the creator. Rather than being a sign of arrogance, this statement seems to me to elevate the reciprocal relationship between the actual flower clock and its image to an ontological level.

The intent for this simultaneous presentation was made more evident in a series of compass-based works produced from 1976 to 1977. *Work '77-D* (1977, cat. no. 48) is a print of a photograph taken of a folded piece of paper that had a perfect circle drawn on it, upon which a perfect circle of exactly the same dimensions is drawn with a felt pen to coincide with the image of the circle distorted by the process. In other words, the artist creates a physically manipulated image of a circle that is transformed by introducing multiple perspectives achieved through folding the picture plane, after which the distorted image is two-dimensionally re-rendered in the form of a printed photograph, enabling the circle to coexist on the same plane as a contrasting perspective. It is a tricky mechanism to say the least.

This may seem like a bit of a leap, but depending on how you think about it, one could say that this overlaps with the multiple perspectives in Cézannean cubism. In Paul Cézanne's still life works, two perspectives coexist: the plate of fruit on the table is depicted as a perfect circle as if viewed directly from above, while the mouth of the vase placed on the same table is in an oval shape as if viewed from diagonally above. The simultaneous presence of the photographic image and the drawn image in Kinoshita's work seems to indicate her awareness of the problem of pictorial space, which also bears connections to cubism.

Incidentally, this trickiness does not call into question the purity of her methodological experimentation. The search for conceptualism often leads to a tricky shift in thinking, and in the case of the above work by Kinoshita, she attempts to reverse the function of photography, which transforms a three-dimensional space into a two-dimensional one, in order to create a three-dimensional image as a pure illusion generated from two-dimensional space. This in essence is nothing but the simultaneous existence of two perspectives on the same plane, which is impossible in reality.

Again, in this respect, the works with the flower clock and compass share the same intention. Kinoshita Kazuyo returned to painting in the 1980s, but the fact that she had been working on series of tension-filled works like this from times prior to that is indeed something that should be highly evaluated. While such works could be regarded as the most radical conceptualist experiments in postwar Japanese art, in retrospect, one might say that they also presented a world permeated with an extremely intellectual and exquisite sense of beauty that could only be conceived through the hands of this particular artist.

Crystallizations of Artistic Thought:
The Photographic Works and Paintings of Kinoshita Kazuyo

Mitsuda Yuri Professor, Tama Art University Graduate School
Director, Tama Art University Art Archives Center
Director, peu/art cottage

I. Duration of Kinoshita's Career

Kinoshita Kazuyo was born in Kobe in 1939, and if one considers her first full-fledged foray into the art world to be her debut photographic exhibition in 1972, she embarked on her career relatively late. Amid the nation's rapid economic growth and an explosion of movements ranging from junk art and anti-art to Pop Art, the 1960s were a vibrant era for Japan's art scene, but Kinoshita's early works, including many sculptures, remain largely unknown.

By 1972, several of Kinoshita's female contemporaries had made significant strides. Tanaka Atsuko, seven years her senior, had left the Gutai Art Association in 1965, navigated a critical phase of her career, and was exhibiting at Minami Gallery. Kanno Seiko, six years older than Kinoshita, had joined Gutai around the time of Tanaka's departure, was producing systematic painting incorporating mathematics, and had a solo exhibition at Gutai Pinacotheca in 1971. Meanwhile, Sawai Yoko, ten years behind Kinoshita at Kyoto City University of Arts, was on the cusp of her career. There had been scant participation by Kansai-based artists in Expo '70 Osaka, a major international event in Senrioka, Osaka Prefecture, leading to a sense that the regional art scene had exerted little lasting impact. Meanwhile, the Trends in Contemporary Japanese Art exhibition series at the National Museum of Modern Art, Kyoto had ended in 1970, marking the close of an era.

Meanwhile, in the late 1960s collectives such as Group "i" and THE PLAY began staging conceptual group performances in outdoor settings. Around 1969, the Kyoto Independent Exhibition at the Kyoto City Museum of Art gained momentum, and there were a variety of other innovative endeavors including film exhibitions led by artist groups. The 1970s saw the emergence of venues in the Kansai region that embraced avant-garde activities, notably with the inauguration of Art Now, a juried contemporary art exhibition at the Hyogo Prefectural Museum of Modern Art (predecessor of the Hyogo Prefectural Museum of Art) that ran from 1975 to 1988. While the involvement of women artists in these collaborative efforts was negligible, Kinoshita pursued her photographic art independently in her hometown of Kobe, showing work in the Kyoto Independent, the Contemporary Art Exhibition of Japan, and various group shows, and held several solo exhibitions in Tokyo while exhibiting consistently at galerie 16 in Kyoto. Kinoshita pursued a tranquil, intellectual photographic vision, and became a widely respected and trusted figure in the art community.

Around the time of the 10th Tokyo Biennale: Between Man and Matter in 1970, the Japanese art scene saw widespread exploration of new forms and media, including silkscreen, video, photography series, and installation, while the traditional media of painting and sculpture were fundamentally reevaluated. In addition to discarded materials, artists incorporated industrial products like fiber-reinforced plastic, acrylic, iron, and stainless steel, as well as technological elements such as lights and motors. This was accompanied by a progressive shift toward using the terms 2D and 3D rather than painting or sculpture. These developments coincided with Kinoshita's photography period.

Kinoshita dedicated herself to the production of photographic works throughout the 1970s, steadily gaining recognition and accolades. Around 1980, she transitioned toward pastel and eventually devoted herself to oil painting. Like her earlier works, her painting was marked by profound contemplation to which she applied rigorous methodologies, but she introduced a more physical and dynamic appeal to her oil paintings. She continued earning acclaim for her innovative pictorial and spatial exploration until her untimely death from illness in 1994. During her years engaged in painting, the discourse around art changed and 2D went back to being called "painting," while the term New Painting came into vogue. However, Kinoshita remained aloof from the prevailing trends of narrative and expressionistic painting. She followed the emergence of the Kansai New Wave in the 1980s and enjoyed interacting with emerging artists, all the while staying on her unique path.

Kinoshita once wrote of her work as follows:

I have always wanted my works to be strong enough to stand the test of time, and not to fade or decay. And I aim to focus solely on artistic issues, and to keep anything extraneous to art out of my work as much as possible.

(Gallery Promenade, solo exhibition at Tor Road Gallery, October 1984, p. 7)

Thirty years after her passing, this exhibition at two museums showcasing the full scope of Kinoshita Kazuyo's work is a long-awaited opportunity. In writing about Kinoshita's work, I will strive as she did to "focus solely on artistic issues" to the greatest possible extent.

II. Photography and Seeing (1)

Kinoshita often released short statements in conjunction with her solo exhibitions, focusing first of all on analyzing the act of seeing, and by extension, the perception of being.

In the exhibition *Futatabi, miru koto ni tsuite* [On Seeing, Revisited] (galerie 16, 1973), she showed the photo series *Untitled* (cat. no. 19). This series, executed with the help of acquaintances, features photos of the Flower Clock, a local landmark in front of Kobe Station, taken by ten different people. It comprises twenty photos in all, in ten pairs. In each pair, a close-up of the Flower Clock is paired with a shot of the person photographing it, taken from behind at a distance. While the photos of the Flower Clock are all similar, the pairing with the distant shots reveals that each photographer is unique, and the two photos taken simultaneously resonate with each other. However, since both the Flower Clock and the photographers were shot from nearly identical positions, the only notable differences between the photo sets are the time indicated on the clock and the photographers' appearance.

In his review of the exhibition, Hirano Shigemitsu interpreted this as an experiment with "the objective existence of things, that is, the existence of things that precedes seeing." Hirano writes that the act of seeing, shaped by "subjects' various ideas, mentalities, and moods," is "clearly divergent from the pre-existing state of things," and thus the work was an inquiry into the "objective existence of things." [1] This implies that the Flower Clock is an entity that transcends and is unaffected by the changing photographers, an interpretation that aligns with the following statement from the artist:

> *Futatabi, miru koto ni tsuite* [On Seeing, Revisited]
>
> When a person "sees" a thing that "exists," that thing appears to manifest more richly and dynamically, reflecting both a universal and an individual character shaped by diverse consciousnesses influenced by general concepts, personal ideas, daily and situational elements, and variations in people's thoughts or perceptions. However, when all intentions related to it are severed, it is recognized simply as existing in itself.
>
> (Exhibition leaflet, 1973)

Perceiving something that simply exists by severing it from intentions entailed, in this case, capturing long-range shots of both the photographer and the thing being photographed, and the role of another *seeing* person (perhaps Kinoshita herself) who shoots from a distance. This seeing person captures both the thing being photographed and the photographers using cameras to see it, along with their surrounding environment. With only the photos of the Flower Clock, the different photographers and the context of the surrounding scenery would remain unknown. The distant shots offer a meta-perspective on the act of seeing.

The question arises, however, of why there is not another photographer, even farther away, behind the photographer shooting from a distance. Why is there no questioning of the identity of the photographer (s), who may or may not have been the same person taking all ten shots from a distance? To me it suggests that Kinoshita assigned two separate roles of photography to the two types of photos in each set. These roles are *recreation of human vision and field of view*, elucidating the act of seeing, and *documentation* made possible by the objectivity of the lens. The Flower Clock photos embody the former and the shots from a distance the latter, with Kinoshita delegating these dual duties of photography to each pair in the series.

III. Photography and Seeing (2)

Placing yet another photographer behind the one shooting from a distance would lead to an endless sequence of photographers capturing each other, which would be an entirely different kind of experiment. This concept is explored in a work from three years later, *Untitled (Some profile or some consciousness)* (1976, cat. no. 35), where a photograph of two people is viewed by one of them, who is then photographed, and the process repeats. The act of seeing oneself being seen is repeatedly layered within the work.

Two people (a couple) facing one another is a rare subject within Kinoshita's body of work, and in this sense intriguing. In the beginning they look at each other, and each one of them is both the observer and the observed. One of them then looked at the photograph of them facing each other, becomes aware of themselves being looked at (photographed), and then looks at that photograph... it is a cycle. There is no way of knowing how the two see each other (there are no photographs showing the field of view). The work comprises layers of photography's objective role in documenting the act of seeing. Paradoxically, the photographs reveal the misalignment in the couple's visual perspectives, perpetuating a cycle of seeing without end.

Untitled (1976, cat. no. 39) is an intriguing work that also functions as a self-portrait. It is a fixed-point observation of the artist's standing figure from the front. In a mechanical sequence taken, on different days, from a stationary point, she divides her body into eight segments and amalgamates them to depict multiple instances of herself at different times. The dates of shooting noted on each segment are at short intervals, implying that the work may be more akin to a temporally sequenced collage than to a fixed-point observation. Despite minor variations in clothing and hairstyle, she stands almost unchanged in the same location, seemingly affirming the stability of her existence. Here, photography is effectively utilized as objective documentation.

At the same time, the self-referential nature of the subject adds an additional layer of complexity, enhancing the work's appeal. That is, people cannot see themselves without the aid of a mirror or photograph. Thus, the automatically triggered self-portrait is not only documentation but also a surrogate for the field of view, and an endeavor to see the unseen self.

_____

IV. Photography and Seeing (3)

___

The art critic Nakahara Yusuke's seminal book *Miru koto no shinwa* [The Mythology of Seeing] (Film Art Inc., 1972) addresses the theme of seeing, as its title suggests. Nakahara, who was commissioner of the 10th Tokyo Biennale: Between Man and Matter (1970), compiled this book of essays from between 1965 and 1971 with seeing as a central concept. Then at the peak of his career, he argued that the latest developments in conceptual art, film, performance, and installation should be seen as efforts to reevaluate the act of seeing. Other critics of the time such as Miyagawa Atsushi and Ishiko Junzo also engaged with this theme, seeking to analyze preconceptions, habits, and personal or historical orientations that subconsciously influence viewers' perspectives. They believed that rendering these visible and consciously addressing them was crucial for fundamentally reassessing both the creation and appreciation of art, a stance widely shared at the time. Ishiko's emphasis on optical illusions in his role as theoretical leader of the group Genshoku, and Nakahara's organization of the *Tricks and Vision* exhibition (Tokyo Gallery, Muramatsu Gallery, 1968), were motivated by the conviction that reexamining illusions produced by artistic techniques could lead to a critical reevaluation of art itself. This analytical approach to seeing was viewed as essential for the evolution of contemporary art.

This was an internationally shared concern. Starting in the late 1960s, Jan Dibbets [Fig. 1] of the Netherlands, Giuseppe Penone [Fig. 2] from Italy, and Vito Acconci [Fig. 3] and Ed

Ruscha [Fig. 4] of the US were at the forefront of a trend of utilizing series of photos to explore and analyze spatial perception, changes in subjects over time, and the relation of actions and spaces. Closer by there were photo series by Japanese artists such as Nomura Hitoshi [Fig. 5] and Kawaguchi Tatsuo.

Kinoshita evidently shared this paradigm in her own way, striving for a pure perception of existence itself. To this end she identified and illuminated various obstacles, necessitating the camera's use and the creation of photographic works. Since her high school days, Kinoshita had imagined a state where all existence is perceived as equal:

> If consciousness could drift throughout the universe like fog, everything could be known. Since my teens, I've harbored the heartfelt desire to remain merely as a unit of consciousness... What I truly aim to see are "things that exist equivalently," be they life forms or mental entities.
>
> ("Interview," in *Kazuyo Kinoshita 1939 – 1994*, AD&A, 1996, p. 91)

> To let consciousness float in space.
>
> (*Kobecco*, vol. 212, December, 1978, p. 60)

She may have longed for a transcendent, divine viewpoint, with clear vision of all things. Such

Fig. 1   Fig. 2   Fig. 3   Fig. 4

Fig. 1 Jan Dibbets *Perspective correction – My studio 1, 2: square*, 1969
Image from *Jan Dibbets*, Kamakura Gallery, 1982

Fig. 2 Giuseppe Penone *Reversing One's Eyes*, 1970
Image from *Giuseppe Penone: The Venis of Stone*, Toyota Municipal Museum of Art, 1997, p. 114

Fig. 3 Vito Accinci *Following Piece*, 1969
Image from *Vito Acconci*, PHAIDON, 2002, p. 38

Fig. 4 Edward RUSCHA *Phillips 66, Flagstaff, Arizona, 1962, from Twentysix Gasoline Stations*, 1963
Image from *Ed Rucha and photography*, Whitney Museum of American Art, 2004, p. 113

Fig. 5 Nomura Hitoshi *Photobook or The Brownian Motion of Eyesight*, photobook, 1972 – 1973, Toyota Municipal Museum of Art
Image from *Seeing: Contingency and Necessity / The Work of Hitoshi Nomura*, AKAAKA, 2006, p. 19

Fig. 5

a vantage point would reinforce the belief in equality of existence that formed the corner-stone of her practice. From this impartial perspective, all that exists, and all that does not, is regarded as equivalent.

Kinoshita endeavored to convey this principle through various means, including creation of transparent sculptures. Her 1970 series *Boundary Thought* (cat.nos.8–10) is clearly an example of this exploration. The series features sliced geometric forms – cubes, cones, cylinders – echoing Cezanne's famous dictum to "treat nature by means of the cylinder, the sphere, and the cone." The interiors of these forms are the same color as the space surrounding them, implying that the interior and exterior of existence are essentially homogeneous and equivalent.

In daily life, we do not perceive all existence as homogeneous and equivalent. Our perception of specific things is colored by our awareness. The series (1975, cat.nos. 24–34), where she silkscreened copies of a single photograph in sequence as a representation of a changing "field of view" over time and then added hand-coloring, highlights the difficulty of viewing subjects as equivalent, or illustrates steps towards this goal.

Photographic works and silkscreen prints exploring the observer-subject relationship were quite common at the time. In part of his *Work* series (circa 1969–74) [Fig. 6], Yoshida Katsuro aimed to represent the observer's perspective through changes in color and imagery. Uematsu Keiji, in his photo series *Seeing–Landscape* (1974) [Fig. 7], repeatedly captured almost the same scene while altering his vantage point. These works, which illustrate the process of forming relationships with subjects over time through changes in perspective, align with Kinoshita's approach. All three artists aimed to render the observer-subject relationship visible, but what differentiates Kinoshita's work is that it seems to reach some sort of conclusion. It suggests that when photography stops time, one can eventually perceive the entirety of a scene while sequentially shifting viewpoints. Kinoshita's clear,

Fig. 6
Yoshida Katsuro *Work 13*, 1971
Courtesy of Yumiko Chiba Associates

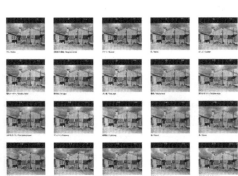

Fig. 7
Uematsu Keiji *Seeing–Landscape*, 1974
Courtesy of Yumiko Chiba Associates

fundamental belief in the equivalence of existence led her to aim for the elimination of all subjective conditions.

V. Photography and Seeing (4)

Kinoshita's next series, in which she photographed geometric shapes on paper, is her most extensive series and can be described as her signature work.

The geometric shapes began with compass-drawn circles and evolved to include diagonals, parallel lines, squares, triangles, and grids in various arrangements. These basic geometric shapes, first hand-drawn on paper, were then photographed, and they would appear distorted due to the angle of the photograph or the warping and folding of the paper. The photographs in this series act as fields of view. Normally, based on our past experience, we unconsciously correct distortions in our field of view, for example perceiving a distorted image of a circle as a perfect circle. However, Kinoshita's rigor does not allow for such ambiguities. She aesthetically challenges our mundane, convention-bound vision and guides us toward new realms of perception.

In these works, she then replicated on the photographs the same shapes that were initially drawn on paper. In this process, the shapes in the photographs and those drawn on the photos' surfaces are aligned in size. This allows the surface of the photograph and the reality underlying it — the paper captured on film shortly before — to merge, causing different temporal layers to interpenetrate. The shapes added to the photos with a felt-tip pen exist in the foreground, in a temporal and spatial dimension distinct from that of the photographed image. Instead, they are lines that have been layered on the surface of the field of vision — i.e., the surface of the photograph. When the shapes in the photographed three-dimensional space and the two-dimensional shapes drawn on the photo surface are superimposed, the discrepancies illuminate distortions in our field of view. They may also reveal the "correct (?)" way for us to see the subject.

In some cases the original paper is shot from farther away, leaving margins around it, and in others the area of photograph's entire surface is nearly identical to that of the original paper. Broadly speaking, Kinoshita seems to have transitioned from the former to the latter. In the first approach, the photograph acts more as objective documentation of the paper. In the second, the photograph's field of view closely aligns with the surface of the actual paper.

Her working process is meticulous. Simple pen lines in well-chosen colors are applied to the black-and-white photographs, conveying a sense of serenity and subtle delight atop a precisely crafted base. This is akin to an intellectual game carefully orchestrated by the artist.

> The production of these works begins with minimizing ideas, images, and anything arbitrary to the greatest possible extent. The next step is to manually alter the selected piece of paper by folding or drawing lines, establishing conditions from which new dimensions can emerge. Subsequently, I expand the scope of actions or interactions in a manner similar to the initially set conditions, advancing as though perpetually establishing mechanisms, and the process ceases (as opposed to concluding) when the paper itself and its altered state seem to be equivalent. My aim is for the work to facilitate an authentic experience of seeing.
>
> (*View Kanzaki*, no. 36, 1981, p. 23)

Kinoshita begins by setting the initial conditions for the paper prior to photographing it, establishing a phase where "the paper itself and its altered state seem to be equivalent," making the act of seeing into a real experience. As the paper is placed on a desk, there are three planes: the surface of the paper as a material, the desktop as a location, and the photograph serving as a proxy for the field of view. The interplay of these planes with their respective settings illuminates the misalignment between the geometric shapes' original forms and the experience of seeing them. Her commitment to precision gives this misalignment a sense of serenity, and her careful exclusion of superfluous details makes it beautiful. There is a paradoxical quality to the lyrical equilibrium achieved by works "minimizing ideas, images, and anything arbitrary."

Altering the initially established conditions enables the creation of diverse variations in viewing patterns. After producing a substantial body of work in this mode, in 1977 Kinoshita began creating installations in gallery spaces, pursuing the same practice of establishing conditions but eliminating photography from the process (pp. 102-103). The installations incorporated drawing paper, a desk, and transparent acrylic sheets, presumably as stand-ins for photographs. From documentary photographs alone, the three-dimensional setup of these installations is not clear to me, and it seems that it may have been a challenge to flawlessly merge the three planes — paper, desk surface, acrylic sheet surface (as a substitute for a photograph) — within an actual physical space. Kinoshita does not seem to have attempted further installations, but this exploration indicates her intent to break free of the constrained equilibrium of photographic space.

In 1981, Kinoshita had a solo exhibition at Heidelberg Kunstverein where her photographic works received significant acclaim, thanks in part to an introduction by Uematsu Keiji, who was living in West Germany at the time. However, by this time Kinoshita was already venturing into new artistic territory, and international art trends were also moving in different directions.

VI. Pictorial Space (1)

The artist who had delved extensively into the act of seeing through photography was now entering a new phase.

> In photographic works the concept took precedence, and as expression threatened to become a mere means to an end, I adopted the practice of direct drawing. This shift in technique seems to have facilitated broader exploration. Colors take on the form of planes fully equivalent to the paper's surface, while lines, devoid of meaning as shapes or function as boundaries, merely add depth to these color planes. My aspiration is for the various expressive elements to coalesce and form a unified pictorial plane.
>
> ("Kinoshita Kazuyo Exhibition," *Bijutsu Techo*, no. 477, February 1981, p. 251)

The practice of drawing began with pastel on paper. By creasing the paper, laying down straight lines, and selectively rubbing pastel along these lines, she produced works such as *Pa '80-74* (cat. no. 80) *and Pa '80-105* (cat. no. 82). Such works on paper were a natural progression from the "establishment of conditions" in her photographic works.

Kinoshita wrote that her pastel works sought to render color "fully equivalent to the paper's surface," taking on the form of "planes of color." This means that areas rubbed with pastel were to be seen as no different from untouched portions of the paper. The black lines drawn were not meant to convey meaning as shapes or function as boundaries. Rather than delineating shapes, these lines were placed on the paper to add "depth to these color planes."

Kinoshita discussed pictorial space using somewhat cryptic language, articulating a vision for a uniquely pictorial space that departs from the illusion of three-dimensionality afforded by perspective. Having delved into the essence of seeing, Kinoshita eschewed the use of perspective to simulate 3D space, and of course avoided the faceted shallow reliefs and tactile illusion of space characteristic of Cubism. Rather, she speaks of a distinct "depth" peculiar to the picture plane, a concept that exists purely in the visual realm.

Fig. 8
Takamatsu Jiro,
Space in Two Dimensions, 1973
Courtesy of Yumiko Chiba Associates

Exploring Kinoshita's artistic intent offers the opportunity to contrast her endeavors with Takamatsu Jiro's more or less concurrent *Space in Two Dimensions* series (1973–86) [**Fig. 8**]. While continuing to exhibit works from the *Shadow* painting series initiated in 1964, Takamatsu broadened his investigation of the interplay between shadow and painting to encompass projection and perspective, and presented the results of this investigation in both two-dimensional and three-dimensional works. Around 1970, he ventured into defining a specifically pictorial spatiality diverging from conventional perspective, which he termed "space in two dimensions."

To circumvent the optical illusions associated with three-dimensional space, it was necessary for Takamatsu to adopt abstraction for this series. Shapes within the picture plane inherently suggest spatial dynamics, but here, lines are not contours surrounding shapes but rather exist as mere marks on the canvas. Takamatsu first explored space in two dimensions in pencil and paper sketches in 1974, and did not incorporate color until he showed paintings on canvas in his solo exhibition at Tokyo Gallery in 1977. He pursued the use of color that did not form shapes, allowing lines to remain open-ended and unconnected while leaving ample space for the ground, thus preventing the emergence of color planes [2]. Takamatsu painstakingly ensured that untouched white areas of the canvas did not suggest depth or establish a figure-ground relationship with the colored sections. Seen in this light, the characteristics of his space in two dimensions are deeply aligned with Kinoshita's initial pastel works and the concepts she articulated.

Kinoshita soon shifted from paper to canvas, narrowing her palette and embarking on the creation of compositions through the dynamic interplay of brushwork. This set her on a path distinct from that of Takamatsu, whose space in two dimensions developed into canvases characterized by parallel color fields and thin planes that also acted as thick lines, and eventually into paintings entirely lacking negative space. His subsequent *Form* series, begun in 1980, saw him saturating the foregrounds of paintings with undulating lines of various colors. While their trajectories did not run parallel, Kinoshita and Takamatsu both pursued their own methodologies to grapple with the challenge of conveying spatiality unique to painting.

VII. Pictorial Space (2)

Viewing Kinoshita's final series, created in 1993–94, with its restrained palette of whites interplaying with reds or blues, one is inevitably drawn to the highly delicate and thoughtful brushwork interwoven between strokes. These works reveal pictorial spaces comprised of complex movements that seem to pull away from each other in every direction.

When Mark Rothko applied vast, simplified color fields to monumental canvases, he took the greatest care with the edges of these color fields. In Rothko's iconic painting from the 1950s through the mid–1960s, the canvases' matte finish, the scumbled brush strokes, and the drips of paint evoke a subtle sense of levitation. Especially at the edges of the color fields, a gentle, "feathery" fluctuation gave rise to a unique spatial effect, seeming neither to recede nor to advance. It is not clear whether Kinoshita had the opportunity to see Rothko's canvases. At first glance, her marks appear to be what could be called paint- erly strokes, but they are neither simple nor single-layered. Rather than moving in one di- rection, they appear to drift in various directions, like strokes akin to color fields, while inter- twining with the white of the foreground. Kinoshita's final works contain elements that invite comparison with Rothko's brushwork.

This approach is also visible in her series from circa 1991–92, in which she laid down brushstrokes and then wiped them off to create shadowy effects before layering on additional strokes. The dynamics and interplay of the initial strokes, which are preserved in their pre-wiping-off form maintained while being submerged into the white ground, attain transparency and buoyancy. By deliberately overlaying strokes of white, which ad- vances into the foreground, and another hue, multifarious, multi-layered motion emerges, transcending the simple dichotomy of foreground and background. This arguably repre- sents a realm exclusive to the domain of painting, which cannot be seen in the tangible, three-dimensional world. Kinoshita's brushstrokes convey a sense of bodily motion while also revealing thoroughly considered relationships of length, proximity, direction, and subtle layering.

Kinoshita evidently sought to create a sense of buoyancy within her paintings, aiming to deepen pictorial space without imposing boundaries. Light with no identifiable point of origin bathes the entire canvas in uniform luminosity.

Viewing these works, one feels a sense of closeness to the artist who strove to seize light itself and infuse it into the canvas, evoking the experience of gazing at sunlight filtering through the leaves of an enormous tree.

All of Kinoshita's art emanates a meticulous, straightforward approach that illus- trates her unwavering artistic intent, and the effect is crisply refreshing. Her determination to exclude elements extraneous to art arose from a desire to refine her artistic thought, un- tainted by personal biases. By confining her creative process strictly to the artistic realm, she aimed to ensure the autonomy of her works. This approach reveals her ambition, unwavering throughout her career, to grapple with the very nature of existence. It is essential that we gain a deeper appreciation of Kinoshita's position in the field of contemporary art as it once existed in Japan, a position of undeniable significance.

*1   Hirano Shigemitsu, "Exhibition Review," *Bijutsu Techo*, no. 373, November 1973, pp. 292–293
*2   Mitsuda Yuri, "A Nowhere Place: The Painter Takamatsu Jirō and His Experiments," (Dallas Museum of Art, scheduled for publication in Takamatsu Jirō exhibition catalogue, 2025)

An interview with Kinoshita Kazuyo

[Edited by Shigihara Haruka]

This is a translation of an interview with artist Kinoshita Kazuyo conducted toward the very end of her life and originally printed in Japanese in the volume *Kazuyo Kinoshita 1939–1994* (1996, AD&A). The interview took place on April 23, 1994, at the AD&A Gallery, with interviewers Ochi Yujiro and Takemura Yoko; Ochi serving as lead editor.

This reprinting includes a note added by Ochi, with typos, missing characters and so on in the original Japanese version of the interview corrected and a very small number of changes made to make the transcript more consistent. Notes and the numbers of works in this exhibition have also been added in brackets by the current editor.

K: Kinoshita / O: Ochi (Shizuoka Prefectural Museum of Art) /
T: Takemura (AD&A)

O You were born in 1939 I believe; in what part of Kobe?

K Nagata-ku, which was obliterated during the war — houses, shops, factories, everything. I was at kindergarten when the war ended. [**Fig. 1**]

O The generation who had to ink out part of textbooks?

K No.

O Do you perhaps recall the black markets?

K No. I do remember, from elementary school, singing for soldiers of the occupation forces in Motomachi, and receiving candy.

O Do you remember going hungry at all?

K Not me personally. Our parents took good care of us. At kindergarten I was evacuated to the Miki area, where I remember eating rice porridge without much rice in it. I don't remember ever feeling hungry.

O Returning to Kobe, did it not feel like there was nothing there?

K Not really. We had gone to seek shelter at Takigawa High School in Suma-ku, and I remember the flares were incredible to watch. We were often told of bombs being dropped. And of times when all the people who sought shelter against school buildings had died, or suchlike. I was fortunate to survive.

O You went on to attend Kyoto City University of Arts. At what age were you first awakened to art?

K I first became properly aware of art in middle school. I'd enjoyed drawing since I was young and was often praised for it. In my second year at middle school I acquired an oil painting set, and joined the fine art club. I remember the first painting I did with that set, with no instruction from any-

Interview 1

An interview with Kinoshita Kazuyo

one. It was my little sister, in profile. Through middle and high school I was in the fine art club, volleyball club, and choir, and often tired from sport, but did always intend to go into art. Although the idea of studying to get into art school didn't even occur to me, and when my teacher in the last year of high school asked if I was really intending to go, I just said "Yes." I hadn't studied any drawing either, and didn't know what I'd do if I failed the entrance exam, so after school was out, I started going by myself to another school that had lots of plaster figures I could draw.

O   Where did you attend middle and high school?

K   Shinwa Gakuen (Shinwa Girls' Junior & Senior High School).

O   Did you get into the Kyoto City University of Arts on your first try?

K   Starting in my year they brought in the system whereby you only got to sit the practical exam if you passed your written exams in other subjects. My year, the intake had a lot of students who were good at studying. I may well have got in due to that new way of doing things.

O   What year did you start university?

K   1958.

O   What were classes like at the Kyoto City University of Arts?

K   In the morning you had your academic classes, then in the afternoon, studio work until about four o'clock; first years would sketch plaster figures, second years nudes. My teachers were Kuroda Jutaro, Tsuda Shuhei, Imai Kenichi, and Suda Kunitaro. I liked Suda's works. I can't say I was especially influenced by my teachers. I was a bit of a teacher's pet of Tsuji [Shindo] and Horiuchi [Masakazu] in the sculpture faculty, but didn't have much to do with the Western painting teachers.

O   Were you a good student at university?

K   A genuinely good student is one who is at university, yet not overly "academic," I suppose. That wasn't me, and after graduation I regretted not sticking out more, doing things too much by the book.

O   What did you do after graduation?

K   I ended up at teaching a huge junior high school in Kobe. It was the era of problems with violence in schools, and I quit, disillusioned as an educator, after just over three years. Then I went to teach art at Shinwa Gakuen. [Fig. 2][Fig. 3]

O   Were you engaged in your own work as an artist by then?

K   I started exhibiting in my second year at university, at group shows, Kyoto City Museum of Art, and so on.

O   What kind of paintings were you producing?

K   School only valued the academic and figurative. My paintings around that time were abstract and borrowed forms from the likes of plants and static objects. I never showed anything representational.

I've always maintained that what people think and feel in their teens

Fig. 1
Kinoshita Kazuyo's birthplace
(Kinoshita Tategu Ten [Kinoshita Joiner Store])

Fig. 2
Photographed in 1962
(the age of a teacher at the Maruyama Middle School)

Fig. 3
Photographed in 1962
(the age of a teacher at the Maruyama Middle School)

tends to stick, and frequently becomes a life-long theme. Thinking back at the age I am now, though not aware of it then, from that point on if someone asked me a particular question, I would always give the same answer. Thus I've realized that for me too, the concerns I had as a teen-ager have become my theme, one I struggle to step beyond. I remember looking at the night sky with friends when I was fifteen or sixteen and dis-cussing whether if you kept going, it would eventually come to an end, and if there was a wall or boundary at the end of the universe, what lay beyond it? Humans are only capable of contemplating the infinity of the cosmos up to a certain point, I think. There may well be a boundary. And even if you believed you'd found it, there may be others. Meaning the whole existence of that universe becomes tenuous and devoid of reality. When the existence of an object, its existence as a relative thing, becomes tenuous, so does one's own existence; a frightening thought. In an effort to dispel my long-felt unease, I managed to plug the gap by confirming my own existence. If consciousness can drift in the cosmos like mist, it can confirm everything. On an emotional level I've hoped since my teens that I would continue to exist as just the smallest unit of consciousness [a mist like presence].

Though not conscious of it at the time, for some reason I painted in abstract style right from the start. Early on I was fascinated by the ground and the earth's interior and tried to depict life in there. Then borrowing plant forms, I starting imbuing my paintings with the message that those life forms can and do exist freely [see *Title Unknown*, 1962, cat. no. 2 etc.] in un-constrained worlds where things have form but are not enclosed; world where they can move freely. From the free-spiritedness of Paul Klee, his idea that art "makes visible," I thought that if we exist in the world of the invisible, we can do so freely. Klee's paintings have both shapes and lines, and when you undo the lines, everything becomes equal planes. He uses color and form to visually express a rich sensibility, but what I am really trying to discern is "something that exists on an equal level." Whether life form or spirit. That way of looking is why I liked Klee, and was influenced by him.

O Tell us about up to 1971 or so, with anything in particular you'd like to add.

K I kept having the same thoughts, talked to those I was closest to [who lived with me], and the first one was interested in Klee, and like me in some ways, different in others. Okuda [Yoshimi] told me that Virginia Woolf said similar things (See Kinoshita Kazuyo, "50 Pairs of Eyes," *Bijutsu-Josen*, no. 3, July 1974, pp. 24-25.)

I've pondered many aspects of "existence," and expressed these thoughts as messages. My approach to existence has been to treat in-side and out equally. Though we too began as dust (the smallest unit of matter) in the air, and are part of that which has been created, we possess powerful desires. To me humans are creatures that confirm their own existence for the sake of their desires, try to ramp up these desires by creating entities, in the manner of gods. Our desires quickly grew more powerful, and the drive to confirm our own existence made us try harder to engender existence itself. One could arrogantly say we attempted to become gods. I think that [generating something that exists] became my method for living, my way of life.

Fig. 4
At "Exhibition of Okuda Yoshimi and Kinoshita Kazuyo" (1972, Shirota Gallery)

Inside and out, right and left, top and bottom. I did paintings in which for example there would be sky in the background, and when you turned over the person rendered in planar fashion, there would be a sky painted inside them; or a geometric form like a sphere or cube painted flat, and when turned over, you could see a piece cut out with the same colors and space as the outside, thus forming a space equal to the outside ["Boundary Thinking" series, 1970, cat. nos. 8–13].

In my 20s I also did a lot of three-dimensional pieces. They had the shapes of things, but to make their existence equal to that of the space I would make them in glass, or spread plaster of Paris directly on my skin, then when the female molds had set, flip them over and line them up together, thus expressing inside and outside as equals. Back then I didn't have the cash to rent gallery space, so entered various competitions, but in most cases, my work wasn't picked. So none of those three-dimensional pieces remain.

I did one work that used 3000 sheets of cellophane to express existence. It's clear and has a form, but only the walls and floor are visible through it. What does it mean to exist? This has always been my focus. Back then I was doing slightly Cubist-style paintings. The idea of splitting a solid, opening it up, making it flat, chimed well with my own ideas. People are segmented into planes, each plane being connected to the two-dimensional plane of the outside space and equal to it. So trying to make everything equivalent. The grid lines ["Saturation" series, 1971, cat. nos. 14–16] show expansion in two dimensions, with lines painted for the existence and expanse of the plane, but as you see, these lines peter out. This is my idea that things should not be bound, are not bound. Everything circulates, and saturates everything else. That is existence. [**Fig. 4**]

O   Tell us about the activities of Group "i" that were going on around you?

K   I was certainly greatly influenced by the existence of Group "i." There was a group in Kobe, and they split into Gutai and anti-Gutai. Back then Kawaguchi [Tatsuo] was featuring frequently in *Bijutsu Techo* magazine, and these people contacted us — there were two classmates of mine in the group — so we ended up being part of it. Somehow it felt like they didn't really want to include women, and back then I had my own struggles with making ends meet, and was not especially bothered about joining as such, but the group's intention was to tackle the question of existence, and that was something I could get on board with. The nine of them [Group "i" members Inoue Haruyuki, Okuda Yoshimi, Kawaguchi Tatsuo, Takeuchi Hirokuni, Toyohara Yasuo, Nakata Makoto, Mukai Takeshi, Murakami Masami, Yoshida Tsutomu] would meet at my place most days to debate things. I've always thought of their activities as part of me. Though it was only for a short time, they would show work when [the thoughts of] all nine coincided, shift to the next thing before that had quite finished, and present something new every few months. I cooperated in all of that.

O   When did you marry Kawaguchi-san?

K   In 1963, I think. Two or three years after leaving university. We both led our respective high school art clubs, and met at a cultural festival. We used to see each other almost daily. We weren't married and living together that long, but I spent the ten years from my late teens that it took to grow into myself in various ways, with him. I think we had a common interest in the nature of existence.

O   How about your work at galerie 16 in 1972?

K   That might have been the series from 1971. Up to then I'd been doing oils, messages about existence still dominating my thoughts. During this period a number of young male artists from Kyoto came together and invited me to work with them as a group, so I discussed this [with Okuda], and we decided to come up with some kind of plan, then take that plan and try to get people together. I put together a plan for photography using my own concept, but on hearing that of the seven or eight who assembled, one didn't want to work with women, I said very well, thanks but no thanks. So instead of artists I assembled ten of my own friends and asked them to help. My plan was one that involved a group working together, and required ten people, so I came up with a method for it using photographs [Untitled / Mu 38 (Flower Clock), 1973, cat. no. 19]. When we tried it, I found the message I wanted to get across was communicated more readily than with a two-dimensional oil painting.

O   Can you explain that message?

K   When it comes to the existence of things, for example, take a floral clock. Even if humanity were to be wiped off the face of the earth, a floral clock would continue to exist for a while. As would the universe. That I view as absolute existence. All other states of existence are relative existence, and to my mind these two were not separate things, but proof of a single existence. You start with a person setting up a camera and taking a shot. Then the next person does the same, so each individual takes a picture. The time will be different for each, and the scene each person sees will be relative, so by rights is different. They should all be different, but all look

Interview 1
—
An interview with Kinoshita Kazuyo

to be the same entity. I'm trying to demonstrate visually that there is absolute existence and relative existence, but that there can only be a single existence. I found it interesting how easy it was to convey this concept, and carried on working in photography.

I liked the "Saturation" series, but it was often seen as having a certain lyricism, which really, was fine, but back then I found it intolerable, being more driven to get my message across.

O   What about your beaker photos [*Untitled / Mu 60 (Beaker)*, 1973, cat. no. 21, presented in January 1974 (solo show at galerie 16)]?

K   There are ten pairs of photos, top and bottom. It's a simple work: the only difference between them is the measurement on the scale. And at first glance all the water looks the same, but in reality the temperature is different in each case. It shows the disjoint between seeing, perceiving, and existing.

I was invited to take part in a photo art exhibition at Gallery Signum ["Photo / Arts – Photography as method" (1974)] and submitted a work containing multiples of the same photo, in which the time was the same but on different days [*Untitled / Mu 59 (Watch)*, 1974, cat. no. 20]. Time is also a part of existence, and time itself is existence. [**Fig. 5**]

O   In September 1974 you presented a work at the Muramatsu Gallery. I seem to remember this involved placing objects one by one in a room, then removing them one by one. [*Mu 61 (Increasing and decreasing of things)*, 1974, cat. no. 22]

K   The first and final spaces appear to be the same entity, but in fact, in the intervening time, these entities, had appeared and then disappeared. Even with a single entity, that of a space, differences in perception, and method, can alter ideas around existence.

O   Was this at your art room on Tor Road?

K   Yes. I was assisted by people who had exhibited alongside me at Gallery Signum. I filmed the work using an 8mm camera, made prints and arranged them in the gallery. In 1992, I remade it as a video at the O Art Museum [The film presented at Gallery Signum [cat. no. 23] was converted to VHS and exhibited as part of "Video – A New World: Possibilities of the Medium" (1992, O Art Museum, Tokyo)]

O   Any comments on this wall work [*Untitled-b / Mu 103 (Stains on the wall (blocks))*, 1972, cat. no. 18]?

K   It's a piece consisting of two photos. Two identical photos / entities, but by marking the wall with chalk, at the moment of recognition, when you see that, the existence of the same wall becomes something different. Really it can only be the same entity, but when perceived by ten people, it will manifest as ten entities, and I wanted to show that a change occurs, using various examples. This was submitted to "Signifying." I took part in a group

Fig. 5
Untitled / Mu 59 (Watch)
from the Installation view of
"Photo / Arts – Photography as method"
(1974, Gallery Signum)

show ["Signifying: Language / Thing — with the Manifestation of Attitude" (1974, Kyoto City Museum of Art)] organized by Mizugami Jun from Nagoya and his associates.

O   Among your works in 1975 is one [*Untitled,* cat. no. 25] in which you hand-color a photo from a bus tour.

K   I colored each part as I saw it, ultimately becoming cognizant of the whole thing. Existence depending on the state of cognition. To see an object means perceiving and becoming conscious of it, and expanding this also means an increase in entities. I wanted to make it start and finish with the fact that humans may think, but an entity is the same thing regardless of whether we see it or not, are cognizant of it or not.

O   You did the whole thing didn't you — made a photographic plate, silk-screened and hand colored it.

T   It's incredibly fresh, this work, but did people get it? What was it like back then?

K   Works using photography were common in the 1970s. Concepts and methodologies the world was very interested in influenced individual artists, doubtless me as well. I don't think I'd have used a photograph here if there hadn't been group shows. For my part I'm glad I did this work, I managed to reconfirm my concept, and I also have the feeling that the change from sending a message about existence, to attempting to create existence itself, one could say, that is a gradual strengthening of my method of expression, was possible because of this project. If this project hadn't come to an end in my mind, I think it would have taken longer.

O   Moving forward to February 1976. Your works at galerie 16 are of a slightly different bent.

K   The way of presenting the message is a little different. I've brought vision, perceiving and recognizing, to the focal point of the photos. The thing in sharpest focus is what can be seen, what is out of focus cannot, and I used this method to photograph various things.

This, [*Untitled (Some profile or some consciousness),* 1976, cat. no. 35] is a slightly different work. Here I have superimposed the way in which a person sees another person and becomes aware of them, and my own objectivity and agency, and captured that in the photo. I made it so you could see everything: this person themselves looking at this, the person themselves looking at this photo, the person in the photo looking at themselves, the person in the photo looking at the other person. Human existence can also become various existences according to the relative perception of the viewer, but there is only one. I took photos and just kept making stuff every day.

However by this stage there were a lot more young artists using photography, and it was becoming a tricky medium in which to offer something fresh that would draw people in. I wondered if there was some way

Interview 1

—

An interview with Kinoshita Kazuyo

to escape the universal nature of photography, and shifted to drawing on paper. Once doing something new, I lost interest in this work. Because I'd become interested in something new, and was churning out lots of it, I didn't show the works of this period. It was only when Takahashi Toru happened to ask me in 1977 to take part in a self-portrait exhibition ["Art Core Contemporary Art 77 Series: Self-Portraits '77" (Art Core, Kyoto)] that I remembered oh yes, I do have some work using my own face, and submitted it [*Untitled*, 1976, cat. no. 39, other]. [**Fig. 6**]

Fig. 6
Installation view of
"Art Core Contemporary Art 77 Series:
Self-Portraits '77" (1977, Art Core)

O   Then you moved to a new kind of work. Any thoughts on work "A" [**Fig. 7**]?

K   I used thread and a pencil to draw a circle, and got someone to photograph this. Visually, the circle is an ellipse, but because you perceive it at the same moment you see it, it is recognized as a circle. The shape you can see is that of an ellipse, and if it were replaced by something else, an ellipse may the only existence you recognize, but actually it is a perfect circle. This was an attempt to get closer to the question of existence by showing discrepancies in perception.

Fig. 7
'76-A (1976)
Image from *Bijutsu Techo*, no. 462, March 1980

O   It's a lovely work with a lot of variations.

K   I think a planar entity has to be attractive. It's no good having people glance at it like an ordinary photo, think "Oh a photo" and move on. I devise a layout for making that plane a more expressive thing; draw it on a small piece of paper, photograph it, and enlarge it so the grain becomes coarser. Using ASA-400 film makes it even grainier. The surface takes on a more pebble-dashed look, giving the photo the texture of a drawing. The idea was to make a space with that kind of texture.

T   When you first started doing photography, did it not have to be that attractive?

K   At the time, what I wanted most to convey was messages about existence, so I wasn't thinking quite that far. Around the time [similar] scenery photos [taken by the growing number of artists using photography] started to come out, photos per se lost their interest for me. It didn't matter much who took them, or whether they were taken well, they were much of a muchness. I wanted to make something visually different. I used colored felt pens for works, and color for the shapes perceived / recognized. The photographic paper used was not the usual sort, but Mitsubishi CH paper.

T   Did you photograph your own hand here?

K   When It's my own hand, I ask someone else to take the picture. All the hands that appear are mine. Although initially there was too much explanation, and it would actually be better without the compass in there.

O   February 1977 you did some work for an independent show, and I see this goes off in a slightly different direction?

K   Alongside my Kobe associates I did a work under the title "Nuru" (Paint). It was basically an informal sort of exhibition organized by artists.

Fig. 8
Installation view of "Art Now '78"
(1978, Hyogo Prefectural Museum of Modern Art)

O   You mention Gallery U?

K   Yes, although It's no longer around. It was run by a sculptor by the name of Kunishima [Seiji].

O   Your style has become more refined over the years?

K   The painting I do now, what it relies on, does not leave the surface to do the work. This work for example is grounded in my thoughts, my way of being, around existence; that's how the expression comes about, so there is a specific foundation. So it was mentally easier than now. [In the interview, Kinoshita was saying "This silkscreen is…" while pointing to a photographic work from ca.1977.]

T   A more design- or construction-centric approach perhaps.

K   Although it is easier to have one concept, and base your expression on that.

     The installation at Kitano Circus in Kobe ["Kinoshita Kazuyo exhibition" (1977, Gallery Kitano Circus, Kobe)]. This was done in thick acrylic, and still exists in its entirety.

     Then there was a work that brings into being a horizon. Usually you would think of it as a line drawn on paper, so if you think of the paper as the main constituent, it is not a horizon. So a difference in perception, makes existence ambiguous. I wanted to put lots of these on the wall as an installation using sheets of paper, with lines as matter. However a French artist was already doing it, so I didn't.

O   You showed works ['77-O, 1977, cat. no. 52, other] at "Art Now '78" [**Fig. 8**] that led to the work you are doing now.

K   From lines to planes. I was becoming more and more ambitious and got the urge to use color. Initially I made these into works that included the space, but then tried to eliminate the space, making works the size of the whole area of the space. By about 1979 I was keen to try different kinds of expression, and began actually drawing on top of photos with colored pencils, rather than spraying. I started doing drawings soon after this, so never exhibited the works from this period, and stopped using a camera about 1979.

O   We're talking about works from your transition period, when you were moving into drawing.

K   To my mind It's not important for an artwork or expression to have obvious human fingerprints, or personal emotion.

     When I was working with photography, it would take ages to tidy up the grain; five or six hours for one photo was probably the longest. I was doing this every day, which inhibited my expression. I wanted to present things in a more physical manner.

O   You had moved to drawing by the 1980 Kyoto Independents Exhibition?

K   I was drawing, but still folding the paper. It was the kind of paper used for fusuma (sliding doors), and I would make planes using lines made by folding and by drawing equally, with pastel color fields. I did a lot of these big works using paper, making forms grounded in my own concept of existence.

O   Did you show these anywhere?

K   Just once, at the City Gallery (Motomachi).

O   This is starting to get closer to the Kinoshita-san we are familiar with, I suspect.

K   Looking at it now like this, though not like the world as Klee thought of it, something of the look of Klee's work seems to have been carried over in me. I show the inside and outside of planes enclosed by lines, but in the end want to convey that these are equal two-dimensional planes. Up to 1980 I made photos, then shut those away and started drawing, but ended up shutting that away too and never having the opportunity to show it.

T   What was your reason for moving to pastels as a material?

K   Rather than bringing into existence planes as fixed forms on a surface, I wanted soft, permeated planes so that the surface of the paper and the plane with color did not end up being in very different dimensions. Pastels were an effective way to achieve that. For the black lines I used what are called Dermatograph pencils, which can draw on anything.

T   You seem to be firmly drawing, rather than smudging.

K   Pastels don't adhere very well so I've diligently rubbed them into the paper. So the colors stick properly. I found myself wanting to draw more and more, and use color. All the while there was something that bothered me: that it was too easy for me, because drawing lines meant the expression was plainly grounded in my own concept. By too easy I mean, I didn't think it would result in very robust works, so as I made these I wondered if there was a way to hide the concept as I expressed it.

O   From 1981 we see a slightly different development. The work you presented at the Okayama Prefectural Cultural Center? [Fig. 9]

K   I used a canvas for water-based paints there. At the time I was moving from pastels to oils on canvas, similar sort of work, but that was destroyed by fire.

O   What were you doing from 1981 to 1983?

K   I was doing the same series, switching from pastels to canvas, but had reached an impasse. It had struck me that my ideas on existence were not as free as they once were. Moving away from the works that got destroyed and reaching this point took ages, and it was a tough period. I would paint, and scrap, paint and scrap. On one occasion I scrapped something concrete I had painted and in doing so, had a realization, and was at that point able to change my method of expression. Not my concept when it came to expression, or the actual concept of a work, but finally change my method of expression. I realized that rather than bringing all

Fig. 9
Installation view of
"the 7th Pan-Setouchi Contemporary Art Exhibition"
(1981, Okayama Prefectural Cultural Center)
(center) Ca-C '81-2, (right) Ca-C '81-13
Both are 1981, oil on canvas, 162.2 × 130.3 cm

of my ontology, all my conceptual baggage to my expression, I should just make existence itself on the picture plane. All I had to do was bring into existence what I expressed. In a sense, I succeeded in taking out a graphical concept. Floating free of my foundations was unsettling, and did take some time to get used to.

'82-CA1 [cat. no. 90]: this was the first work in a series, an important one for me, a work with something removed.

O   October 1982. '82-CA1. At galerie 16, wasn't it?

K   From this point I started giving my works serial numbers.

O   So as the number is now up to 700, you've painted 700?

K   This work was done by initially painting with a brush, then wiping with a cloth. The wiping means that the plane of the canvas and plane with the paint on it are of equal value. I did this because in my own mind, this is the same as it has always been, because I have a constant desire to make two-dimensional planes equal. Adopting that method, making the work itself an entity. All entities, like stars in the heavens, were created by the gods and may appear to be random, but exist in a specific relative order. But as far as we can tell, they exist naturally, and that existence is incredibly powerful. I want the painting to be an entity like that. In other words, I want to be the creator god.

T   One senses a world in the background, or a different world.

K   For me It's a method of expression, and the question is how to make a limited plane stand on its own, actively bring it into existence. This contrast is essential to that. The power of the tiny plane to exist and that of the color block to exist, are equal in my mind. So it is a limited two-dimensional entity. If I could explain completely in words what I've brought into existence, what is emitted by it, it would be the same as before, all explainable in words, but I believe that which can be fully explained in words, is as an entity very weak. To make something worthy of the term creation requires some entity beyond words, something that has an effect on you, or it cannot be a creation. The need for that aspect prompted me to excise my own conceptual stuff. In previous works too, I had without a doubt been aiming for expression with a sense of existence beyond words, so It's not that they lacked that aspect entirely, but it had to be greater, or the work could not count as a creation.

O   You went to Germany in 1981, I believe.

T   How were things going conceptually at this point, in Germany?

K   The director of the museum in Germany [Hans Gercke of the Kunstverein] liked works that used photography, and the plan from the start was to present some work with photos, so at this point I wasn't showing [my new conceptual approach] very much. But an artist wants to show, as the mood takes them, what they are doing at present. There was a need there to appeal in a pow-

Interview 1

An interview with Kinoshita Kazuyo

erful way. Specifically, I think I've taken an approach that gives a strong look to the color fields. It's no good having something that you pass by and forget, or with no obvious differences. Offering calm, stable works may also be important, but in my case I wanted to excite the consciousness into rethinking a little; to make a person feel discomfort, to make them pause in their awareness. I wanted to be free. Up to that point I'd been basing things on a single concept, so I suppose I was constrained in a sense.

O   1983 seems different to '82.

K   Bringing a "slant" to the picture plane, was an inevitable part of the expression, of its strength.

O   What came next after the wiping in 1986?

K   I do some wiping here and there, but a lot more actual painting. I like the work from around this time myself.

T   Your colors here were indigo and so forth.

K   A lot in one color, yes. I'm more interested in the spaces I paint [the spaces that emerge from my painting] than planes arising from a harmonizing of color and color, so I didn't need to use a lot of colors. Even if one is ostensibly painting freely, an image of some kind starts to form, and the viewer also seeks an image as they look. But for me, it was necessary that the painting not stand as a single image. One might seem to appear, but soon disappear, but all the same, it will exist. In my case, the painted part, and the unpainted, must be made on a single, equal plane. Lines, colors, forms executed that look like nothing, form no image, create the tension in the space, the work being completed when each becomes inevitably there of necessity. Not image becoming painting, but existing as painting.

O   At first glance your spatial composition also looks quite Eastern.

K   I'm not aware of thinking in an especially "Eastern" way. I use oil painting, but have no desire to adhere slavishly to traditional European painting. I think there is a thing whereby no matter what materials an artist uses, when you look at a work of theirs, the culture of the times they lived in, their ethnicity and suchlike, has to seep out somewhere. For example, an Asian and a European will even paint lines differently. I prefer to point in a way that the brushstrokes don't show, to "make something free" so that what becomes visible could be painted by any person using a brush. If you get into the groove as you paint with the brush, you can probably find yourself able to express even the momentum of the stroke, or something spiritual. That's risky, so I prefer to preserve where possible that awkwardness of first holding the brush. I have never, ever painted a comfortable, mentally disciplined line in a single stroke.

O   I admire though, how you have managed to fill each individual work with so much tension, while doing so much work over the years.

Fig. 10
Installation view of
Kinoshita Kazuyo solo exhibition
(1989, AD&A Gallery)
Courtesy of AD&A, photo by Karamatsu Minoru.
Image from *Kazuyo Kinoshita 1939—1994*,
AD&A, 1996, p.54

K   When it comes to color, even, I challenge myself to use different colors to see if I can make my usual same things in different colors, but find myself at times bound by the picture planes I create. When that happens, I need to find a way to avoid it.

T   You did an exhibition in 1989 at AD&A [**Fig. 10**], but '89 was in a sense a peak for you, wouldn't you agree?

K   It was my second breakthrough phase, with oils, having earlier done it with pastels, and I was feeling a little more at ease.

O   Next, 1988. Was *'88-CA487* [cat.no.111] the turning point? *'88-CA488* and *'88-CA489* are the breakaway works.

K   To a similar degree to existence, I couldn't afford to determine shapes or lines with a natural inevitability myself; they came about by me being moved in response to a thing placed there, going on to find the next thing, and repeating this over and over.

O   So was 1989 when things started to come together again?

K   Yes, when I was struggling a bit less.

O   How long does it take you to do each painting?

K   Usually from a day to a week to do 80 percent of it, then anything from a week to a couple of months for the last 20 percent.

O   There's a feeling of something built up inside the artist, overflowing.

K   I did my best to trust the picture plane completely, and once I had one thing on there, be moved by what was already painted, which meant I could paint fairly freely.

T   If someone said to you for example, works from this era were good, so can you please paint them again, you wouldn't be able to, right? Occasionally I get inquiries about that.

K   I could paint something similar up to a point, but the sensation that was occurring of necessity at the original time, might not return.

T   At your exhibition at AD&A in 1991, the reds were striking.

K   I was able to use red like I did blue. To my mind the picture plane has to be vital and dynamic, has to have tension, but in saying that, I don't want to make shapes from the painted surface and unpainted surface. I want each to simply be there, so that together they form a single, highly charged two-dimensional space.

T   Tell us about the 1992 LA series.

K   I am quite secure in myself generally, and it never occurred to me that my works could be influenced in any manner and change because I went to the US. But living there for a year it seems the environment of California did in fact have an impact. In Japan I need more time meditating before I first put brush to canvas, and to be mentally still to some extent before I move the brush, but in LA that wasn't really necessary. I was able to wield the brush in a more carefree way; paint without worrying about the ten-

Interview 1

An interview with Kinoshita Kazuyo

sion of the spaces formed when I placed the brush, I guess, or the weight of existence. I could think about everything, paint everything, with a certain lightness. In a sense I suppose the seriousness had been taken out of it. The way the spaces are is also a little different. The environment there affected even the smallest things; I found myself for example unable to wear the clothing I'd brought from Japan. It's like it didn't fit the landscape. [Fig. 11]

Fig. 11
At Los Angeles (1992)

O   We were surprised to see your work evolve in new ways once again. In April 1994 at AD&A you showed some work of extraordinary power, work of compelling strength. [Fig. 12] Tell us about that.

K   I'd like to be able to do strokes with as much freedom as possible. Painting repeatedly is how form and color come about. Although I was trying not to produce paintings by executing strokes, but pursuing inevitability as I painted, so that shapes and spaces formed. I strived to give myself up more to the canvas, to ensure nothing intentional of mine found its way in. I hadn't managed to complete the works I did in Los Angeles, or throw them all out, so had brought them back, and left them to one side ever since. I was studying them, unable to continue painting and thinking of scrapping them, when it occurred to me that I could put what I was currently doing over the top, and thus made them part of a new way of working. They have an in-between quality, and a different feel. What I initially intended had been destroyed, nor could I complete the approach I had here. It was as if a free space divorced from my own intentions was created, as if what was willed, was removed.

Fig. 12
Installation view of
Kinoshita Kazuyo solo exhibition
(1994, AD&A Gallery)
Courtesy of AD&A, photo by Karamatsu Minoru.

T   How about the green in this work?

K   This is a work I was unsure about exhibiting right up to the end. I complete my paintings by entrusting myself to the canvas, and considering the whole of the picture plane, by letting it seek from me what is necessary as I proceed, but with this work, to some extent I ignored that careful consideration. If you think carefully as you paint, there will always be somewhere that should be painted a little more, but here I didn't do that for the most part, instead painting to the rhythms of my body. So I finished this without deeming it "complete" myself, and thus wasn't sure if I wanted ed to show it.

It's hard even for me to describe the work I'm doing right now. I have this strong urge to make things that can't be grasped in words, which makes what I'm doing even harder to describe. If you asked me to explain my canvases in terms of theory or structure, it would probably be too difficult. I guess I could only say that this is my real, inevitable expression. If you were to ask me why I did this, or why this color is here, I could only reply that it turned out that way because it was necessary for the expression, and I didn't paint it to look like that. As expression, the picture plane demanded it of me. These days that is the only way I can describe my work. All I can say is, I've gained more freedom than ever before.

T   Does that include freedom from how the world sees you?

K   Not that; freedom when it comes to expressing on the canvas. Previously there were times when a kind of pattern would take hold and become order, and I'd be bound by that and lose my freedom, in turn diminishing the nature of my expression. I had to break that somehow. In that sense, in the work I'm doing now there is far less constraint on the canvas. In that sense, I think I've gained my freedom.

(April 23, 1994, at the AD&A Gallery)

Editor's note

This interview took place on the occasion of Kinoshita Kazuyo's final solo exhibition, at AD&A, with the gallery's cooperation and when the artist's health had already deteriorated considerably. At the time it was clear to anyone who saw Kinoshita that the cancer had advanced to a point where she was not long for this world, and that this would be the last opportunity to record her own comments on her work. The interview was undertaken in a conversation while looking at a file containing a chronological list of her works, compiled by her, and was conducted over of a period in excess of four hours, which was as long as she could manage. Kinoshita's lack of stamina by this stage, combined with the drugs she was on to fight the cancer, was affecting her faculty for thought, so there may be errors in this interview with regard to timing or names, due to her mixing things up or mis-remembering. As the main aim of the interview was to record Kinoshita's own comments on her work for posterity, we hope anyone affected by such errors will be understanding. We ask you also please to let myself as lead editor, or AD&A know of any such factual discrepancies.

Ochi Yujiro (1996)

from the left: Ochi Yujiro, Kinoshita (Image from video of the interview, 1994)

Interview 1
—
An interview with Kinoshita Kazuyo

An interview with Uematsu Keiji

[Edited by Sato Ayuka]

This interview with prominent, internationally active artist Uematsu Keiji was conducted on October 17, 2023, at his studio in Minoh, Osaka Prefecture. The three curators of this exhibition (Oshita Yuji, Nakamura Fumiko, and Sato Ayuka) spoke with Uematsu, who was a close friend of Kinoshita Kazuyo, about his interactions with her and his insights into her creative process.

Meeting Kinoshita Kazuyo

How did you come to know Kinoshita Kazuyo?

We met in university. In 1967, Okuda Yoshimi, who later became Kinoshita Kazuyo's partner, won the Japan Cultural Forum Prize at the International Young Artists Show[1]. His work, which was titled *Container (Provocative Negative I)*, had a white negative image of a container at the center, surrounded by blue and red paint applied with a roller. After this, Okuda was in a group exhibition[2] at Tor Road Gallery in Kobe, along with Mukai Shuji from the Gutai group and another guy, Higashiyama Akira, who was ahead of me at university. When I went to see the show, I met Okuda. He was very talkative, a highly logical mind, and even though we were meeting for the first time, he spoke about his own work and contemporary art in general with great enthusiasm. In fact he was so intense, it made me wonder why he felt compelled to speak so much, but there was this passion and energy to him that contrasted with the cool, conceptual, intellectual sensibility of his work. So that was when I first met Okuda Yoshimi. Later in 1967, I saw him again at an outdoor show of happenings[3] [the First PLAY Exhibition], organized by Ikemizu Keiichi and others in Kobe East Park. And that was where I met Kinoshita for the first time.

In 1969, I showed some work in the 1st International Exhibition of Modern Sculpture at the Hakone Open-Air Museum, and Yoshimi [Okuda Yoshimi, referred to below by given name] was also exhibiting. At the time, Kazu [nickname for Kinoshita Kazuyo, used below] and Yoshimi were running a coffee shop in Yamamoto-dori, Kobe, which I used to go to a lot. [**Fig. 1**] Yoshimi was usually making coffee and doing this and that, and I think Kazu was helping out as well. I was living in Kobe, in walking distance of the coffee shop, so it was around that time that we got to know each other properly.

An interview
with Uematsu Keiji

Fig. 1
At the coffee shop

Fig. 2
Kinoshita painting a still life in the art class

Fig. 3
Direct mail for
*Kinoshita Kazuyo: Existence and Perception...
And to Another Reality 1979—1991*
(1991, galerie 16)

Was the coffee shop a kind of gathering place for fellow artists?

—

Well, I don't remember meeting any other artists at the coffee shop. It was only a few years later, after Kazu and Yoshimi bought a house on Tor Road, that Kobe artists began getting together at Yoshimi's place. The house was also their studio, it had a wood-floored workspace on the first floor and their living quarters on the second and third floors. Artists liked and trusted Kazu and Yoshimi so much, so there were always people coming and going. They started an art class called Art Room Tor in their studio, and the students mainly painted still lifes, they weren't necessarily focusing on abstract art. [**Fig. 2**] Kazu was actually busier dyeing kimonos, painting sashes and fabrics and things at home, which they would then take to Kyoto. The students in their art classes all began by learning representational art, but a lot of people were influenced by the two of them and eventually evolved into abstract painters and sculptors. Many went on to have solo shows at venues like Shinanobashi Gallery. Kazu and Yoshimi treated their students with respect as fellow artists. There were others who visited not as students but as friends, like Tatsuno Toeko, who I heard was also doing kimono painting and dyeing, and Kodama Yasue, who I think looked up to Kazu in a way. There were so many young artists who admired Kazu and Yoshimi, and I think a lot of them were inspired by their dedication to art and their lifestyle as artists.

Kinoshita's Works in Uematsu's Collection
You own some of Kinoshita's works, three of which you're kindly lending to this exhibition. How did you come to acquire them?

—

'91-CA645 (cat. no. 118) is one that I bought. In 1991, when I was temporarily back in Japan from Germany, I went to Kazu's show at galerie 16[*4] in Kyoto. On the invitation was written, "Existence and Perception...And to Another Reality." [**Fig. 3**] Oil paintings from quite a few years were on view, but I was particularly taken with the latest work. It looked like a really fresh development in her use of space, brushwork, and sense of freedom, and I really wanted to acquire it. Of course there were larger works that were really impressive, but my budget was limited, so I went with this. It's not too large, but I feel like it condenses all these different aspects of Kazu's world. I remember how happy I was to acquire it.

'78-4-B (cat. no. 58) and '79-5-A (cat. no. 64) were gifts from Kazu when she was going back to Japan after her 1981 solo exhibition in Heidelberg. She had brought a lot of works from Japan and selected some to exhibit. Afterwards, she said I could choose some works from among those she showed and the others, and I selected two. They're really great pieces. Her series from that time, those photographs inscribed with felt pens, captured the essence of seeing and perceiving in such a compelling way. I was lucky to obtain two of those incredible works.

The collection of the Otani Memorial Art Museum, Nishinomiya City contains some of Kinoshita's works that you previously owned.

Yes, I got that ['85-CA287 (cat. no. 104)] through a trade. Kazu, Yoshimi, and I used to exchange works, their paintings for my sculptures or photographs. My collection of works by Yoshimi and Kazu was displayed at an Otani Memorial Art Museum, Nishinomiya City show of new acquisitions,[5] alongside my works that I had given them. The things I had given were inscribed with messages like "To Yoshimi" or "To Kazu." Eventually, I decided to donate all of their works that I owned. It seemed more meaningful for them to be viewed by a wider audience than to just stay at my place, where there's so much other stuff as well. I felt it was better to have Kazu and Yoshimi's art together in one location, so I donated it to the Nishinomiya museum.

I also got '86-CA358 (cat. no. 108) in a trade with Kazu. She gave it to me around 1986, when I began renting a house in Japan. At my house, I displayed two works each by Kazu and Yoshimi in a single room. The energy and force of their art gave the room a real vibe.

Interactions with Kinoshita

When did you start trading artworks with Kinoshita?
I understand that there was a box of materials[6] that Kinoshita entrusted to AD&A Gallery before she died, saying "Please don't let anybody throw away my works," and it included many plan drawings and photographs that you had evidently given her.

I moved to Germany in September 1975, but whenever I was back in Japan, I made sure to visit Kazu and Yoshimi. During these visits I would discuss my forthcoming projects, sharing plans and sketches, telling them "I'm thinking of doing something like this next," that kind of thing. I often consulted them about my work. I rarely seek advice from others, but when I felt really uncertain about what to do next, they were the ones I trusted and confided in. I often left drawings at their house, and that's why Kazu had so much of my stuff, I'm sure. It was less about trading works and more about me giving them things. I was really happy to hear that there was so much of my stuff, and deeply touched that it was so well taken care of.

The photographic works Untitled-a / Mu 102 (Books) (cat. no. 17) and
Untitled-b / Mu 103 (Stains on the wall (blocks)) (cat. no. 18), which are included
in this exhibition, were created at an early phase, when Kinoshita had
just begun incorporating photography. I understand you introduced her to
the lab where they were developed.

—

Actually, I was the one who printed those two. Alongside sculpture and installation, I was also working with photography, video, film, and other media. I
started with photography around 1972. Anyway, Kazu approached me about
developing photos for her art. At the time I was working in the design department at Hyogo Prefectural Technical High School, which had a marvelous
photo studio and darkroom. I used to print my own pictures there, and when
Kazu asked if I could process hers, I said I'd be happy to. There are two large
panels, right? I produced four of those in all. Kazu was there too, and we
mounted the photos on the panels together.

   Not long ago, there was a show of art from 1972[7] at the Otani Memorial
Art Museum. I had forgotten about helping her back then, but when I went to
see the show, I saw Kazu's photo work there and it struck me, "Hey, I printed
that." Kazu had submitted it to the Japan Art Festival[8], but it wasn't selected
and was returned to her, and I don't think she showed it anywhere else. Seeing it again brought back memories, it was a real blast from the past. I think
It's an important early work that questions the nature of viewing, and It's a
precursor to her later series where she drew on photos with felt pens. As for
the labs where she printed her photos later on, I did introduce those to her.

Solo Exhibition in Germany

In 1981, Kinoshita had a solo exhibition at
the Heidelberger Kunstverein, Germany. It seems that her last works
on paper were from around this period. Can you tell us about meeting her
in Germany during this time?

—

I came back to Japan around October 1981 and had a solo show as part of
the *Today's Artists* series at the Osaka Contemporary Art Center. Later, when
I went back to Germany, I flew over with Kazu. She brought her works with
her, rolled up, and out of those she chose which ones to exhibit. The show
was titled *Kazuyo Kinoshita 1976−1980,* and it was part of a series called
Angebote zur Wahrnehmung. The German word *Wahrnehmung* means "perception," and the series title could be translated as something like "Proposals
for Perception" or "Presentations to Perception." Hans Gercke, the director of
the Heidelberger Kunstverein, selected three artists per year for this series,
each of them showing at different times, but all with the "Proposals for Perception" theme. Gercke was fond of photography, and as part of this series,

Interview 2

—

An interview with Uematsu Keiji

he was one of the first in Germany to show things like photos by the conceptual artist Jan Dibetts. The series wasn't just for photographers, though, it also included sculptors. I first participated in 1979, I think it was. There were three of us, a German artist, a Swiss artist and me. I had the opportunity to introduce a number of Japanese artists. The next year there was a show of Takeoka Yuji, who was based in Düsseldorf, and the year after that there was Kazu's show. It was interesting, the director was fond of Japan and he would feature one Japanese artist every year. That was quite extraordinary. He was quick to recognize Kazu's talent too. The venue has since been entirely renovated, but documentary photos from her exhibition there still exist. These photos give you a good idea of what the venue was like. [**Fig. 4**] It was a well-planned exhibition, with natural lighting and works displayed neatly, giving it an intellectual kind of atmosphere. I took all those photos, and printed them at my darkroom in Düsseldorf.

As the title suggests, Kinoshita's solo exhibition in Germany featured her works from 1976 to 1980, which were predominantly photographic works, is that right?

—

I believe that period was just before she pivoted to painting. Naturally, as an artist, she was keen to present her latest works, and I think she particularly wanted to exhibit her pastels and paintings. However, when it comes to overseas exhibitions, It's wise to narrow the scope of what you present in order to gain viewers' understanding, and the venue director was more taken with the photographic works. Also, she asked Nakahara Yusuke to write a text[9], and he told Kinoshita that she should focus on one medium, for example photography, and concentrate on a specific time frame as well. [**Fig. 5**] She was eager to exhibit her most recent things, not past works, but since she was completely unknown in Germany, she opted for the photography route. She was basically on board with this decision, and the exhibition turned out really well.

Kazu was in Germany for a month, and after the Heidelberg exhibition, she made contact with the Städtische Galerie im Lenbachhaus in Munich. The Lenbachhaus Kunstforum had a large underground venue in the city center, and there was a proposal for her to do a solo installation there. Unfortunately it fell through. That was a really a shame.

—

Archival photos still exist that document the small models she created when planning the exhibition at the Städtische Galerie im Lenbachhaus.

—

Yes, I took those photographs. She built the models in my studio. After brainstorming and discussing things, she would create a model, bring it to meetings and present a proposal. However, for some reason, the discussions ceased

Fig. 4
Installation view of
Kazuyo Kinoshita 1976—1980
(1981, Heidelberger Kunstverein),
photo by Uematsu Keiji.

Fig. 5
from the left: Uematsu Keiji, Nakahara Yusuke,
Kinoshita

after she went back to Japan. She also went to meet with a curator at the Musée d'art moderne de la Ville de Paris. Kazu was invited to participate in a show of works on paper somewhere in France, as well as the exhibition *Das Foto als autonomes Bild — Experimentelle Gestaltung 1839—1989*[10], marking 150 years since the invention of photography, in Bielefeld, Germany. Other Japanese artists like Wakae Kanji and me also showed works. We were prominently featured in the *Bildgebende Fotografie* book published by DuMont.

From Photography to Painting

Around the time of her solo show in Germany, Kinoshita shifted from photography to painting. What were your thoughts on her works at the time?

—

I was really close with Kazu and Yoshimi, but I don't remember us talking much about their works. I often asked for their advice, but neither of them ever really approached me for guidance. I don't know to what extent they shared things between them, but if you look at Yoshimi's work from the early days onward and also track Kazu's development over the years, you'll notice that they both shifted to painting around the same time. I think they must have consulted each other about this. There's a consistent thread running through Kazu's work, whether she was moving from photography to drawing, or transitioning to painting, it all ties together. When I compare that with my own practice, I recall that when I was young I wanted to experiment with all kinds of things, and I began working with installation, sculpture, photography and film, around 1972. I guess Kazu wanted to try out lots of different media too. That's why she got into photography, and I think her way of thinking was aligned with Yoshimi's. Kazu wasn't part of Kawaguchi Tatsuo's Group "i," but she was always spending time with them, and Yoshimi was a member. The Group "i" people often talked about topics like "existence," and they used these kinds of words in their exhibition titles. Kazu started out with photography in 1972, but before that she was painting, with biological or geometric themes. Personally I think photography worked better for her, it was the best medium to convey her ideas clearly. Take her works with circle motifs, like *'76-C* (cat. no. 42) or *Work '77-D* (cat. no. 48), which deal with the nature of "seeing." She would draw a circle on a flat surface, bend it a bit, take a photo, and then draw the same circle on the photograph, which produces a dual perception of space. This was a great way to explore through photography what "seeing" means and how we perceive circles. She stayed with photography a pretty long time, until 1979.

Interview 2

—

An interview with Uematsu Keiji

In 1980, Kinoshita began experimenting with pastels in her series where she folded paper, photographed it, and then drew on it.

———

Well, as for me, I started working with photography around 1972 and stopped around 1976. That was because I was figuring out what I really wanted to focus on, and coming from a background in sculpture, I wanted to continue with three-dimensional work. So, despite having all kinds of ideas, I decided "All right, that's enough of that," and quit other things completely. I wanted to focus on my core practice, and not spread myself too thin across different media. Looking at Kazu's work, I see photography as a medium that conveys her ideas clearly. Folding paper in one place, drawing lines, then unfolding it — the concept comes across right away. Yoshimi also started out with painting, then explored photography and sculpture, and then he went back to painting around the same time as Kazu. I guess that around 1980, they probably talked things over and arrived at what they really wanted to do. They may have felt they had done enough with photography and it was time to move on.

Fig. 6
'86-CA362 (1986)
Image from *Kazuyo Kinoshita 1939 – 1994*,
AD&A, 1996, p. 46

———

Kinoshita mentioned in an interview that in 1980 and 1981,
she shifted from the narrowly focused mode of photography to
experimenting with pastels, and then when she began working on canvas,
she felt she had finally succeeded in changing her mode of expression.

———

I can understand that sentiment. One time when I was back in Japan and saw Kazu's work [*Pa-C '80-117* (cat. no. 85)], I was really surprised to discover that she had moved from photography to pastel. I could see the connection with her earlier work, but I wasn't very taken with it. After that, she began making these works where she wiped off oil paint, and her way of interpreting space started to intrigue me. Her works from around 1986 with layers of color, like *'86-CA362* [**Fig. 6**] and *'86-CA363*, didn't appeal to me much, but clearly, it was from then on that she began reducing her use of color lines. Her evolution during this period was quite extraordinary.

Her photographic works that involved folding paper, or the ones where she blurred edges with pastels, had kind of a systematic approach. She had a clear vision of the final outcome, and within these bounds, she was gauging how she could develop the work and how many works she could produce. I guess that got monotonous after a while, and that was probably why she felt she had done as much as she could with photography. Painting allowed her to be more spontaneous, the decisions about where to wipe away and when to stop were entirely up to her. Then she started working with line, deciding where to place each line... in painting, just adding lines can completely trans-form the pictorial space, right? It becomes a process of figuring out how to create something new in painting, and that gives you an enormous amount of freedom.

One time when I was back in Japan and visited Kazu's studio, she was working on a huge painting, and I told her, "Wow, this is really great." She thought it was good too, but she struggled with how long to keep going and when to stop. With works like these, knowing when to stop is crucial and also challenging. Sometimes she would spend a whole week just looking at the same unfinished piece. Still, I believe this uncertainty gave her a sense of freedom, it opened up new possibilities within her. So, embracing painting late in her career was a great step for her. Kazu died in 1994, and I often wonder what she would have created if she had lived longer.

Battling Cancer and Painting Until the End

In her final years, Kinoshita repeatedly visited Los Angeles for
cancer treatment, while continuing to produce works. Could you tell us
about that time?

—

I think it was in the fall of 1990 that I learned Kazu had cancer. I remember it well. She was very open about it, even asking me if I wanted to feel the lump. We talked about a lot of things around that time, but one thing I recall is that the cancer was already pretty far along when they discovered it. She wasn't sure about having surgery, questioning whether it would make a difference, wondering if it might be better just to leave it. She figured it would be a waste, undergoing surgery and having it not make a difference, so she was inclined not to have it. After she talked it over with Yoshimi, eventually they seemed to agree that Kazu should live life on her own terms. She continued painting right up to the end, and was admitted to the hospice at Kobe Adventist Hospital in 1994. I used to visit her about once a week. She spent most of her time in the hospital organizing her materials, or else painting watercolors. The last watercolor she worked on, which was untitled and unfinished (cat. no. 133), was made into a print and given out at her funeral. I donated my copy to Nishinomiya [Otani Memorial Art Museum, Nishinomiya City]. Kazu hung onto life fiercely, always eager to work more, even while she was undergoing cancer treatment. If she had had surgery and it hadn't been successful, she wouldn't have been able to paint again. In that sense, not having surgery and continuing to paint until the end was probably the best decision. She stayed an active artist right up to her final days. I'm so glad this retrospective is happening, and I think she would have been delighted with it too.

Interview 2

—

An interview with Uematsu Keiji

*1 The 4th International Young Artists Show: Japan-America (March 4 –14, 1967, Seibu Department Store SSS Hall, organized by Japan Cultural Forum).

*2 *Three-Person Exhibition: Mukai Shuji, Okuda Yoshimi, Higashiyama Akira* (April 4 [?] – 16, 1967, Tor Road Gallery, organized by the Kobe Shimbun Co.).

*3 The First PLAY Exhibition was an outdoor happening / exhibition by the Kansai-based artist collective The PLAY, founded in 1967 and led by Ikemizu Keiichi. Participants staged happenings for one hour each day over three days in Kobe East Park, Sannomiya, Kobe.

*4 *Kinoshita Kazuyo: Existence and Perception...And to Another Reality 1979 –1991* (July 23 – August 4, 1991, galerie 16).

*5 *Collection: godai* [Works from the Collection: Five Themes] (January 22 – March 13, 2022, Otani Memorial Art Museum, Nishinomiya City).

*6 This box of materials is currently in the collection of Nakanoshima Museum of Art, Osaka

*7 *Back to 1972 – How Japanese Contemporary Art Looked 50 Years Ago* (October 8 – December 11, 2022, Otani Memorial Art Museum, Nishinomiya City).

*8 The Japan Art Festival was an exhibition series lasting from 1966 to 1977, with the goal of presenting Japanese contemporary art overseas. It was organized by the Japan Art Festival Association, Inc. (now the Japan Art and Culture Association).

*9 The art critic Nakahara Yusuke contributed a text to the catalogue for Kinoshita's solo exhibition in Germany.

*10 *Das Foto als autonomes Bild — Experimentelle Gestaltung 1839 –1989 (The photograph as an autonomous image: Experimental design 1839 –1989),* (September 3 – November 12, 1989, Kunsthalle Bielefeld / December 15, 1989 – January 28, 1990, Bayerische Akademie der Schönen Künste).

年譜

（編：中村史子）

——

本年譜は、『木下佳通代 1939–1994』(AD&A、1996年) 掲載の年譜 (編集：熊田司) を底本とし、追記、再編集したものである。

1939年	4月18日、神戸市林田区 (現・長田区) に、父・義雄、母・綾子の長女として生まれる。家業は建具店で、次女・美智子、長男・陽一、次男・竹雄の4人兄弟であった。
1945年	幼稚園の頃、三木市に疎開。実家と、店・工場すべてを戦火で失う。
1946年	4月、神戸市立真陽小学校に入学。
1952年	4月、神戸の親和学園親和中学校に入学。2年生のとき、油絵具のセットを買ってもらい美術部に入部。
1955年	4月、親和学園親和女子高等学校に進学。
1958年	4月、京都市立美術大学 (現・京都市立芸術大学) 西洋画科に入学。黒田重太郎や須田国太郎に師事するが、むしろ彫刻科の辻晋堂・堀内正和両教授に親しむことが多かった。
1962年	3月、京都市立美術大学西洋画科を卒業。4月、神戸市立丸山中学校に美術の教師として勤務。
1963年	10月、河口龍夫と結婚。
1964年	4月、新たに開校した神戸市立吉田中学校に移る。
1965年	3月、神戸市立吉田中学校を退職。その後、母校の親和学園で美術を教える。6月、河口龍夫、奥田善巳らによって、前衛美術集団・グループ〈位〉が結成され、メンバーには属さなかったが行動を共にする。
1968年	この頃までグループ〈位〉は活動を続けるが、木下は河口龍夫と袂を分かつ。
1970年	2月25日、奥田善巳と結婚、神戸市生田区山本通4丁目に住む。

1971年	10月、神戸市生田区山本通3丁目に移転し、奥田善巳とともに美術教室アートルーム・トーアを開設、主宰する。
1977年	第13回現代日本美術展の出展作品《作品'77-D》が、兵庫県立近代美術館賞を受賞。渡欧し、カッセルにてドクメンタ6を見学。
1981年	11月30日、渡欧しパリ経由でハイデルベルクに入り、翌年1月29日に帰国。
1982年	2月、『月刊神戸っ子』が各分野で活躍する新人に贈る、「ブルーメール賞」美術部門の第11回受賞者に選ばれる。
1983年	6月14日、春から使っていた中山手通4丁目のアトリエが火災にあい、作品50点余を焼失。
1985年	3月1日、神戸市中央区新港町の三菱倉庫にアトリエを構える。
1986年	3月、同志社大学（京田辺キャンパス）ラーネッド記念図書館ロビー壁面のための作品を制作、設置。11日から14日まで韓国に旅行し、当地の作家と交流。
1987年	8月9日から11日まで、韓国に滞在。
1990年	9月10日、神戸中央市民病院で乳がんを告知される。翌月にかけ、治療法を求めて国内の各病院を訪ねる。
1991年	5月31日、知人を頼ってロサンゼルスに渡航、6月17日に帰国。 12月26日、ふたたびロサンゼルスに渡り、1992年3月9日に帰国するまで複数の病院を訪ねる。 1991年から1994年まで、合計7回、ロサンゼルスに渡航し、治療を受けつつ制作に励む。
1994年	1月に約1週間、2月から3月にかけて1カ月強、ロサンゼルスに滞在。 4月11日、韓国に渡り李医学博士に面会するとともに、美術館・画廊をまわって14日に帰国。 5月27日、最後のロサンゼルス渡航。 6月14日、帰国し、21日神戸アドベンチスト病院に入院。 9月19日、神戸アドベンチスト病院で逝去。

主な展覧会歴

1960年	グループ〈ケゴ〉展（開催月日不明、京都書院画廊）
1961年	グループ〈ケゴ〉展（開催月日不明、大阪画廊）
1962年	グループ〈ケゴ〉展（開催月日不明、京都市美術館）

| 1963年 | 3月「1963 京都アンデパンダン展」(6−12日、京都市美術館) |
| | 2人展 (開催月日不明、ヌーヌ画廊、大阪) |

| 1966年 | 木下佳通代展 (開催月日不明、ウィンナ画廊、神戸) |
| | 2人展 (開催月日不明、会場不明、神戸) |

| 1971年 | 3月「1971 京都アンデパンダン展」(3−16日、京都市美術館) |

| 1972年 | 2月 奥田善巳・木下佳通代作品展 (7−13日、シロタ画廊、東京) |
| | 7月 木下佳通代展 (11−16日、ギャラリー16、京都) |

| 1973年 | 2月「1973 京都アンデパンダン展」(25日−3月9日、京都市美術館) |
| | 8月 木下佳通代展「再び、「みる」ことについて・展」(28日−9月2日、ギャラリー16、京都) |

1974年	1月「PHOTO / ARTS −方法としての写真−」(11−19日、ギャラリーシグナム、京都)
	1月 木下佳通代展「「みる」ことについて」(15−20日、ギャラリー16、京都)
	4月「ヴィデオ / 京都 / 1974」(28日−5月11日、ギャラリーシグナム、京都)
	9月 木下佳通代展 (9−15日、村松画廊、東京)
	11月「シグニファイング − 言語・事物 / 態度の表明とともに」(企画：水上旬、6−10日、京都市美術館)

1975年	2月 木下佳通代展 (25日−3月2日、ギャラリー16、京都)
	2月「1975 京都アンデパンダン展」(26日−3月9日、京都市美術館)
	7月「私のポスター展」(8−20日、アートコア・ギャラリー、京都)
	9月 木下佳通代展 (8−14日、村松画廊、東京)
	11月「美術の祭典・東京」展 (1−20日、東京都美術館)

1976年	2月 木下佳通代展 (24−29日、ギャラリー16、京都)
	4月「第12回現代日本美術展」(28日−5月14日、東京都美術館 / 6月9−22日、京都市美術館)
	11月 木下佳通代展 (8−14日、村松画廊、東京)

1977年	2月「第8回国際青年美術家展」(8−20日、東京都美術館)
	2月「1977 京都アンデパンダン展」(14−23日、京都市美術館)
	2月 木下佳通代展 (22−27日、ギャラリー16、京都)
	3月「第6回兵庫県美術祭」(8−27日、兵庫県立近代美術館)
	3月 木下佳通代展 (28日−4月2日、ギャラリーU、名古屋)
	4月「表現技法シリーズその2＝ぬる」展 (12−17日、神戸三越5階ギャラリーL&C)
	4月「第13回現代日本美術展」(28日−5月14日、東京都美術館 / 6月1−12日、京都市美術館)
	5月「アート・コア現代美術77シリーズ『自画像'77』」
	(企画：高橋亨、17−22日、アートコア・ギャラリー、京都)
	10月 自選展シリーズ・木下佳通代展 (4−16日、ギャラリー・サードフロア、京都)
	11月 木下佳通代展 (1−12日、ギャルリーキタノサーカス、神戸)

1978年	2月 「アート・ナウ '78」(4–26日、兵庫県立近代美術館)
	3月 「20年を迎えた京都アンデパンダンの方向」(8–19日、京都市美術館)
	4月 木下佳通代展 (17–22日、村松画廊、東京)
	4月 「第12回日本国際美術展」(25日–5月10日、東京都美術館 / 6月6–18日、京都市美術館)
	8月 木下佳通代展 (15–26日、ギャラリー16、京都)
	10月 「いま、ドローイングは….」展 (企画：乾由明、2–7日、今橋画廊、大阪)
	12月 「第1回エンバ賞美術展」(13–18日、芦屋市民センターほか)
	12月 「EXPERIENCE BOOK」展 (25–31日、真木画廊、東京)

1979年	3月 木下佳通代展 (5–10日、鞆ギャラリー、大阪)
	3月 「第2回現代美術入札オークション展」(5–10日、今橋画廊、大阪)
	3月 「1979 京都アンデパンダン展」(8–18日、京都市美術館)
	4月 「第14回現代日本美術展」(25日–5月9日、東京都美術館 / 6月7–20日、京都市美術館)
	6月 「イメージのルーツ《物体》」(16–29日、ギャラリーウエストベス、名古屋)
	7月 アグネス・マーチン・木下佳通代 二人展 (20–29日、トアロード画廊、神戸)
	7月 木下佳通代展 (23–28日、不二画廊、大阪)
	12月 「ART IN WESTBETH '79」(15–23日、ギャラリーウエストベス、名古屋)

1980年	1月 「現代美術 – 入札 – オークション展 '80」(21–30日、番画廊、大阪)
	3月 「1980 京都アンデパンダン展」(6–16日、京都市美術館)
	5月 木下佳通代展 (5–24日、村松画廊、東京)
	11月 木下佳通代展 (11–22日、ギャラリー16、京都)
	11月 木下佳通代作品展 (15–30日、神戸時代ギャルリー)

1981年	1月 「100mm からの拡大展」(12–24日、ギャラリーU、名古屋)
	2月 「コラージュ展」(16–26日、ギャラリー・プチフォルム、大阪)
	2月 木下佳通代展 (17日–3月7日、ギャラリーウエストベス、名古屋)
	2月 「第8回郷土美術総合展 – 兵庫県美術祭」(14日–3月1日、兵庫県立近代美術館)
	3月 「1981 京都アンデパンダン展」(5–15日、京都市美術館)
	7月 「兵庫現代美術展 – 海 –」(11日–8月9日、兵庫県立近代美術館)
	8月 「兵庫県立近代美術館名品展」(15日–9月15日、兵庫県立近代美術館)
	10月 「神戸招待現代美術展 – 平面へのアプローチ」(15–27日、神戸国際交流会館・画廊ポルティコ)
	10月 「第7回汎瀬戸内現代美術展」(21日–11月1日、岡山県総合文化センター)
	12月 「Kazuyo Kinoshita 1976–1980」
	(13日–82年1月10日、ハイデルベルク・クンストフェライン、西ドイツ)
	12月 「WESTBETH ART SHOW '81」(14–23日、ギャラリーウエストベス、名古屋)

1982年	3月 「1982 京都アンデパンダン展」(4–14日、京都市美術館)
	4月 木下佳通代 Part I ['76–'80] (5–14日、シティギャラリー、神戸)、
	同 Part II ['79–'81] (15–24日、シティギャラリー、神戸)
	5月 木下佳通代展 (開始日不明–31日、神戸時代ギャルリー)
	6月 木下佳通代展 (21日–7月3日、村松画廊、東京)

10月 木下佳通代展 (19−31日、ギャラリー16、京都)

10月 「チャリティ神戸美術」展 (28日−11月2日、ギャラリーさんちか、神戸)

12月 木下佳通代展 (3−12日、トアロード画廊、神戸)

12月 「Travaux sur papier, objets, photos」 (4日−83年1月30日、文化活動センター、パリ、フランス)

1983年 2月 「SQUARE PARTY」 (22日−3月3日、シティギャラリー、神戸)

3月 「1983 京都アンデパンダン展」 (3−13日、京都市美術館)

5月 「WESTBETH ART EXHIBITION MAY 83」 (3−14日、ギャラリーウエストベス、名古屋)

7月 木下佳通代展 (11−23日、村松画廊、東京)

9月 「積極的なタブロー展」 (企画：ヨデン・マモル、6−18日、神戸現代美術ギャラリー)

9月 木下佳通代展 (26−10月8日、信濃橋画廊、大阪)

10月 「現代美術における写真：70年代の美術を中心として」

　　　(7日−12月4日、東京国立近代美術館 / 12月13日−84年1月23日、京都国立近代美術館)

10月 「第8回汎瀬戸内現代美術展」 (26日−11月6日、岡山県総合文化センター)

1984年 1月 「兵庫現代美術展 −都市−」 (26日−2月19日、兵庫県立近代美術館)

1月 「HARVEST」 (30日−2月10日、シティギャラリー、神戸)

3月 「1984 京都アンデパンダン展」 (1−11日、京都市美術館)

7月 「GET THIRTYS」 (23日−8月4日、不二画廊、大阪)

10月 木下佳通代展 (9−18日、トアロード画廊、神戸)

1985年 2月 「積極的なタブロー展」 (企画：ヨデン・マモル、18日−3月2日、信濃橋画廊、大阪)

2月 「1985 京都アンデパンダン展」 (28日−3月10日、京都市美術館)

6月 「兵庫現代美術展 −音楽−」 (1−23日、兵庫県立近代美術館)

8月 「昭和59年度 新収蔵作品展」 (8日−9月16日、国立国際美術館、大阪)

10月 「実験芸術国際展」 (21日−12月21日、ペーテフィ・レジャーセンター、ブダペスト、ハンガリー)

10月 「第9回汎瀬戸内現代美術展」 (23日−11月3日、岡山県総合文化センター)

12月 木下佳通代展 (1−13日、トアロード画廊、神戸)

1986年 1月 「9・個の視点」 (6−18日、村松画廊、東京)

8月 木下佳通代展 (17−30日、トアロード画廊、神戸)

11月 「ARTS OF TODAY」 (28日−87年1月4日、ブダペスト・ヒルトン、ハンガリー)

1987年 9月 木下佳通代展 (6−18日、トアロード画廊、神戸)

9月 「7人のアーティストによる現代美術展 木下佳通代展」 (23日−10月4日、ギャラリィミュ、大津)

10月 「第10回汎瀬戸内現代美術展」 (14−25日、岡山県総合文化センター)

1988年 1月 「'88兵庫の美術家」 (5日−2月7日、兵庫県立近代美術館)

2月 「TOR ROAD 20+1」 (14−25日、トアロード画廊、神戸)

8月 木下佳通代展 (28日−9月8日、トアロード画廊、神戸)

11月 木下佳通代展 (9−20日、ギャラリィミュ、大津)

11月 「第24回今日の作家展 多極の動態」 (企画：中村英樹、11−26日、横浜市民ギャラリー)

1989年　1月 木下佳通代展 (9−21日、不二画廊、大阪)

　　　　1月 「drawing '89」 (30日−2月4日、ギャラリー・ラ・ポーラ、大阪)

　　　　2月 「中田実郎コレクションによる木下佳通代・奥田善巳展」 (3−5日、ラポルテホール、芦屋)

　　　　3月 「TOR ROAD 20+2」 (19−30日、トアロード画廊、神戸)

　　　　4月 「現代美術の中の写真」 (8日−6月18日、兵庫県立近代美術館)

　　　　5月 「ギャラリィミユ企画展」 (開催日不明、ギャラリィミユ、大津)

　　　　6月 「Japon 89 Petit format de papier」
　　　　　　 (9日−7月2日、クル・デ・サール、ベルギー / ミュゼ・ドゥ・プティ・フォルマ、ベルギー)

　　　　6月 「AZコレクション展」 (12−7月15日、アートサロンロロ、加古川)

　　　　7月 「Recent Paintings '89」 (17−29日、信濃橋画廊、大阪)

　　　　9月 「Das Foto als autonomes Bild: Experimentelle Gestaltung 1839−1989」
　　　　　　 (3日−11月12日、ビーレフェルト・クンストハレ、西ドイツ / 12月15日−1990年1月28日、ミュンヘン・ヴァイ
　　　　　　 ヤリッシュ・クンスト・アカデミー、西ドイツ)

　　　　11月 木下佳通代展 (5−16日、トアロード画廊、神戸)

　　　　11月 木下佳通代展 (6−30日、AD&Aギャラリー、大阪)

　　　　11月 「KOBE現代美術展5−中田実郎、コンテンポラリー・アート・コレクション、木下佳通代・
　　　　　　 奥田善巳展」 (13−19日、画廊ポルティコ、神戸)

　　　　12月 「Miniature Exhibition '89」 (12−24日、ギャラリーココ、京都)

1990年　1月 「EMA−12分の1−」 (1−28日、布忍神社、大阪)

　　　　2月 「20+3」展 (18−3月1日、トアロード画廊、神戸)

　　　　2月 「利岡誠夫コレクション展」 (19−24日、AD&Aギャラリー、大阪)

　　　　3月 「'90兵庫の美術家」 (3−25日、兵庫県立近代美術館)

　　　　7月 「Flash Point 木下佳通代・館勝生・野田広人展」 (企画：中谷至宏、17−29日、ギャラリーココ、京都)

　　　　9月 「視点・平面」 (3−28日、AD&Aギャラリー、大阪)

　　　　9月 木下佳通代展 (30日−10月11日、トアロード画廊、神戸)

　　　　12月 「Miniature Exhibition '90」 (11−23日、ギャラリーココ、京都)

1991年　1月 「EMA−12分の1−」 (1−27日、布忍神社、大阪)

　　　　1月 「20+4」展 (20−31日、トアロード画廊、神戸)

　　　　3月 木下佳通代展 (25−4月5日、AD&Aギャラリー、大阪)

　　　　3月 木下佳通代展 (26−4月11日、トアロード画廊、神戸)

　　　　5月 「海岸通りレンガ倉オープニング」展 (17日−6月28日、AD&Aギャラリー、大阪)

　　　　6月 「BACK AND FORTH '70年代からの航跡」 (18日−7月7日、ギャラリー16、京都)

　　　　7月 「木下佳通代展−実在と認識…そしてもう一つのリアリティーへ・1979−1991」
　　　　　　 (23−8月4日、ギャラリー16、京都)

　　　　7月 「現代美術オカダコレクション展」 (2−13日、アートスペースモーブ、神戸)

1992年　1月 「EMA−12分の1−」 (1−26日、布忍神社、大阪)

　　　　1月 「'92兵庫の美術家」 (25−2月23日、兵庫県立近代美術館)

　　　　4月 「新収蔵品展」 (3−4月12日、静岡県立美術館)

5月「トアロード・コレクション」(17日−6月7日、トアロード画廊、神戸)

6月「いま絵画は−OSAKA '92」(29日−7月11日、大阪府立現代美術センター)

9月「現代絵画女流作家展」(開始日不明−9日、アートサロンロロ、加古川)

11月「ビデオ・新たな世界−そのメディアの可能性」(3−25日、O美術館、東京)

11月 木下佳通代展 (9−21日、AD&Aギャラリー、大阪)

12月「Miniature Exhibition '92」(8−20日、ギャラリーココ、京都)

12月「9作家のグループ・ショウ」(14−19日、不二画廊、大阪)

1993年　1月「EMA−12分の1−」(1−31日、布忍神社、大阪)

4月「新収蔵品展」(3日−4月11日、静岡県立美術館)

8月「Open House Gallery in Karuisawa」(5−22日、会場不明、長野)

10月「WOMEN'S 93」

(1−6日、近鉄アート館、大阪 / 1994年5月12日−6月3日、ギャラリーEMORI、東京)

12月「現代日本の版画と写真」(3日−26日、静岡県立美術館)

1994年　1月「EMA−12分の1−」(1−31日、布忍神社、大阪)

1月「現代美術における空間」(22日−2月20日、兵庫県立先端科学技術支援センター)

2月「プライベート・コレクション、コレクターの‥‥」(25日−3月9日、ABCギャラリー、大阪)

4月 木下佳通代展 (4−16日、AD&Aギャラリー、大阪)

4月「関西の美術 1950's−1970's −創造者たちのメッセージ−」

(9日−5月8日、兵庫県立近代美術館)

7月「Osaka・M, C・コレクション展 −5人の現代美術コレクションより−」

(22日−8月6日、集雅堂ギャラリー、大阪)

以降は没後の展示となる

1995年　11月「こどもたちへのプレゼント−いくつもの顔」(11日−12月3日、兵庫県立近代美術館)

1996年　1月「円の造形」(26日−3月25日、兵庫県立先端科学技術支援センター)

5月「収蔵品展 現代の版画」(14日−6月14日、静岡県立美術館)

10月 木下佳通代展 (1日−31日、AD&Aギャラリー、大阪)

1997年　6月「開館20周年記念展 国立国際美術館の20年 日本の水彩・素描と版画」

(19日−9月2日、国立国際美術館、大阪)

9月「〈私〉美術のすすめ: 何故〈WATAKUSHI〉は描かれるのか」

(6日−10月19日、板橋区立美術館)

1998年　6月「線の表情」(4日−7月28日、国立国際美術館、大阪)

1999年　4月「所蔵名品展1999-1 新収蔵作品を中心にして」(13日−6月13日、京都市美術館)

2000年　6月「新収蔵品展」(20日−7月30日、静岡県立美術館)

8月「所蔵作品展 写真と美術の対話」(8日−9月23日、東京国立近代美術館フィルムセンター)

9月「大阪市立近代美術館(仮称)コレクション展2000 写真/絵画/平面」

(23日−11月5日、ATCミュージアム、大阪)

2001年　8月「コレクション展第3期 多様な平面」(14日−10月28日、京都市美術館)

9月「兵庫県立美術館・移動美術館、画家とモデル−人物画からのメッセージ」

(19日−30日、ひがしうら文化館/10月3−14日、おおやホール/
10月17−28日、兵庫県立先端科学技術支援センター)

木下佳通代展(開催月日不明、アートギャラリーK、神戸)

2002年　4月「常設展示第I期」(6日−7月21日、兵庫県立美術館)

8月「20世紀。美術は虚像を認知した−モナ・リサとマンモンのあいだで−」

(3日−9月23日、平塚市美術館)

2003年　3月「所蔵作品展 近代日本の美術」(14日−5月11日、東京国立近代美術館)

7月「収蔵品展 今日の美術−彩」(19日−8月31日、静岡県立美術館)

9月「コレクション展第3期」(2日−10月13日、京都市美術館)

2004年　3月「コレクション展I」(13日−6月27日、兵庫県立美術館)

6月「コレクション展第2期 前衛の意識・表現の前進」(12日−8月29日、京都市美術館)

9月「コレクション展第3期 題名考」(4日−11月7日、京都市美術館)

11月「コレクション展第4期 連続と反復」(13日−2005年1月16日、京都市美術館)

2005年　2月 木下佳通代展 (18日−3月1日、ギャラリー島田、神戸)

10月「収蔵品展 版画と写真−複製芸術の可能性−」(12日−11月13日、静岡県立美術館)

12月「所蔵作品展 近代日本の美術」(24日−2006年3月5日、東京国立近代美術館)

2006年　3月「コレクション展 I」(18日−7月9日、兵庫県立美術館)

4月「コレクション展第1期 京都美術地誌案内−反・官展/反・画壇の系譜」

(4日−5月21日、京都市美術館)

5月「コレクション展第2期 線を探しに」(26日−7月23日、京都市美術館)

7月「木下佳通代&奥田善巳展」(22日−8月1日、ギャラリー島田、神戸)

7月「コレクション展第3期 表面への意志」(29日−10月1日、京都市美術館)

12月「コレクション展第4期 春を待つ」(20日−2007年2月25日、京都市美術館)

2007年　12月「コレクション展III」(1日−2008年3月9日、兵庫県立美術館)

2008年　1月「写真の美術 美術の写真」(26日−3月23日、大阪市立近代美術館(仮称)心斎橋展示室)

3月「コレクション展I」(22日−6月29日、兵庫県立美術館)

3月「所蔵作品展 近代日本の美術」(29日−5月18日、東京国立近代美術館)

4月「中田実郎コレクションと木下佳通代展」(5−16日、ギャラリー島田、神戸)

4月「線の発見」(26日−6月8日、大阪市立近代美術館(仮称)心斎橋展示室)

11月「コレクション展第3期 ふたつで一つ」(15日−2009年1月18日、京都市美術館)

2009年	3月「コレクション展 I」(28日–7月12日、兵庫県立美術館)
	4月「コレクション展第1期 時空を旅する 美術にみる物語」(4日–6月7日、京都市美術館)
	7月「コレクション展第2期 作家の一言、見人の一言、美術館での一会」
	(11日–10月11日、京都市美術館)
	7月「県美プレミアム II」(19日–12月2日、兵庫県立美術館)
	10月「所蔵品展 II 答えのない質問」(3日–11月23日、伊丹市立美術館)
2010年	4月「コレクション展第1期 円と方」(10日–6月20日、京都市美術館)
	4月「かたちのちから」(29日–6月20日、大阪市立近代美術館(仮称)心斎橋展示室)
	7月「コレクション展 II」(17日–11月7日、兵庫県立美術館)
2011年	2月「木下佳通代 & 奥田善巳展」(20日–3月2日、ギャラリー島田、神戸)
2012年	6月「対話する美術 / 前衛の関西」(9日–7月29日、西宮市大谷記念美術館)
2013年	4月「日本の絵画の50年」(20日–6月16日、和歌山県立近代美術館)
	7月「アート・アーチ・ひろしま2013 ピース・ミーツ・アート」(10日–10月18日、広島県立美術館)
2014年	1月 木下佳通代展 (25日–2月5日、ギャラリー島田、神戸)
	3月「県美プレミアム I」(22日–7月6日、兵庫県立美術館)
	6月 個展 (20日–2015年12月31日、木下佳通代記念館、神戸)
	8月「夏のクールスポット展 垂直の夢・水平の意志」(6–21日、京都市美術館)
	12月「コレクション展 2014 / 2015 – 冬」(16日–2015年2月22日、和歌山県立近代美術館)
2015年	3月「For a New World to Come: Experiments in Japanese Art and Photography,
	1968–1979」(7日–7月12日、ヒューストン美術館、アメリカ /
	10月9日–2016年1月11日、ジャパン・ソサエティー、ニューヨーク、アメリカ)
	7月「県美プレミアム II」(18日–11月8日、兵庫県立美術館)
	2月 木下佳通代展「『存在に対するメッセージ』から『存在そのものの創造』へ」
2016年	(企画: 森下明彦、20日–3月2日、ギャラリー島田、神戸)
	3月「県美プレミアム I」(19日–6月19日、兵庫県立美術館)
	6月「時代をこえて beyond the time」(28日–7月3日、ギャラリー16、京都)
	7月「県美プレミアム II」(2日–11月6日、兵庫県立美術館)
	9月「平成28年度第4回コレクション展」(22日–12月11日、京都国立近代美術館)
2017年	1月「名品コレクション III: 現代の美術 (前期) 円 (まる)」(14日–2月26日、名古屋市美術館)
	3月「木下佳通代 等価に存在する何か。」
	(18日–4月28日、Yumiko Chiba Associates viewing room shinjuku、東京)
	6月「Japanese conceptual photography from the 70's」
	(6日–7月29日、GALERIE CHRISTOPHE GAILLARD、パリ、フランス)

6月「木下佳通代 もうひとつの実在」(17日–7月8日、ギャラリーヤマキファインアート、神戸)

9月「Becoming & Dissolving」(15日–11月16日、ALICE BLACK、ロンドン、イギリス)

2018年　1月「日本の戦後美術展」(13–27日、ギャラリーヤマキファインアート、神戸)

3月「象る、象られる。」(3–31日、Yumiko Chiba Associates viewing room shinjuku、東京)

3月「コレクション展I」(17日–6月24日、兵庫県立美術館)

6月「所蔵作品展 MOMAT コレクション」(5日–9月24日、東京国立近代美術館)

11月「ニュー・ウェイブ 現代美術の80年代」(3日–2019年1月20日、国立国際美術館、大阪)

11月「県美プレミアム III」(17日–2019年3月3日、兵庫県立美術館)

2019年　3月「コレクション展I」(16日–6月23日、兵庫県立美術館)

6月「奥田善巳・木下佳通代の相克」(8日–19日、ギャラリー島田、神戸)

8月「名品コレクションII: 現代の美術 反復と連続」(1日–12月15日、名古屋市美術館)

11月「コレクション展III」(23日–2020年3月1日、兵庫県立美術館)

2020年　1月「コレクション－現代日本の美意識」(7日–2月28日、国立国際美術館、大阪)

6月「コレクション展I」(2日–9月22日、兵庫県立美術館)

9月「コレクションルーム秋期」(26日–11月29日、京都市美術館)

10月「京都の美術 250年の夢 第1部-第3部 総集編－江戸から現代へ－」
　　　(10日–12月6日、京都市美術館)

10月「コレクション展II」(10日–12月27日、兵庫県立美術館)

2021年　2月「奥田善巳・木下佳通代の相克」(20日–3月3日、ギャラリー島田、神戸)

4月「疎密考」(24日–5月30日、和歌山県立近代美術館)

6月「もうひとつの世界」(8日–7月18日、和歌山県立近代美術館)

11月「Demonstration展」(2–14日、トアロード画廊、神戸)

11月「Metamorphosis and Evolution 変容と進化」(20日–12月25日、emmy art +、東京)

2022年　1月「コレクション・五題」(22日–3月13日、西宮市大谷記念美術館)

4月「GYFA ショー part II 戦後の女性アーティスト－1970–2017－」展
　　　(16日–5月14日、ギャラリーヤマキファインアート、神戸)

10月「常設展 特集: 大きな版画」(8日–11月27日、名古屋市美術館)

10月「Back to 1972－50年前の現代美術へ」(8日–12月11日、西宮市大谷記念美術館)

2023年　1月「コレクション展I」(21日–7月23日、兵庫県立美術館)

9月「女性と抽象」(20日–12月3日、東京国立近代美術館)

2024年　4月 木下佳通代展〈pre-〉(26–29日、5月3–6日、トアロード画廊、神戸)

Profile: Kinoshita Kazuyo

1939   Born on April 18 in Kobe, Hyogo Prefecture.

1958   Enrolled in the Western-style painting department at Kyoto City University of Arts.

1962   Graduated from the same department. While working as a teacher,
she began to energetically devote herself to her artistic practice.

1965   Joined in the activities of Group "i" (formed by Kawaguchi Tatsuo, Okuda Yoshimi, and others).
Participated until 1968.

1977   Received the Hyogo Prefectural Museum of Modern Art Prize in
the 13th Contemporary Art Exhibition of Japan, in which she showed *Work '77-D* (cat. no. 48).

1994   Died of breast cancer in Kobe.

Solo Exhibitions

1972   galerie 16, Kyoto (also 1973–1978, 1980, 1982, 1991)

1974   Muramatsu Gallery, Tokyo (also 1975, 1976, 1978, 1980, 1982, 1983)

1979   Tor Road Gallery, Kobe, Hyogo (also 1982, 1984–1991)
(Note: The 1979 exhibition was a two-person show with Agnes Martin; the other were solo shows.)

1981   *Kazuyo Kinoshita 1976–1980*, Heidelberger Kunstverein, West Germany

1989   AD&A Gallery, Osaka (also 1991, 1992, 1994, 1996)

2005   Gallery Shimada, Kobe, Hyogo (also 2014, 2016)

2017   *In Search of Substantiality — Unifying the Absolute and the Relative*,
Yumiko Chiba Associates Viewing Room Shinjuku, Tokyo
ANOTHER EXISTENCE, Gallery Yamaki Fine Art, Kobe, Hyogo

Group Exhibitions

1963   Kyoto Independents Exhibition, Kyoto City Museum of Art (also 1971, 1973, 1975, 1977–1985)

1976   Contemporary Art Exhibition of Japan, Tokyo Metropolitan Art Museum &
Kyoto City Museum of Art (also 1977, 1979)

1978   *ART NOW '78*, Hyogo Prefectural Museum of Modern Art (now the Hyogo Prefectural Museum of Art)

1982   *Travaux sur papier, objets, photos*, Centre d'action Culturelle, Paris, France

1983   *Photography in Contemporary Art*, The National Museum of Modern Art, Tokyo &
The National Museum of Modern Art, Kyoto

1988   The 24th Artists Today Exhibition: *Phases Multiplar Movement*,
Yokohama Civic Art Gallery, Kanagawa

1989   *Das Foto als autonomes Bild: Experimentelle Gestaltung 1839–1989*, Kunsthalle Bielefeld,
West Germany & Bayerische Akademie der Schönen Künste, München, West Germany

2015   *For a New World to Come: Experiments in Japanese Art and Photography, 1968–1979*,
Museum of Fine Arts, Houston, USA & Japan Society Gallery, New York, USA

2018   *New Wave: Japanese Contemporary Art of the 1980s*, The National Museum of Art, Osaka

35.7 (~~93~~
(92, (8.45)

半径 9.75
(25.35)

(23.27)
8.95 →

→ 9.9 ←
(25.74)

16.75
43.55)

— 18.95 —
(49.27)

←1.95→
(5.07)

12.55
(32.63)
75

18.95
16.75
35.70

← 11.1 (28.86)

11.7
(30.42)

2 (6.76)

参考文献
（編：中村史子、奥野桃子、浦川慶子）

———

本リストは、『木下佳通代 1939-1994』(AD&A、1996年) 掲載の文献リスト（編集：越智裕二郎）を底本とし、
追記、再編集したものである。

個展カタログ、単行本
— 『Kazuyo Kinoshita: 1976-1980』展覧会図録、ハイデルベルク・クンストフェライン (西ドイツ)、1981年
— 『木下佳通代 1939-1994』AD&A、1996年

自筆（逐次刊行物等）
— 木下佳通代「五十対の眼」『美術情宣』7月号 No.3、美術情宣編集委員会、1974年、pp. 24-25
— 「表紙・作者のことば」『朝日ジャーナル』7月号、vol.19、No.27、1977年、p. 4
— 「制作の断片より」『U通信』No.4、ギャラリーU、1978年、p. 2
— 『Japanskt kalejdoskop』Tormag Fotosätteri (ロンマ、スウェーデン)、1980年
— 「展覧会案内 木下佳通代展」『美術手帖』2月号 No.477、美術出版社、1981年、p. 251
— 「KANZAKI'S Gallery 木下佳通代」『VIEW かんざき』No.36、1981年、p. 23
— 木下佳通代「ハイデルベルクの想い出」『神戸っ子』4月号 No.252、1982年、p. 31
— 木下佳通代「LUCY ESSAY「女と美術家」」『Lucy』No.2、1983年8月
— 木下佳通代「私の好きな作品 19世紀ヨーロッパ風景画展」神戸新聞、1983年11月15日
— 木下佳通代「好意の溢れた贈り物を 日頃の不義理を補う お礼の気持を伝えたい」日本経済新聞(夕)、1983年12月2日
— 「トアロード画廊 木下佳通代展」『画廊プロムナード』1984年10月
— 木下佳通代「うまいもん情報 とっておきの味 香辛料のきいた手作りソーセージが好評」『あまから手帖』2月号、
  京阪神エルマガジン社、1985年、p. 92
— 「関西横文字職業図鑑 時代 人間 画家・木下佳通代 いい作品をつくりたい、です。」『QTAI週刊求人タイムズ』7月号 vol.120、
  学生援護会関西本社、1986年、pp. 19-23
— 木下佳通代「今宵もなじみの顔がある わが愛しの"とまり木"たち」『神戸っ子』2月号 No.322、1988年、p. 59
— 木下佳通代「『都市計画の日』シンポジゥム基調講演より 神戸の人々が創造的になれる生活環境を」『神戸っ子』12月号 No.332、
  1988年、p. 60
— 木下佳通代「抽象と感性」『建築と社会』4月号、丹青社、1992年、p. 37
— 木下佳通代「私の夢ホテル・105 宇宙ステイション」『週刊文春』1993年1月14日、p. 69

自筆（パンフレット・リーフレット等）
— 木下佳通代個展「再び、「みる」ことについて・展」印刷物、ギャラリー16 (京都)、1973年
— 木下佳通代個展「「みる」ことについて」印刷物、ギャラリー16 (京都)、1974年
— 「文承根展」印刷物、ギャラリーQ (東京)、1984年
— 「兵庫現代美術展「音楽」」兵庫県立近代美術館、1985年

インタビュー / アンケート
— 岩井昭三「ひと 第13回現代日本美術展に地元女性で入賞」毎日新聞(朝)、1977年6月1日
— 木下佳通代「神戸っ子'77 時間をもった存在との関わり」『神戸っ子』9月号 No.197、1977年
— 木下佳通代「おんなの初夢 汐の香に気づく街」『神戸っ子』1月号 No.201、1978年、p. 34
— 木下佳通代「アンケート わたしの趣味三昧」『神戸っ子』12月号 No.212、1978年、p. 60
— 木下佳通代「イメージの神戸」『神戸っ子』10月号 No.222、1979年
— (知)「おんな who's who ハイデルベルクで個展を開いた木下佳通代さん 西独市民の反響にびっくり 幼時から絵が大好き」
  毎日新聞(朝)、1982年2月27日
— 「こうべの女 変わり続ける作風 画家木下佳通代さん」産経新聞(夕)、1982年6月7日
— 木下佳通代「美術教育を考える アンケート 何もかも刺激的」『美術手帖』7月号増刊 No.529、美術出版社、1984年、pp. 30-31

座談会
— 赤根和生、小西保文、南和好、松本宏、木下佳通代「キャンペーン 国際文化都市神戸を考える "現代美術館"を神戸に」『神戸っ子』
  2月号 No.238、1981年、pp. 58-62
— 増田洋、小林陸一郎、今井祝雄、大森一樹、木下佳通代、小林郁雄「キャンペーン 国際文化都市神戸を考える 空間リサイクルで芸
  術を街なかへ 芸術センターの設立を目指して」『神戸っ子』6月号 No.290、1985年、pp. 52-56

グループ展カタログ

— チハーコヴァー・ヴラスタ『Experience Book』1978年
— 『アート・ナウ'78』兵庫県立近代美術館、1978年
— 『神戸招待現代美術展1981 平面へのアプローチ』画廊ポルティコ・ギャラリーさんちか、1981年
— Dany Bloch『Travaux sur papier, objets, photos』Centre d'action culturelle (パリ、フランス)、1982年
— 『現代美術における写真: 1970年代の美術を中心として』東京国立近代美術館・京都国立近代美術館、1983年
— 『International Experimental Art Exhibition Budapest』Fiatal Művészek Klubja (ブダペスト、ハンガリー)、1985年
— 『Art of Today International Exhibition Budapest』Budapest Hilton (ブダペスト、ハンガリー)、1986年
— 『第24回今日の作家「多極の動態」横浜市民ギャラリー、1988年
— 『現代美術メッセージ'88』京都国際芸術センター、1989年
— Gottofried Jäger『Das Foto als autonomes Bild: Experimentelle Gestaltung 1839–1989』
  Kunsthalle Bielefeld, Bayerische Akademie München (西ドイツ)、1989年
— 『Japon 89 Petit format de papier』Cul-Des-Sarts (クーヴァン、ベルギー)、Musée du Petit Format (ニスム、ベルギー)
— 『いま絵画は－OSAKA'92』大阪府立現代美術センター、1992年
— 『ビデオ・新たな世界－そのメディアの可能性』O美術館 (東京)、1992年
— 『WOMEN'S 93』近鉄アート館 (大阪)、1993年
— 『関西の美術 1950's–1970's: 創造者たちのメッセージ』兵庫県立近代美術館、1994年、pp. 86-92
— 『国立国際美術館の20年: 開館20周年記念展』国立国際美術館 (大阪)、1997年
— 『線の表情』国立国際美術館 (大阪)、1998年
— 『20世紀。美術は虚像を認知した－モナ・リサとマンモンのあいだで』平塚市美術館、2002年
— 『対話する美術 / 前衛の関西』西宮市大谷記念美術館、2012年
— 『For a New World to Come: Experiments in Japanese Art and Photography, 1968–1979』
  Museum Fine Arts Houston, Japan Society (アメリカ)、2015年
— 『ニュー・ウェイブ: 現代美術の80年代』国立国際美術館 (大阪)、2018年
— 『Back to 1972 50年前の現代美術へ』西宮市大谷記念美術館、2022年

逐次刊行物

— 「展覧会メモ」京都新聞 (朝)、1972年7月4日
— (藤)「展評」京都新聞 (朝)、1973年8月31日
— 平野重光「展評 映像表現'73 木下佳通代個展から」『美術手帖』11月号 No.373、美術出版社、1973年、pp. 291-294
— (潤)「展評」京都新聞 (朝)、1974年1月19日
— 平野重光「展評」『美術手帖』4月号 No.380、美術出版社、1974年、pp.231-233
— 「展覧会案内 (東京)」木下佳通代展 (9・9-15 村松画廊)『美術手帖』9月号 No.385、美術出版社、1974年、p.299
— 平井亮一+たにあらた「展評 木下佳通代個展から」『美術手帖』12月号 No.388、美術出版社、1974年、pp.226-237
— (藤)「展評 変貌する風景写真」「写真を使った魅力的な表現も」京都新聞 (朝)、1975年3月1日
— 乾由明「MIZUE JOURNAL 5 京都アンデパンダンの20年」『みづゑ』5月号 No.842、1975年、pp.116-117
— 藤慶之「展評・関西」『美術手帖』5月号 No.394、美術出版社、1975年、p.238
— 「おもしろい試み 木下佳通代展」毎日新聞 (夕)、1975年9月11日
— (潤)「見た、見えた」京都新聞 (朝)、1976年2月28日
— 高橋亨「展評 木下佳通代個展 (ギャラリー16、2・24-29)」『美術手帖』5月号 No.407、美術出版社、1976年、pp.260-264
— 「美術 評F&T コンパスの円で」京都新聞 (朝)、1977年2月26日
— 高橋亨「展評」『美術手帖』5月号 No.420、美術出版社、1977年、pp.230-234
— 小川正隆「春の公募展から 自由でしかもナウ」朝日新聞 (夕)、1977年5月12日
— 「評F&T 合成写真の自画像」京都新聞 (朝)、1977年5月21日
— 中原佑介「平面評 第13回現代日本美術展 受賞に輝く作品 "絵画離れ"少ない」毎日新聞 (朝)、1977年5月24日
— 平野重光「"技術"の発展を期待－現代日本美術に寄せて－」毎日新聞 (夕)、1977年6月11日
— 高橋亨「展評 木下佳通代展」『美術手帖』8月号 No.423、美術出版社、1977年、pp.250-254
— (T)「評F&T 見て、認識すること」京都新聞 (夕)、1977年10月8日
— 安黒正流「展評 木下佳通代展」『美術手帖』1月号 No.428、美術出版社、1978年、pp.264-269
— 「「アート・ナウ」展あす開幕 新進気鋭の28人が出品 県立近代美術館」朝日新聞 (朝)、1978年2月3日
— 「単純に素直に 木下佳通代さん (アート・ナウ'78開幕)」朝日新聞 (朝)、1978年2月5日
— (草)「美術 アート・ナウ'78 自由、新鮮な発想で造形化 層厚い関西現代美術作家」神戸新聞 (朝)、1978年2月17日
— (藤)「アート・ナウ'78展 新鮮、自由な試み」京都新聞 (朝)、1978年2月18日
— 村田慶之輔「美術 アート・ナウ'78展 臨場感を演出 "もの"とのかかわり追う」読売新聞 (夕)、1978年2月21日
— 「展覧会案内 (東京)」『美術手帖』4月号 No.432、美術出版社、1978年、p.237
— 「[画廊]京都・他 展覧会案内」『美術手帖』8月号 No.437、美術出版社、1978年、p.311
— (T)「評F&T 紙に引かれた直線のズレ」京都新聞 (朝)、1978年8月19日
— 中村敬治「美術 見ることのあいまいさ－木下佳通代展」読売新聞 (夕)、1978年8月24日
— 山村悟「現代造形の諸傾向を網ら エンバ賞美術展」毎日新聞 (夕)、1978年12月26日
— 山村悟「若返り共同作品目立つ 京都アンデパンダン展」毎日新聞 (夕)、1979年3月15日
— 山村悟「1979 京都アンデパンダン展」『京都市美術館ニュース』No.112、1979年3月
— 針生一郎「現代日本美術展を見る 真摯な模索や思いがけない展開 立体部門の方に活気」毎日新聞 (夕)、1979年5月2日
— 山脇一夫「展評 木下佳通代展」『美術手帖』5月号 No.449、美術出版社、1979年、pp.250-252
— 「ギャラリー 明快な観念芸術 A・マーチンと神戸の木下佳通代二人展」神戸新聞 (夕)、1979年7月24日

— 「美術 真の姿を問いかける 木下佳通代展」朝日新聞(夕)、1979年7月25日
— (山)「一枚の紙が作る空間と存在感と－木下佳通代展」毎日新聞(夕)、1979年7月26日
— 工藤順一「展評」『美術手帖』9月号 No.454、美術出版社、1979年、pp.266-269
— 「[特集]美術に拠る写真 写真に拠る美術 photography by art, art by photography」『美術手帖』3月号 No.462、
  美術出版社、1980年、p.49
— 赤根和生、乾由明、増田洋、草野拓郎「第9回ブルーメール賞美術部門 選考座談会 榎忠の発想と個性を評価」『神戸っ子』
  3月号 No.227、1980年、pp.56-57
— 高橋亨「三つの節約」、中原佑介「1980年 京都アンデパンダン展を見て」『京都市美術館ニュース』No.117、1980年3月
— 熊田司「あらわれて集合し現在する－一九八〇年京都アンデパンダン展」『美術手帖』5月号 No.465、美術出版社、1980年、
  pp.14-15
— 「兵庫県立近代美術館10周年 国際的に評価される彫刻と版画の収集」『神戸っ子』7月号 No.231、1980年
— (山)「木下佳通代展 拡散した色彩に新鮮な情感(22日まで、ギャラリー16)」毎日新聞(夕)、1980年11月14日
— (T)「評F&T 直線と色面と」京都新聞(朝)、1980年11月15日
— (安)「美術 意欲作 実りの晩秋 街の画廊の新作個展」読売新聞(夕)、1980年11月17日
— 建畠晢「展評 関西」『美術手帖』1月号 No.475、美術出版社、1981年、pp.214-216
— 「美術 パステル画の新たな追求 木下佳通代展」新聞社不明、1981年3月2日
— 建畠晢「1981 京都アンデパンダン展」『京都市美術館ニュース』No.122、1981年3月
— 中村英樹「展評 名古屋 木下佳通代展」『美術手帖』5月号 No.481、美術出版社、1981年、pp.226-228
— 乾由明「関西における第一線版画作家 絶えず明確な問題意識を提示」『版画芸術』7月号 No.34、阿部出版、1981年、
  pp.151-153
— 「Angebote zur Wahrnehmung VIII: Kazuyo Kinoshita」掲載誌不明、1981年
— 「季村さん(詩人)ら5人「ブルーメール賞」きまる」毎日新聞(朝)、1982年2月20日
— 「神戸の木下佳通代さん 好評だった西独での個展 活発に動く美術家に刺激受ける」神戸新聞(夕)、1982年2月20日
— 「ブルーメール賞決まる 詩人・季村敏夫氏ら 五部門の気鋭の新人に」神戸新聞(朝)、1982年2月24日
— 「'82ブルーメール賞 美術部門受賞者 平面に知性と情感を表象 木下佳通代(画家)」『神戸っ子』3月号 No.251、1982年
— 愛宕出「1982 京都アンデパンダン展」『京都市美術館ニュース』No.126、1982年3月
— (草野)「ギャラリー 写真とドローイングに独特のイメージ 木下佳通代展」神戸新聞(夕)、1982年4月13日
— 中島徳博「展覧会レポート 内輪のクサミに抗するもの '82京都アンデパンダン展」『美術手帖』5月号 No.496、美術出版社、
  1982年、pp.126-127
— 「郷土の美術家」『兵庫教育』6月号 No.375、1982年
— 「Artist Gallery」『神戸からの手紙』1982年6月号、p.124
— 赤津侃「展評 東京」『美術手帖』9月号 No.501、美術出版社、1982年、pp.162-168
— 「展覧会」毎日新聞(夕)、1982年6月24日
— 藤慶之「評F&T 絵の具をふき取り、削り」京都新聞(朝)、1982年10月23日
— 山脇一夫「木下佳通代展 過去の抽象画抜け出す試み」読売新聞(夕)、1982年10月26日
— 山村悟、毎日新聞(夕)、1982年10月29日
— 「ギャラリー 異色のイリュージョン 木下佳通代展」神戸新聞、1982年12月(掲載日不明)
— 里信邦子「木下佳通代論」『Le clebs』4月号 No.20、1983年6月、pp.37-38
— 土肥美夫「リアリティー失った写真 記号化し概念表現 「現代美術における写真」展」毎日新聞(夕)、1984年1月12日
— 井上明彦「新鮮な可能性を示した企画展1983・関西の個展から」『美術手帖』1月号増刊、美術出版社、1984年、pp.25-28
— 田原由紀雄「1984 京都アンデパンダン展」『京都市美術館ニュース』No.134、1984年3月
— 中村英樹「1985 京都アンデパンダン展」『京都市美術館ニュース』No.139、1985年4月
— (草野)「文化 ギャラリー 純粋な絵画の表現 木下佳通代展」神戸新聞(夕)、1985年12月7日
— 「文化 「9・個の視点」(18日まで、村松画廊)」毎日新聞(夕)、1986年1月16日
— 「色調への小気味よい挑戦 木下佳通代展開く」『神戸っ子』1月号 No.297、1986年、p.142
— 中村英樹「未分化なものの記述」『ART '86』No.116、マリア書房、1986年8月14日、pp.18-19
— 草野「ギャラリー 絵画の原点に返る 木下佳通代展」神戸新聞、1986年8月22日
— 草野「文化 洋画中堅50人が力作 水準高い '88兵庫の美術家」神戸新聞(朝)、1988年1月27日
— 草野「ギャラリー 自由な空間処理 木下佳通代展」神戸新聞(夕)、1988年9月2日
— 「ART CALENDAR 木下佳通代展」産経新聞(朝)、1988年11月16日
— 「N氏の部屋で色と形は限りなく音楽に近づく」『新住宅』4月号 No.524、新住宅社、1991年、pp.88-89
— F「展評」京都新聞(朝)、1991年6月22日
— F「展評」京都新聞(朝)、1991年7月27日
— 吉賀好之「展評KYOTO」『三彩』10月号 No.529、三彩社、1991年、pp.120-121
— 竹村楊子「抽象芸術の成熟」『建築と社会』4月号、丹青社、1992年、pp.36-37
— 「女性5人で現代絵画展 独特の抽象世界 稲美町の画廊 鴨下さん(高砂)ら14点」神戸新聞、1992年9月5日
— 中谷至宏「Reviews 京阪神」『美術手帖』7月号 No.690、美術出版社、1994年、pp.150-152
— 有本忠浩「あるき目です ギャラリー 木下佳通代回顧展」毎日新聞(大阪夕刊)、1996年10月19日
— 中島徳博「紙上美術館 木下佳通代「Untitled」」『兵庫県立近代美術館ニュース ピロティ』No.109、1998年12月、p.1
— 出原均「神戸の名品」『神戸商工だより』2021年4月
— 武澤里映「神戸の名品」『神戸商工だより』2023年3月

パンフレット・リーフレット
— 「奥田善巳・木下佳通代 作品展」展覧会印刷物、シロタ画廊(東京)、1972年

— 「ヴィデオ / 京都 / 1974」展覧会印刷物、ギャラリーシグナム (京都)、1974年
— 「シグニファイング (意味化)－言語 事物/態度の表明とともに」展覧会記録集、京都市美術館、1974年
— 「第8回国際青年美術家展」パンフレット、1977年
— 「第1回エンバ賞美術展」パンフレット、1978年
— チハーコヴァー・ヴラスタ「イメージのルーツ展」展覧会印刷物、ギャラリーウエストベス (名古屋)、1979年
— 「岡山県・岡山市芸術祭 第7回汎瀬戸内現代美術展」展覧会印刷物、岡山県総合文化センター、1981年
— 「ポートピア '81協賛 兵庫県立近代美術館名品展」出品目録、兵庫県立近代美術館、1981年
— 「岡山県・岡山市芸術祭 第8回汎瀬戸内現代美術展」展覧会印刷物、岡山県総合文化センター、1983年
— 「岡山県・岡山市芸術祭 第9回汎瀬戸内現代美術展」展覧会印刷物、岡山県総合文化センター、1985年
— 「9・個の視点 The 9 Visional Points」リーフレット、村松画廊 (東京)、1986年
— 「岡山県・岡山市芸術祭 第10回汎瀬戸内現代美術展」展覧会印刷物、岡山県総合文化センター、1987年
— 「日本アートフェア '87」図録、1987年11月、pp. 44-45
— 「drawing '89」展覧会印刷物、ギャラリー ラ・ポーラ (大阪)、1989年
— 「EMA－12分の1－「午」」リーフレット、布忍神社 (大阪)、1990年
— 「'90 兵庫の美術家 兵庫県立近代美術館招待展」展覧会印刷物、兵庫県立近代美術館、1990年
— 「EMA－12分の1－「未」」リーフレット、布忍神社 (大阪)、1991年
— たにあらた「70年代が今を語る」「BACK AND FORTH '70年代からの航跡」展覧会印刷物、ギャラリー16 (京都)、1991年
— 「EMA－12分の1－「申」」リーフレット、布忍神社 (大阪)、1991年
— 「'92兵庫の美術家 兵庫県立近代美術館招待展」展覧会カタログ、兵庫県立近代美術館、1992年
— 「EMA－12分の1－「酉」」リーフレット、布忍神社 (大阪)、1993年
— 「EMA－12分の1－「戌」」リーフレット、布忍神社 (大阪)、1994年
— 「所蔵品展II 答えのない質問」リーフレット、伊丹市立美術館、2009年
— 森下明彦「「存在に対するメッセージ」から「存在そのものの創造へ」」展覧会印刷物、ギャラリー島田 (神戸)、2016年
— 「女性と抽象」展覧会印刷物、東京国立近代美術館、2023年

関連書籍

— Gottfried Jäger 『Bildgebende Fotografie』Du Mont, Köln, 1988, pp. 224-225
— 『アート・ナウ全記録1973－1990』兵庫県立近代美術館、1992年
— 『DOCUMENTS 30 years of the Yokohama citizen's gallery 1964－1994』横浜市民ギャラリー、1995年
— 『50 years of galerie 16 1962－2012』ギャラリー16、2014年
— 『兵庫県立美術館所蔵作品選』兵庫県立美術館、2001年、p. 174
— 『兵庫県立美術館所蔵作品選』兵庫県立美術館、2016年、pp. 168-169

作品画像掲載

— 平井亮一「展覧会短評」『三彩』286号、三彩社、1972年4月、p. 111
— 坂本慶一「現代のことば 自動販売機」カット、京都新聞 (夕)、1977年8月23日
— 池井望「現代のことば 出歯亀君のなげき」カット、京都新聞 (夕)、1977年8月26日
— 笠原芳光「現代のことば 幻の建築」カット、京都新聞 (夕)、1977年9月3日
— 目次用カット『神戸っ子』1月号 No. 225、1980年
— 目次用カット『神戸っ子』2月号 No. 226、1980年
— 目次用カット『神戸っ子』3月号 No. 227、1980年
— 目次用カット『神戸っ子』4月号 No. 228、1980年
— 目次用カット『神戸っ子』5月号 No. 229、1980年
— 目次用カット『神戸っ子』6月号 No. 230、1980年
— 目次用カット『神戸っ子』7月号 No. 231、1980年
— 目次用カット『神戸っ子』8月号 No. 232、1980年
— 目次用カット『神戸っ子』9月号 No. 233、1980年
— 木下佳通代「私の泊ったハイデルベルグのホテル」カット『神戸っ子』4月号 No. 252、1982年、p. 31

出品リスト / List of Works

作品データは、原則として
以下の通り記載した。

作品番号
—
タイトル（日／英）
—
制作年
—
技法・材質（日／英）
—
サイズ
—
所蔵者（日／英）
—
初出展覧会

———

In principle, the data of the works
were described as follows.

Catalogue number
—
Title of work
(in Japanese and English)
—
Year of production
—
Material and technics
(in Japanese and English)
—
Size
—
Collection (in Japanese and English)
—
Exhibition history

1
題不詳／む76
Title Unknown / Mu76
1960
油彩, カンヴァス
Oil on canvas
103.5×84.0 cm
The Estate of Kazuyo Kinoshita

2
題不詳
Title Unknown
1962
油彩, カンヴァス
Oil on canvas
72.2×60.6 cm
個人蔵
Private Collection

3
題不詳
Title Unknown
1962
油彩, カンヴァス
Oil on canvas
47.3×39.3 cm
The Estate of Kazuyo Kinoshita

4
題不詳／む80
Title Unknown / Mu80
ca.1961-62
油彩, カンヴァス
Oil on canvas
65.0×80.0 cm
The Estate of Kazuyo Kinoshita

5
題不詳
Title Unknown
ca.1961-62
油彩, カンヴァス
Oil on canvas
91.0×65.0 cm
The Estate of Kazuyo Kinoshita

6
無題
Untitled
1962
油彩, カンヴァス
Oil on canvas
76.0×64.0 cm
The Estate of Kazuyo Kinoshita

7
無題
Untitled
1962
油彩, カンヴァス
Oil on canvas
91.0×73.5 cm
The Estate of Kazuyo Kinoshita

8
境界の思考・A
Boundary Thinking A
1970
油彩, カンヴァス
Oil on canvas
91.0×116.5 cm
ギャラリーヤマキファインアート
Gallery Yamaki Fine Art

9
境界の思考・B
Boundary Thinking B
1970
油彩, カンヴァス
Oil on canvas
91.0×116.5 cm
ギャラリーヤマキファインアート
Gallery Yamaki Fine Art

10
境界の思考・C
Boundary Thinking C
1970
油彩, カンヴァス
Oil on canvas
91.0×116.5 cm
個人蔵
Private Collection

11
境界の思考・D
Boundary Thinking D
1970
油彩, カンヴァス
Oil on canvas
91.0×116.5 cm
ギャラリーヤマキファインアート
Gallery Yamaki Fine Art

12
境界の思考・E
Boundary Thinking E
1970
油彩, カンヴァス
Oil on canvas
91.3×117.2 cm
個人蔵
Private Collection

13
境界の思考・F
Boundary Thinking F
1970
油彩, カンヴァス
Oil on canvas
91.0×116.5 cm
ギャラリーヤマキファインアート
Gallery Yamaki Fine Art

14
[滲触] む95
[Saturation] Mu95
1971
油彩, カンヴァス
Oil on canvas
116.5×91.0 cm
ギャラリー島田
Gallery Shimada
「奥田善巳・木下佳通代作品展」
(1972年, シロタ画廊)

15
[滲触]
[Saturation]
1971
油彩, カンヴァス
Oil on canvas
116.5×91.0 cm
The Estate of Kazuyo Kinoshita

16
[滲触]
[Saturation]
1971
油彩, カンヴァス
Oil on canvas
161.0×130.5 cm
個人蔵
Private Colleciton
「奥田善巳・木下佳通代作品展」
(1972年, シロタ画廊)

17
Untitled-a / む102 (本数冊)
Untitled-a / Mu102 (Books)
1972
ゼラチンシルバープリント, パネル
Gelatin silver print on panel
103.0×147.0 cm
大阪中之島美術館
Nakanoshima Museum of Art, Osaka
「シグニファイング―言語・事物 / 態度の表明とともに」(1974年, 京都市美術館)

18
Untitled-b / む103 (壁のシミ(ブロック))
Untitled-b / Mu103
(Stains on the wall (blocks))
1972
ゼラチンシルバープリント, パネル
Gelatin silver print on panel
103.0×147.0 cm
大阪中之島美術館
Nakanoshima Museum of Art, Osaka
「シグニファイング―言語・事物 / 態度の表明とともに」(1974年, 京都市美術館)

19
Untitled / む38 (花時計)
Untitled / Mu38 (Flower Clock)
1973
ゼラチンシルバープリント
Gelatin silver print
各51.2×72.3 cm, 20点組
兵庫県立美術館
Hyogo Prefectural Museum of Art
個展「再び、「みる」ことについて・展」
(1973年, ギャラリー16)

20
Untitled / む59 (腕時計)
Untitled / Mu59 (Watch)
1974
ゼラチンシルバープリント
Gelatin silver print
各52.6×42.5 cm, 5点組
京都市美術館
Kyoto City Museum of Art
「PHOTO / ARTS―方法としての写真―」
(1974年, ギャラリーシグナム)

21
Untitled / む60 (ビーカー)
Untitled / Mu60 (Beaker)
1973
ゼラチンシルバープリント
Gelatin silver print
各52.6×42.4 cm, 20点組
大阪中之島美術館
Nakanoshima Museum of Art, Osaka
個展「「みる」ことについて」
(1974年, ギャラリー16)

22
む61 (物の増加と減少)
Mu61 (Increasing and decreasing of things)
1974
ゼラチンシルバープリント
Gelatin silver print
各53.0×42.8 cm, 21点組
大阪中之島美術館
Nakanoshima Museum of Art, Osaka
個展 (1974年, 村松画廊)

23
題不詳
Title Unknown
1974
シングルチャンネル・ビデオ (1/2インチオープンリールビデオからデジタル化), モノクロ, サウンド
Single-channel video (digitization from the original 1/2-inch open reel video tape) monochrome, sound
13 min
大阪中之島美術館
Nakanoshima Museum of Art, Osaka
「ヴィデオ / 京都 / 1974」
(1974年, ギャラリーシグナム)

24
無題
Untitled
1975
シルクスクリーン・水性インク, 紙
Silkscreen, ink on paper
各40.9×54.8 cm, 17点組
静岡県立美術館
Shizuoka Prefectural Museum of Art
個展 (1975年, ギャラリー16)

25
無題
Untitled
1975
シルクスクリーン・水性インク, 紙
Silkscreen, ink on paper
各40.7×54.0 cm, 14点組
静岡県立美術館
Shizuoka Prefectural Museum of Art
「1975 京都アンデパンダン展」
(1975年, 京都市美術館)

26
無題 A
Untitled A
1975
シルクスクリーン・フェルトペン, 紙
Silkscreen, felt pen on paper
111.5×79.0 cm
京都市美術館
Kyoto City Museum of Art
個展 (1975年, 村松画廊)

27
無題 C
Untitled C
1975
シルクスクリーン・フェルトペン, 紙
Silkscreen, felt pen on paper
111.5×79.0 cm
京都市美術館
Kyoto City Museum of Art
個展 (1975年, 村松画廊)

28
無題 D
Untitled D
1975
シルクスクリーン・フェルトペン, 紙
Silkscreen, felt pen on paper
111.5×79.0 cm
京都市美術館
Kyoto City Museum of Art
個展 (1975年、村松画廊)

29
無題 E
Untitled E
1975
シルクスクリーン・フェルトペン, 紙
Silkscreen, felt pen on paper
111.5×79.0 cm
AD&A
個展 (1975年、村松画廊)

30
無題
Untitled
ca.1975
シルクスクリーン・フェルトペン, 紙
Silkscreen, felt pen on paper
96.5×59.0 cm
大阪中之島美術館
Nakanoshima Museum of Art, Osaka
個展 (1975年、村松画廊)

31
無題
Untitled
1975
シルクスクリーン・フェルトペン, 紙
Silkscreen, felt pen on paper
96.5×59.0 cm
和歌山県立近代美術館
The Museum of Modern Art,
Wakayama
個展 (1975年、村松画廊)

32
無題
Untitled
1975
シルクスクリーン・フェルトペン, 紙
Silkscreen, felt pen on paper
96.5×59.0 cm
和歌山県立近代美術館
The Museum of Modern Art,
Wakayama
個展 (1975年、村松画廊)

33
無題
Untitled
ca.1975
シルクスクリーン・フェルトペン, 紙
Silkscreen, felt pen on paper
102.5×60.0 cm
ギャラリーヤマキファインアート
Gallery Yamaki Fine Art
個展 (1975年、村松画廊)

34
Untitled B
Untitled B
1975
シルクスクリーン・フェルトペン, 紙
Silkscreen, felt pen on paper
111.4×79.0 cm
名古屋市美術館
Nagoya City Art Museum
個展 (1975年、村松画廊)

35
Untitled
(Some profile or some consciousness)
Untitled
(Some profile or some consciousness)
1976
ゼラチンシルバープリント
Gelatin silver print
各58.0×85.0 cm、5点組
兵庫県立美術館
Hyogo Prefectural Museum of Art
個展 (1976年、ギャラリー16)

36
む36
Mu36
1976
フォトコラージュ, 感光紙
Photo collage, photographic paper
28.2×23.0 cm
大阪中之島美術館
Nakanoshima Museum of Art, Osaka
「アート・コア現代美術77シリーズ『自画
像'77』」(1977年、アートコア・ギャラリー)

37
む37
Mu37
1976
フォトコラージュ, 感光紙
Photo collage, photographic paper
20.6×16.3 cm
大阪中之島美術館
Nakanoshima Museum of Art, Osaka
「アート・コア現代美術77シリーズ『自画
像'77』」(1977年、アートコア・ギャラリー)

38
Untitled
Untitled
1976
フェルトペン, 感光紙
Felt pen on photographic paper
72.2×102.2 cm
兵庫県立美術館
Hyogo Prefectural Museum of Art
「アート・コア現代美術77シリーズ『自画
像'77』」(1977年、アートコア・ギャラリー)

39
Untitled
Untitled
1976
フェルトペン, 感光紙
Felt pen on photographic paper
103.0×72.2 cm
兵庫県立美術館
Hyogo Prefectural Museum of Art
「アート・コア現代美術77シリーズ『自画
像'77』」(1977年、アートコア・ギャラリー)

40
無題 / む40
Untitled / Mu40
1977
フェルトペン, 感光紙
Felt pen on photographic paper
24.5×120.3 cm
大阪中之島美術館
Nakanoshima Museum of Art, Osaka
「アート・コア現代美術77シリーズ『自画
像'77』」(1977年、アートコア・ギャラリー)

41
無題
Untitled
1977
フェルトペン, 感光紙
Felt pen on photographic paper
105.3×26.0cm
大阪中之島美術館
Nakanoshima Museum of Art, Osaka
「アート・コア現代美術77シリーズ『自画
像'77』」(1977年、アートコア・ギャラリー)

42
'76-C
'76-C
1976
フェルトペン, 感光紙
Felt pen on photographic paper
71.8×101.8 cm
大阪中之島美術館
Nakanoshima Museum of Art, Osaka
個展 (1976年、村松画廊)

43
'76-D
'76-D
1976
フェルトペン, 感光紙
Felt pen on photographic paper
72.0×101.7 cm
AD&A
個展 (1977年、ギャラリーU)

44
'76-E
'76-E
1976
フェルトペン, 感光紙
Felt pen on photographic paper
72.0×102.5 cm
京都市美術館
Kyoto City Museum of Art
個展 (1976年、村松画廊)

45
'76-F
'76-F
1976
フェルトペン, 感光紙
Felt pen on photographic paper
66.7×96.8 cm
大阪中之島美術館
Nakanoshima Museum of Art, Osaka
個展 (1976年、村松画廊)

46
'76-H
'76-H
1976
フェルトペン, 感光紙
Felt pen on photographic paper
70.2×99.8 cm
大阪中之島美術館
Nakanoshima Museum of Art, Osaka
個展 (1976年、村松画廊)

47
'76-I
'76-I
1976
フェルトペン, 感光紙
Felt pen on photographic paper
72.2×102.2 cm
大阪中之島美術館
Nakanoshima Museum of Art, Osaka
個展 (1976年、村松画廊)

48
作品 '77-D
Work *'77-D*
1977
フェルトペン, 感光紙
Felt pen on photographic paper
72.4×102.8 cm
兵庫県立美術館
Hyogo Prefectural Museum of Art
「1977 京都アンデパンダン展」
(1977年、京都市美術館)

49
'77-E
'77-E
1977
フェルトペン, 感光紙
Felt pen on photographic paper
70.0×100.3 cm
大阪中之島美術館
Nakanoshima Museum of Art, Osaka

50
'77-H
'77-H
1977
フェルトペン, 感光紙
Felt pen on photographic paper
67.9×91.6 cm
大阪中之島美術館
Nakanoshima Museum of Art, Osaka
個展 (1977年、ギャラリーU)

51
'77-J
'77-J
1977
フェルトペン, 感光紙
Felt pen on photographic paper
71.8×102.2 cm
大阪中之島美術館
Nakanoshima Museum of Art, Osaka
個展 (1977年、ギャラリーU)

52
'77-O
'77-O
1977
フェルトペン, 感光紙
Felt pen on photographic paper
70.3×100.0 cm
大阪中之島美術館
Nakanoshima Museum of Art, Osaka
「Kazuyo Kinoshita 1976−1980」
(1981年、ハイデルベルク・クンストフェライン)

53
'77-R
'77-R
1977
フェルトペン, 感光紙
Felt pen on photographic paper
59.0×83.5 cm
大阪中之島美術館
Nakanoshima Museum of Art, Osaka
「Kazuyo Kinoshita 1976−1980」
(1981年、ハイデルベルク・クンストフェライン)

54
'77-T
'77-T
1977
フェルトペン, 感光紙
Felt pen on photographic paper
66.8×96.0 cm
大阪中之島美術館
Nakanoshima Museum of Art, Osaka
「自選展シリーズ・木下佳通代展」
(1977年、ギャラリー・サードフロア)

55
'77-Y
'77-Y
1977
フェルトペン, 感光紙
Felt pen on photographic paper
58.6×83.5 cm
ギャラリー島田
Gallery Shimada
「アート・ナウ '78」
(1978年、兵庫県立近代美術館)

56
'77-27
'77-27
1977
フェルトペン, 感光紙
Felt pen on photographic paper
59.1×83.6 cm
和歌山県立近代美術館
The Museum of Modern Art,
Wakayama

57
'78-1
'78-1
1978
フェルトペン, 感光紙
Felt pen on photographic paper
69.8×97.8 cm
大阪中之島美術館
Nakanoshima Museum of Art, Osaka
「20年を迎えた京都アンデパンダンの方
向」(1978年、京都市美術館)

58
'78-4-B
'78-4-B
1978
フェルトペン, 感光紙
Felt pen on photographic paper
46.0×64.1 cm
植松奎二氏
Uematsu Keiji Collection
個展 (1978年、ギャラリー16)

59
'78-7
'78-7
1978
フェルトペン, 感光紙
Felt pen on photographic paper
70.2×98.4 cm
大阪中之島美術館
Nakanoshima Museum of Art, Osaka
個展 (1978年、村松画廊)

60
'78-11
'78-11
1978
フェルトペン, 感光紙
Felt pen on photographic paper
57.0×85.3 cm
The Estate of Kazuyo Kinoshita
個展 (1978年、村松画廊)

61
'78-35-A
'78-35-A
1978
アクリル, 感光紙
Acrylic on photographic paper
70.2×70.1 cm
名古屋市美術館
Nagoya City Art Museum
「Kazuyo Kinoshita 1976−1980」
(1981年、ハイデルベルク・クンストフェライン)

62
'79-1-C
'79-1-C
1979
アクリル, 感光紙
Acrylic on photographic paper
62.8×89.5 cm
名古屋市美術館
Nagoya City Art Museum

63
'79-2-A
'79-2-A
1979
アクリル・フェルトペン, 感光紙
Acrylic, felt pen on
photographic paper
67.9×95.7 cm
AD&A
「1979 京都アンデパンダン展」
(1979年、京都市美術館)

64
'79-5-A
'79-5-A
1979
アクリル・フェルトペン, 感光紙
Acrylic, felt pen on
photographic paper
67.6×96.2 cm
植松奎二氏
Uematsu Keiji Collection
個展 (1979年、靫ギャラリー)

65
'79-7-A
'79-7-A
1979
アクリル・フェルトペン, 感光紙
Acrylic, felt pen on
photographic paper
59.5×85.2 cm
個人蔵
Private Collection
個展 (1979年、靫ギャラリー)

66
Pa-fold '79-21
Pa-fold '79-21
1979
パステル, 紙
Pastel on paper
55.5×75.7 cm
AD&A

67
'79-38-A
'79-38-A
1979
アクリル, 感光紙
Acrylic on photographic paper
51.0×72.0 cm
東京国立近代美術館
The National Museum of
Modern Art, Tokyo
「イメージのルーツ《物体》」
(1979年、ギャラリーウエストベス)

68
'79-39-A
'79-39-A
1979
アクリル, 感光紙
Acrylic on photographic paper
51.0×72.3 cm
東京国立近代美術館
The National Museum of
Modern Art, Tokyo
「イメージのルーツ《物体》」
(1979年、ギャラリーウエストベス)

69
'79-40-A
'79-40-A
1979
アクリル, 感光紙
Acrylic on photographic paper
50.6×72.2 cm
東京国立近代美術館
The National Museum of
Modern Art, Tokyo
「Kazuyo Kinoshita 1976−1980」
(1981年、ハイデルベルク・クンストフェライン)

70
Ph '80-5
Ph '80-5
1980
色鉛筆, 感光紙
Colored pencil on
photographic paper
66.6×84.3 cm
国立国際美術館
The National Museum of Art, Osaka
「Kazuyo Kinoshita 1976−1980」
(1981年、ハイデルベルク・クンストフェライン)

71
Ph '80-10
Ph '80-10
1980
色鉛筆, 感光紙
Colored pencil on
photographic paper
73.8×75.5 cm
国立国際美術館
The National Museum of Art, Osaka
「Kazuyo Kinoshita 1976−1980」
(1981年、ハイデルベルク・クンストフェライン)

72
Ph '80-11
Ph '80-11
1980
色鉛筆, 感光紙
Colored pencil on
photographic paper
62.9×62.2 cm
国立国際美術館
The National Museum of Art, Osaka
「Kazuyo Kinoshita 1976−1980」
(1981年、ハイデルベルク・クンストフェライン)

73
Ph '80-14
Ph '80-14
1980
色鉛筆, 感光紙
Colored pencil on
photographic paper
68.6×68.9 cm
国立国際美術館
The National Museum of Art, Osaka
「Kazuyo Kinoshita 1976−1980」
(1981年、ハイデルベルク・クンストフェライン)

74
Ph '80-21
Ph '80-21
1980
フェルトペン, 感光紙
Felt pen on photographic paper
65.1×74.0 cm
国立国際美術館
The National Museum of Art, Osaka
「Kazuyo Kinoshita 1976−1980」
(1981年、ハイデルベルク・クンストフェライン)

75
Ph '80-30
Ph '80-30
1980
フェルトペン, 感光紙
Felt pen on photographic paper
69.0×91.8 cm
国立国際美術館
The National Museum of Art, Osaka
「Kazuyo Kinoshita 1976−1980」
(1981年、ハイデルベルク・クンストフェライン)

76
Ph '80-44
Ph '80-44
1980
フェルトペン, 感光紙
Felt pen on photographic paper
71.4×99.4 cm
国立国際美術館
The National Museum of Art, Osaka
「Kazuyo Kinoshita 1976−1980」
(1981年、ハイデルベルク・クンストフェライン)

77
Pa-fold '80-35
Pa-fold '80-35
1980
パステル, 紙
Pastel on paper
97.0×179.0 cm
大阪中之島美術館
Nakanoshima Museum of Art, Osaka

78
Pa-fold '80-36
Pa-fold '80-36
1980
パステル, 紙
Pastel on paper
96.5×185.0 cm
大阪中之島美術館
Nakanoshima Museum of Art, Osaka

79
Pa-fold '80-37
Pa-fold '80-37
1980
パステル, 紙
Pastel on paper
94.0×187.0 cm
大阪中之島美術館
Nakanoshima Museum of Art, Osaka

80
Ph '80-74
Ph '80-74
1980
パステル, 紙
Pastel on paper
96.5×187.0 cm
大阪中之島美術館
Nakanoshima Museum of Art, Osaka

81
Pa '80-86
Pa '80-86
1980
パステル, 紙
Pastel on paper
187.5×96.5 cm
大阪中之島美術館
Nakanoshima Museum of Art, Osaka

82
Pa '80-105
Pa '80-105
1980
鉛筆・パステル, 紙
Pencil, pastel on paper
63.0×97.7 cm
個人蔵
Private Collection

83
Pa-C '80-99
Pa-C '80-99
1980
パステル, 紙
Pastel on paper
79.0×55.0 cm
AD&A
個展 (1996年、AD&Aギャラリー)

84
Pa-C '80-111
Pa-C '80-111
1980
パステル, 紙
Pastel on paper
75.8×56.0 cm
名古屋市美術館
Nagoya City Art Museum
個展 (1981年、ギャラリーウエストベス)

85
Pa-C '80-117
Pa-C '80-117
1980
パステル, 紙
Pastel on paper
76.0×56.0 cm
名古屋市美術館
Nagoya City Art Museum

86
Pa-C '80-120
Pa-C '80-120
1980
パステル, 紙
Pastel on paper
75.2×56.2 cm
ギャラリー島田
Gallery Shimada

87
Pa-C '81-6
Pa-C '81-6
1981
パステル, 紙
Pastel on paper
76.0×56.0 cm
名古屋市美術館
Nagoya City Art Museum

88
Pa-C '81-8
Pa-C '81-8
1981
パステル, 紙
Pastel on paper
75.5×51.6 cm
AD&A

89
題不詳
Title Unknown
ca.1981
油彩, カンヴァス
Oil on canvas
52.8×40.7 cm
個人蔵
Private Collection

90
'82-CA1
'82-CA1
1982
油彩, カンヴァス
Oil on canvas
45.5×38.0 cm
大阪中之島美術館
Nakanoshima Museum of Art, Osaka
個展 (1982年、ギャラリー16)

———

91
'82-CA7
'82-CA7
1982
油彩, カンヴァス
Oil on canvas
91.5×73.0 cm
ギャラリー島田
Gallery Shimada

———

92
'82-CA26
'82-CA26
1982
油彩, カンヴァス
Oil on canvas
116.5×90.0 cm
The Estate of Kazuyo Kinoshita
個展 (1982年、ギャラリー16)

———

93
'82-CA62
'82-CA62
1982
油彩, カンヴァス
Oil on canvas
130.5×97.0 cm
個人蔵
Private Collection

———

94
'83-CA74
'83-CA74
1983
油彩, カンヴァス
Oil on canvas
145.5×90.0 cm
個人蔵
Private Collection
個展 (1996年、AD&Aギャラリー)

———

95
'83-CA77
'83-CA77
1983
油彩, カンヴァス
Oil on canvas
162.5×97.5 cm
個人蔵
Private Collection
個展 (1996年、AD&Aギャラリー)

———

96
'83-CA88
'83-CA88
1983
油彩, カンヴァス
Oil on canvas
162.0×130.5 cm
The Estate of Kazuyo Kinoshita
「第8回汎瀬戸内現代美術展」
(1983年、岡山県総合文化センター)

———

97
'83-CA90
'83-CA90
1983
油彩, カンヴァス
Oil on canvas
162.0×130.0 cm
個人蔵
Private Collection
「第8回汎瀬戸内現代美術展」
(1983年、岡山県総合文化センター)

———

98
'84-CA233
'84-CA233
1984
油彩, カンヴァス
Oil on canvas
50.0×60.6 cm
AD&A

———

99
'85-CA251
'85-CA251
1985
油彩, カンヴァス
Oil on canvas
162.0×130.5 cm
個人蔵
Private Collection
「1985 京都アンデパンダン展」
(1985年、京都市美術館)

———

100
'85-CA257
'85-CA257
1985
油彩, カンヴァス
Oil on canvas
162.0×130.5 cm
個人蔵
Private Collection
「第10回汎瀬戸内現代美術展」
(1987年、岡山県総合文化センター)

———

101
'85-CA261
'85-CA261
1985
油彩, カンヴァス
Oil on canvas
162.0×130.5 cm
個人蔵
Private Collection

———

102
'85-CA262
'85-CA262
1985
油彩, カンヴァス
Oil on canvas
182.0×227.0 cm
大阪中之島美術館
Nakanoshima Museum of Art, Osaka
個展 (1996年、AD&Aギャラリー)

———

103
'85-CA267
'85-CA267
1985
油彩, カンヴァス
Oil on canvas
22.8×15.5 cm
AD&A

———

104
'85-CA287
'85-CA287
1985
油彩, カンヴァス
Oil on canvas
72.8×60.5 cm
西宮市大谷記念美術館
(植松奎二氏旧蔵)
Otani Memorial Art Museum,
Nishinomiya City
(former Uematsu Keiji Collection)

———

105
'86-CA323
'86-CA323
1986
油彩, カンヴァス
Oil on canvas
250.0×550.0 cm
北川貞大氏 (大阪中之島美術館寄託)
Nakanoshima Museum of Art,
Osaka deposited by
Kitagawa Sadahiro

106
奥田善巳
Okuda Yoshimi
CO-310
CO-310
1986
油彩, カンヴァス
Oil on canvas
250.0×550.0 cm
北川貞大氏（大阪中之島美術館寄託）
Nakanoshima Museum of Art,
Osaka deposited by
Kitagawa Sadahiro
—

107
'86-CA350
'86-CA350
1986
油彩, カンヴァス
Oil on canvas
91.0×72.8 cm
The Estate of Kazuyo Kinoshita
個展 (1986年、トアロード画廊)
—

108
'86-CA358
'86-CA358
1986
油彩, カンヴァス
Oil on canvas
45.8×38.2 cm
西宮市大谷記念美術館
（植松奎二氏旧蔵）
Otani Memorial Art Museum,
Nishinomiya City
(former Uematsu Keiji Collection)
—

109
'86-CA375
'86-CA375
1986
油彩, カンヴァス
Oil on canvas
91.0×72.8 cm
The Estate of Kazuyo Kinoshita
—

110
'87-CA391
'87-CA391
1987
油彩, カンヴァス
Oil on canvas
162.0×130.5 cm
ギャラリーヤマキファインアート
Gallery Yamaki Fine Art
—

111
'88-CA487
'88-CA487
1988
油彩, カンヴァス
Oil on canvas
218.2×291.0 cm
大阪中之島美術館
Nakanoshima Museum of Art, Osaka
—

112
'88-CA517
'88-CA517
1988
油彩, カンヴァス
Oil on canvas
181.8×227.3 cm
京都市美術館
Kyoto City Museum of Art
—

113
'89-Pa537
'89-Pa537
1989
水彩, 紙
Watercolor on paper
16.4×22.5 cm
大阪中之島美術館
Nakanoshima Museum of Art, Osaka
—

114
'89-CA554
'89-CA554
1989
油彩, カンヴァス
Oil on canvas
182.0×227.0 cm
大阪中之島美術館
Nakanoshima Museum of Art, Osaka
個展 (1989年、AD&A ギャラリー)
—

115
'89-CA557
'89-CA557
1989
油彩, カンヴァス
Oil on canvas
181.5×228.0 cm
大阪中之島美術館
Nakanoshima Museum of Art, Osaka
個展 (1989年、AD&A ギャラリー)
—

116
'90-CA603
'90-CA603
1990
油彩, カンヴァス
Oil on canvas
130.5×162.0 cm
個人蔵
Private Collection
—

117
'90-CA605
'90-CA605
1990
油彩, カンヴァス
Oil on canvas
218.2×290.9 cm
名古屋市美術館
Nagoya City Art Museum
—

118
'91-CA645
'91-CA645
1991
油彩, カンヴァス
Oil on canvas
21.8×27.0 cm
植松奎二氏
Uematsu Keiji Collection
個展 (1991年、ギャラリー16)
—

119
'91-CA652
'91-CA652
1991
油彩, カンヴァス
Oil on canvas
181.8×227.3 cm
京都市美術館
Kyoto City Museum of Art
個展 (1991年、AD&A ギャラリー)
—

120
LA '92-CA681
LA '92-CA681
1992
アクリル, カンヴァス
Acrylic on canvas
181.2×225.0 cm
大阪中之島美術館
Nakanoshima Museum of Art, Osaka
—

121
LA '92-CA700
LA '92-CA700
1992
アクリル, カンヴァス
Acrylic on canvas
218.2×290.0 cm
国立国際美術館
The National Museum of Art, Osaka
個展 (1992年、AD&A ギャラリー)
—

122
LA '92-CA711
LA '92-CA711
1992
アクリル, カンヴァス
Acrylic on canvas
218.5×290.8 cm
和歌山県立近代美術館
The Museum of Modern Art,
Wakayama
個展 (1992年、AD&A ギャラリー)
—

123
LA '92-CA712
LA '92-CA712
1992
アクリル, カンヴァス
Acrylic on canvas
162.2×130.3 cm
The Estate of Kazuyo Kinoshita
個展 (1992年、AD&Aギャラリー)

124
LA '92-CA713
LA '92-CA713
1992
油彩, カンヴァス
Oil on canvas
146.0×112.0 cm
ギャラリーヤマキファインアート
Gallery Yamaki Fine Art

125
LA '92-CA714
LA '92-CA714
1992
アクリル・油彩, カンヴァス
Acrylic, oil on canvas
218.5×290.8 cm
個人蔵
Private Collection

126
LA '92-CA716
LA '92-CA716
1992
アクリル, カンヴァス
Acrylic on canvas
181.8×227.3 cm
京都市美術館
Kyoto City Museum of Art
個展 (1992年、AD&Aギャラリー)

127
LA '92-CA717
LA '92-CA717
1992
アクリル, カンヴァス
Acrylic on canvas
227.3×181.8 cm
京都市美術館
Kyoto City Museum of Art
個展 (1992年、AD&Aギャラリー)

128
LA '92-CA729
LA '92-CA729
1992
アクリル, カンヴァス
Acrylic on canvas
193.9×259.1 cm
京都国立近代美術館
The National Museum of Modern Art,
Kyoto
個展 (1992年、AD&Aギャラリー)

129
'93-CA786
'93-CA786
1993
油彩, カンヴァス
Oil on canvas
290.9×218.2 cm
京都市美術館
Kyoto City Museum of Art
個展 (1996年、AD&Aギャラリー)

130
'93-CA792
'93-CA792
1993
油彩, カンヴァス
Oil on canvas
227.0×181.5 cm
大阪中之島美術館
Nakanoshima Museum of Art, Osaka
個展 (1994年、AD&Aギャラリー)

131
'93-CA793
'93-CA793
1993
油彩, カンヴァス
Oil on canvas
223.5×182.0 cm
大阪中之島美術館
Nakanoshima Museum of Art, Osaka
個展 (1994年、AD&Aギャラリー)

132
'93-CA799
'93-CA799
1993
油彩, カンヴァス
Oil on canvas
145.4×112.1 cm
名古屋市美術館
Nagoya City Art Museum
個展 (1994年、AD&Aギャラリー)

133
無題 (絶筆・未完)
Untitled (Last work, unfinished)
1994
水彩, 紙
Watercolor on paper
23.8×33.4 cm
大阪中之島美術館
Nakanoshima Museum of Art, Osaka

木下佳通代資料
Material of
Kinoshita Kazuyo

p. 100
1
インスタレーションのためのドローイング
Drawing for installation works
1978
鉛筆・インク・フェルトペン, 紙
Pencil, ink, felt pen on paper
大阪中之島美術館
Nakanoshima Museum of Art, Osaka

2
インスタレーションプラン '77
Installation plan '77
1977
鉛筆・インク・パステル, 紙
Pencil, ink, pastel on paper
大阪中之島美術館
Nakanoshima Museum of Art, Osaka

3
インスタレーションプラン '77
Installation plan '77
1977
鉛筆・インク・パステル, 紙
Pencil, ink, pastel on paper
大阪中之島美術館
Nakanoshima Museum of Art, Osaka

4
ギャラリーキタノサーカスのための
インスタレーションプラン
Installation plan for
Gallery Kitano Circus
1977
インク, 紙
Ink on paper
大阪中之島美術館
Nakanoshima Museum of Art, Osaka

p. 101
5
インスタレーションプラン
Installation plan
ca.1977
鉛筆, 紙
Pencil on paper
大阪中之島美術館
Nakanoshima Museum of Art, Osaka

6
インスタレーションプラン
Installation plan
ca.1977
鉛筆・インク, 紙
Pencil, ink on paper
大阪中之島美術館
Nakanoshima Museum of Art, Osaka

p.108
作品プランのためのコンタクトシート
Contact sheet for work plan
1978
ゼラチンシルバープリント・
鉛筆・インク, 紙
Gelatin silver print, pencil,
ink on paper
大阪中之島美術館
Nakanoshima Museum of Art, Osaka

—

作品プランのためのコンタクトシート
Contact sheet for work plan
1978
ゼラチンシルバープリント・
鉛筆・インク, 紙
Gelatin silver print, pencil,
ink on paper
大阪中之島美術館
Nakanoshima Museum of Art, Osaka

p.113
「Pa-fold」シリーズのための
ドローイング
Drawing for the "Pa-fold" series
ca.1979
パステル・フェルトペン, 紙
Pastel, felt pen on paper
大阪中之島美術館
Nakanoshima Museum of Art, Osaka

「Pa-fold」シリーズのための
ドローイング
Drawing for the "Pa-fold" series
ca.1979
パステル・フェルトペン, 紙
Pastel, felt pen on paper
大阪中之島美術館
Nakanoshima Museum of Art, Osaka

p.116
作品プランのためのドローイング
Drawing for work plan
ca.1979
インク・鉛筆・フェルトペン, 紙
Ink, pencil, felt pen on paper
大阪中之島美術館
Nakanoshima Museum of Art, Osaka

作品プランのためのマケット
Maquette for work plan
ca.1979
インク, 紙
Ink on paper
大阪中之島美術館
Nakanoshima Museum of Art, Osaka

—

p.117
左上:
Top left:
作品プランのためのマケット
Maquette for work plan
ca.1979
インク, 紙
Ink on paper
大阪中之島美術館
Nakanoshima Museum of Art, Osaka

—

左下:
Bottom left:
作品プランのためのマケット
Maquette for work plan
ca.1979
紙
Paper
大阪中之島美術館
Nakanoshima Museum of Art, Osaka

—

右上:
Top right:
作品プランのためのマケット
Maquette for work plan
ca.1979
鉛筆, 紙
Pencil on paper
大阪中之島美術館
Nakanoshima Museum of Art, Osaka

右下:
Bottom right:
作品プランのためのマケット
Maquette for work plan
ca.1979
紙
Paper
大阪中之島美術館
Nakanoshima Museum of Art, Osaka

p.122
左上:
Top left:
「Ph」シリーズのためのマケット
Maquette for the "Ph" series
ca.1980
鉛筆・インク, 紙
Pencil, ink on paper
大阪中之島美術館
Nakanoshima Museum of Art, Osaka

—

左下:
Bottom left:
「Ph」シリーズのためのマケット
Maquette for the "Ph" series
ca.1980
鉛筆・インク, 紙
Pencil, ink on paper
大阪中之島美術館
Nakanoshima Museum of Art, Osaka

—

右上:
Top right:
「Ph」シリーズのためのマケット
Maquette for the "Ph" series
ca.1980
鉛筆・インク, 紙
Pencil, ink on paper
大阪中之島美術館
Nakanoshima Museum of Art, Osaka

右下:
Bottom right:
「Ph」シリーズのためのマケット
Maquette for the "Ph" series
ca.1980
鉛筆・インク, 紙
Pencil, ink on paper
大阪中之島美術館
Nakanoshima Museum of Art, Osaka

p.123
「Ph」シリーズのためのマケット
Maquette for the "Ph" series
ca.1980
鉛筆・インク, 紙
Pencil, ink on paper
大阪中之島美術館
Nakanoshima Museum of Art, Osaka

「Ph」シリーズのためのマケット
Maquette for the "Ph" series
ca.1980
鉛筆・インク, 紙
Pencil, ink on paper
大阪中之島美術館
Nakanoshima Museum of Art, Osaka

pp. 102-103
画像のオリジナルプリントや
ネガフィルムは現時点で確認されていない。
The original prints and
negatives remain unknown
at present.

没後30年
木下佳通代

KAZUYO KINOSHITA
A Retrospective

［展覧会］

企画・構成
大下裕司、中村史子
（大阪中之島美術館）
佐藤あゆか、鴫原悠
（埼玉県立近代美術館）

作品輸送
カトーレック株式会社

[Exhibition]

Curators
Oshita Yuji, Nakamura Fumiko
(Nakanoshima Museum of Art, Osaka)
Sato Ayuka, Shigihara Haruka
(The Museum of Modern Art, Saitama)

Transportation
Katolec Corporation

撮影
加藤成文
cat.nos. 104, 108
柳場大
cat.nos. 1, 3, 4, 5, 6, 7, 15, 60, 92, 96, 107, 109, 123

撮影者不明の写真につきましても、
資料的価値を鑑みて掲載しております。
撮影者についてご存じの方は、どうぞ情報を
お寄せください。

Photo Credit
Kato Shigefumi
cat.nos. 104, 108

Yanagiba Masaru
cat.nos. 1, 3, 4, 5, 6, 7, 15, 60, 92, 96, 107, 109, 123

[カタログ]

2024年5月25日発行

執筆
大下裕司
熊田司
佐藤あゆか
建畠哲
光田ゆり

インタビュー
木下佳通代（再掲）
植松奎二

デザイン
大西正一

編集
大下裕司、中村史子、奥野桃子、浦川慶子
（大阪中之島美術館）
佐藤あゆか、鴫原悠
（埼玉県立近代美術館）

翻訳
クリストファー・スティヴンズ
Essay 2、Essay 4、Interview 2、References 2
パメラ・ミキ・アソシエイツ
Introduction、Essay 1、Chapter 1、Chapter 2、Chapter 3、Interview 1
ベンジャー桂
Essay 3
英文校閲
有限会社フォンテーヌ
Essay 1、Essay 2、Essay 3、Essay 4、
Interview 1、Interview 2、References 2、Notes

助成
公益財団法人 小笠原敏晶記念財団

印刷・製本
株式会社八紘美術

発行人
姫野希美
発行
株式会社赤々舎

カバー
《LA '92-CA711》1992年、
和歌山県立近代美術館蔵

公益財団法人
小笠原敏晶記念財団

大阪中之島
美術館
NAKANOSHIMA MUSEUM OF ART, OSAKA

埼玉県立近代美術館
The Museum of Modern Art, Saitama

[Catalogue]

Published on May 25, 2024

Authors
Oshita Yuji
Kumada Tsukasa
Sato Ayuka
Tatehata Akira
Mitsuda Yuri

Interviewees
Kinoshita Kazuyo
Uematsu Keiji

Designer
Onishi Masakazu

Editors
Oshita Yuji, Nakamura Fumiko,
Okuno Momoko, Urakawa Keiko
(Nakanoshima Museum of Art, Osaka)
Sato Ayuka, Shigihara Haruka
(The Museum of Modern Art, Saitama)

Translation
Christopher Stephens
Essay 2, Essay 4, Interview 2, References 2
Pamela Miki Associates
Introduction, Essay 1, Chapter 1, Chapter 2, Chapter 3, Interview 1
Benger Kei
Essay 3

English translation proofreading
Fontaine Ltd.
Essay 1, Essay 2, Essay 3, Essay 4,
Interview 1, Interview 2, References 2, Notes

Granted by
Toshiaki Ogasawara Memorial Foundation

Printing and Binding
Hakko Bijutsu Co.,Ltd.

Publisher
Himeno Kimi
Published by
AKAAKA Art Publishing, Inc.

Cover
LA '92-CA711, 1992,
Collection of the Museum of Modern Art, Wakayama